Tracy Maylett, Ed.D.

ENGAGEMENT
MAGIC

Five Keys for Engaging People, Leaders, and Organizations

GREENLEAF
BOOK GROUP PRESS

Published by Greenleaf Book Group Press
Austin, Texas
www.gbgpress.com

Copyright ©2014, 2019 DecisionWise, LLC

Distributed by Greenleaf Book Group

For ordering information or special discounts for bulk purchases, please contact Greenleaf Book Group at PO Box 91869, Austin, TX 78709, 512.891.6100.

Design and composition by Greenleaf Book Group
Cover design by Greenleaf Book Group
Cover image: iStockphoto/4771306/Hypergon Inc.; Shutterstock/67686535/Yuriy Boyko

Publisher's Cataloging-in-Publication data is available.

Print ISBN: 978-1-62634-617-8

eBook ISBN: 978-1-62634-618-5

Part of the Tree Neutral® program, which offsets the number of trees consumed in the production and printing of this book by taking proactive steps, such as planting trees in direct proportion to the number of trees used: www.treeneutral.com

TreeNeutral®

Printed in the United States of America on acid-free paper

19 20 21 22 23 24   10 9 8 7 6 5 4 3 2 1

Second Edition

To family, friends, valued client partners,
and colleagues . . . my *magic*.

CONTENTS

Beyond MAGIC

In the fall of 2014, my colleague, Dr. Paul Warner, and I released the book *MAGIC: Five Keys to Unlock the Power of Employee Engagement*. But the book didn't start there; it began nearly twenty years prior, as our organization, DecisionWise, conducted our first employee engagement survey.

At that time, the concept of "employee engagement" was largely unknown. Companies had just begun to understand the idea of employee satisfaction and the notion that maybe, just maybe, the employee experience had some impact on the bottom line. If it truly did impact the bottom line, wouldn't it make sense to measure what employees felt? And thus, the idea of the employee survey began to catch on.

As our firm spent the next decade knee-deep in employee survey administration and data, themes began to emerge. First, it was clear that engagement *does* impact the bottom line. There is no doubt that organizations with higher levels of employee engagement tend to outperform other organizations in financial measures, customer service, employee retention, quality, innovation, and a host of other key performance indicators.

Second, an excellent customer experience (CX) is the direct result of a superlative employee experience (EX). Thus, if an organization wishes to drive customer satisfaction, it has to first start with the employee experience. From this concept, my colleague Matthew Wride and I released the book *The Employee Experience: How to Attract Talent, Retain Top Performers, and Drive Results*. That book was an instant success and best seller, largely because organizations resonated with the concept that EX = CX.

Third, we discovered that engagement is a competency. This was a monumental find, as it meant that engagement can be learned, practiced, taught, measured, and even expected of employees and managers, and that they can be held accountable for engagement. This also meant that engagement isn't something that's simply felt; it requires action. A feeling without action is just that—a feeling. But feelings aren't results, and organizations aren't hiring people simply to feel. Engagement involves both feeling *and* acting.

In 2014, our research database was made up of 14 million employee survey responses. Over the past four years, that database has more than doubled to over 32 million survey responses. That's a lot of data! Which brings me to the final point.

With the doubling of the research database, the concepts in the first book—the idea that the keys to employee engagement could be explained by the acronym MAGIC—were validated time and time again, both by research and the practical experience of our clients.

In 2018, DecisionWise finished another chapter in the ongoing journey to understand employee engagement, and brought this updated research to this new book, *Engagement MAGIC*. Written as an update to the first book, and including these new findings, *Engagement MAGIC* provides updated case studies, stories, examples, and research. I am confident that you will find these keys as essential in your individual and organizational engagement as our clients have discovered them to be in theirs.

So, bring the magic.
Tracy M. Maylett, Ed.D.

Introduction

IMAGINE IF ONE-THIRD of the people at your company felt that they could not speak up at work for fear of negative consequences. What would that say about your organization? Would it suggest an environment that stifles free expression? Most important, what would be the consequences of such a "culture of silence"?

Many organizations don't have to imagine this scenario, because it's happening right under their noses. Analysis of more than 30 million DecisionWise Employee Engagement assessments revealed something shocking: 34 percent of all employees are afraid to speak up at work because they believe they will be subject to retribution. That's a major symptom of disengagement. And what if *you* were one of these employees—or have you "been there, done that"?

The outcome? Impaired innovation, reduced safety, and poorer-quality work, for starters. When employees can't speak up about dysfunctional policies or processes, they wind up feeling powerless to direct their work in a way that makes the company competitive.

Okay, so what happens when employees are fully engaged in their work? When we analyzed the publicly traded companies that scored in the top 10 percent and bottom 10 percent of our Employee Engagement assessments, the results were just as dramatic . . . but a lot more favorable. The companies that scored in the top 10 percent in employee engagement were considerably more profitable, grew faster, and had lower turnover than the companies in the bottom 10 percent.

Example: CHG Healthcare Services is at the top of our list with an incredible engagement score that consistently exceeds 90 percent (meaning that over 90 percent of survey question responses are favorable). They have been ranked as high as number three on *Fortune*'s "100 Best Companies to Work For" list, in the same league as titans like Google and SAS. They are the most profitable company in the health-care-staffing industry.

However, before CHG launched its "Putting People First" program and transformed its moderately engaged corporate culture, the company's turnover rate was negatively impacting growth. Today, turnover is half the industry average, and CHG even managed to grow revenue and profits during the 2008–2011 recession while their industry peers saw profitability plummet.

CHG Healthcare Services didn't change on a dime. It took extensive planning, conscious effort, hard work by leaders and teams, and consistent follow-through to gain the trust of employees and transform the company's culture. But the results speak for themselves.

WE CAN'T GET NO SATISFACTION

With results like those, it's no wonder that organizations around the world are investing heavily in order to find ways to "get employees more engaged." The trouble is, they're wasting most of that money. In fact, it is estimated that the market for employee engagement-related programs exceeds $1.5 billion in the United States alone.[1]

By most accounts, employee engagement at work is at dangerously low levels. Depending on the source, you'll read that anywhere from 63 to 80 percent of American workers are not fully engaged in their jobs, and results are similar outside the United States. It's becoming rare to attend a conference or pick up an engagement-related article that doesn't begin with some type of perpetuated myth like, "78 percent of employees are disengaged and unlikely to be making a positive contribution to the workplace." Come on. Do I really need to walk past four employees in the hall before I find a fifth who is actually engaged in her job? Why not fire the 78 percent and let the remaining 22 percent do the work? It would certainly be a lot more efficient (and probably a lot happier place to work).

Because of the research our firm, DecisionWise, has done over the past two decades, we understand that it's not human nature to disengage. In fact, we *want* to engage. So, we don't put a lot of stock in this sort of hand-wringing data (for reasons I'll explain later), but it does drive home two important points:

- Employee engagement is a serious concern in the United States, and that problem is echoed across the globe.
- Companies are spending a lot of money trying to "drive engagement," but all they're really doing is measuring it year to year, rather than impacting it. They're not getting much for their investment.

Even more telling is the fact that employers can't even agree on what engagement is or what it looks like when employees are more engaged. So, we're spending 1.5 billion dollars a year to cultivate something without knowing what it is. Is anybody surprised that most of those efforts fail?

One of the biggest reasons for that failure is that while organizations think they are enacting programs to increase employee engagement, their changes are really all about employee *satisfaction*. Engagement and satisfaction are *not* the same. When you install an espresso machine in every break room, provide each floor with its own air-hockey table, and open an on-site gym, you might get a temporary bump in employee satisfaction. But it doesn't last. You don't win hearts and minds with shade-grown coffee and arcade games.

Most organizations don't understand engagement, so they can't create it. One of the biggest misapprehensions is that engagement is something the organization imposes on employees—that it's transactional. *If I give you this, that, and the other, you'll become engaged in your work*. It's as if engagement were something done *to* employees, something inflicted upon them.

And this is another reason most engagement efforts fail—they assume the responsibility for engagement rests solely on the shoulders of the organization. But in reality, engagement is a 50-50 proposition—a two-way street. Yes, the organization is responsible for creating an environment where engagement can flourish—tilling and amending the soil so that engagement can grow, so to speak. But the employee has an equal responsibility to *be* engaged. Engagement is collaborative: The organization must create the environment in which employees can choose to engage, but it's up to the employee to say, "I'm in!"

THE PURPOSE OF THIS BOOK

You may notice that throughout this book I switch between "I" and "we." That's because the words may be mine, but the findings are the result of nearly two decades of research by a stellar DecisionWise team of industrial psychologists, technology gurus, assessment analysts, and industry experts. We've designed this book as a tool to help both employers and employees shed the many fallacies and myths about engagement and learn to leverage it for what it is: a secret weapon that, when unlocked, can turn a faltering company into a healthy one and a good organization into a great one.

In these pages, you will find insights that our team has accumulated over years of surveying millions of employees and working with hundreds of organizations throughout the world, ranging from small not-for-profits in Uganda, to state and national governments, to the world's largest and most respected corporations. While we've worked hard to teach those clients what we know, we have also learned from them. One of the most important lessons we've taken away is this:

> Engagement is a fundamental human need. It is a power that resides in most people, waiting to be unlocked. People want to be engaged in what they do. If employers build the foundation, employees will do the rest.

That was a critical discovery for us, and it's been a game changer for the organizations we work with. When senior executives find out that the burden for engagement doesn't rest entirely on their shoulders, a weight lifts. Suddenly, the unmanageable becomes manageable. This book is a "what's next" manual of sorts—a guide to using the extraordinary power of engagement to take your organization to the next level, whether that means growth, greater profitability, lower turnover, a more enjoyable workplace, all of the above, or something we haven't thought of.

WHO WE ARE

This book is constructed on a foundation of academic scholarship, psychology, and real-world experience. Our company, DecisionWise, is a management consulting firm specializing in leadership and organization development using assessments, feedback, coaching, and training. Using our Leadership Intelligence® process, we help clients across the world cultivate higher levels of employee engagement and improved business performance. Rather than focusing exclusively on the operational components of business (how to design assembly lines, read profit-and-loss statements, etc.), our focus is on how human capital drives performance.

Simply put, we eat, breathe, and write about employee engagement and the employee experience. We're neck-deep in the topic, from popular culture and mainstream media to academic journals and leading-edge thinkers. We know how to tell the fact from the fabrication, the real issues from the false alarms, and the sound investments from the money pits. So I've filled these pages with that same experience and judgment.

WHY THIS BOOK IS DIFFERENT

But what sets this book apart is the methodology. It's based on data. Lots and lots of data. Over the years, we have deployed our Leadership Intelligence assessments in thousands of corporations and government agencies in more than seventy countries (and in more than thirty languages). From these assessments, we've built an engagement database of more than 30 million responses. This book reflects that research.

I've used that data to make this a book built on reams of empirical facts. No cherry-picking data to support a predetermined conclusion. No neat suppositions supported by nothing more than a few wonky articles from the mainstream press and personal blogs. These assertions and prescriptions are based on a data set with unprecedented statistical power: millions of employees sharing, via precision-designed surveys, their candid opinions about the factors that make their work either intolerable or inspiring.

That means the advice delivered isn't opinion, though I'll offer up a fair amount of that as well. It's field-tested truth. This is both an organizational and a personal approach to engagement. In short, it's about what makes an organization tick, and what ticks people off.

THE PROMISE

Benjamin Franklin said, "Wise men don't need advice. Fools won't take it." This book may respectfully disagree with the founding father: Wise men (and women) are the first to recognize what they don't know and enthusiastically seek advice from people who know what they are talking about. The goal of this book is to make you wiser about employee engagement—what it is, why it matters, how you can foster it in your organization and what it can do to benefit you and the people you work with, and how you can personally engage in your work.

To achieve that goal, *Engagement MAGIC* is an updated follow-up to our first book, *MAGIC: Five Keys to Unlock the Power of Employee Engagement*. Based on additional research, client accounts, and mounds of additional data, this updated book is written in a way that allows readers to dip in and out of the material at will and always come away with something of value. It would be great if you had four undisturbed hours on a cross-country flight to read every paragraph in detail, but that's not likely. So, this book is packed full of useful items:

- Each chapter concludes with a succinct one-page summary of the salient topics, findings, and recommendations.
- At the end of chapters three through seven, you'll find a set of provocative questions designed to get you thinking about what creates engagement for you, your team, or your organization.
- Each chapter features at least one "Egghead Alert" sidebar. When you see it, I'm about to share some academic or scientific theory (remember, this book is based on both academic research and business experience). If that's not your cup of tea, skip it.
- Chapter eight contains an abbreviated version of our Personal Engagement Self-Assessment. Take this simplified 10-minute Engagement MAGIC® Self-Assessment to get a sense of your own level of engagement.

Bottom line, my team and I have updated this book so that senior executives, department managers, and individual employees across all industries and geographies can put concrete action to the research our firm has done. If you're responsible for the health of your entire organization, you'll find big-picture theory and strategy that you can use to plant and grow a culture that will help your people engage meaningfully with their work, increasing productivity, job satisfaction, and profitability. Whether you're managing a team of five or a department of two hundred, you'll find tactics and tools that will help you increase your personal level of engagement while helping your direct reports find connection and autonomy in their work, reduce attrition, and encourage innovation.

And if you're an individual contributor, with only yourself to manage, you'll gain insight into your own level of engagement (or lack thereof) in your current position. More important, you'll discover the many ways in which making the commitment to become more fully engaged in your job will benefit both you and your employer—not just financially, but in the form of greater fulfillment, deeper personal connection, and improved quality of life. Keep in mind that, although most of these examples involve workplace settings, these principles aren't limited to the workplace. These are principles of human psychology, not just business concepts.

In reading any book, you invest your valuable time with the hope of a substantial payoff. This book promises to deliver that. You'll find actionable advice that delivers genuine return on investment (ROI)—data-driven conclusions that have already helped hundreds of industry-leading organizations reduce costs, attract the best and brightest, and grow at unprecedented rates. These same concepts will help you in your personal life.

When you focus on the right things, your business improves. Your life also improves. Let me share with you the means to not only improve the satisfaction level of employees but transform your culture in a way that also transforms your bottom line. You might even find that you are a better person because of it.

PART ONE

Engagement Versus Satisfaction

CHAPTER ONE
Myths of Engagement

"A man's delight in looking forward to and hoping for some particular satisfaction is a part of the pleasure flowing out of it, enjoyed in advance. But this is afterward deducted, for the more we look forward to anything the less we enjoy it when it comes."
—Arthur Schopenhauer

THIS IS A WORK of empirical fact, constructed on the bedrock of behavioral science and hard data. So, I'd like to start off by referencing perhaps the best movie ever made about the modern workplace, *Office Space*.

Yes, it's a counterintuitive beginning, but bear with me.

You probably know this 1999 movie. I'll refer to it throughout the book. It's humorous, but it's also a blistering commentary on what can happen when an employer actively thumbs its nose at engagement.

There may not be a less engaged company than Initech, the fictional software concern where most of the film plays out. Management treats the employees like drones. The employees either stare at their desks, war with printers, or kill time by shuffling papers from one place to another. The company's efforts at creating culture—for example, Hawaiian-shirt day—are pathetic. Nothing illustrates Initech's total lack of engagement better than a scene where the employees celebrate the boss's birthday by standing board-stiff and singing "Happy Birthday" in a monotone, with the blank, slack faces of people being led on a death march.

Initech might be an extreme example of the dangers of disengagement (spoiler alert: At the end of the film, the most egregiously mistreated employee burns down the company headquarters), but unfortunately, it's not entirely fictional. Plenty of well-meaning companies have tried to find ways to get their people engaged and failed:

- In 2011, Wells Fargo, worried that its recent announcement of a $3.8 billion profit wasn't sexy enough for Wall Street, launched Project Compass. It was a "bottom-up initiative" that would ask employees to produce ideas that would trim costs and increase efficiency. Sounds great . . . until you consider that the main expense employees were asked to help cut was their own jobs. By June 2012, Wells Fargo had announced that it would be outsourcing more than a thousand jobs to places like India and the Philippines in order to help cut $1.7 billion in quarterly expenses.[2] It's hard to make employees feel empowered when you're asking them to help decide which of their friends will be let go.

- Torbay Hospital in England had just been awarded the prestigious Acute Healthcare Organization of the Year Award. Twenty of its leaders enjoyed a lavish dinner and an awards ceremony in London. How did they reward the four thousand employees who'd made the honor possible? They gave them Kit Kats. Actually, they didn't even bother to buy the chocolate bars—the staff got vouchers. The clueless gesture infuriated employees and made the hospital's management a laughingstock.[3]

- DecisionWise Employee Experience survey data shows a clear increase in the amount of money spent on employee perks from 2013 to 2018. Yet, in many of these companies, the amount spent on perks is actually inversely proportional to levels of engagement.

- More companies seem to be spending money on incentive bonuses to try to keep their people from leaving. The Society for Human Resource Management reported that in 2017, 96 percent of private companies used some type of short-term incentive plan, up from 94 percent in 2016[4] These figures show a stark increase compared to the findings from the salary data website PayScale, which indicate that in 2012, 72 percent of employers awarded incentive bonuses, compared to only 53 percent in 2010.[5] The improved job market is a big motivator, because people who have more choices are more apt to leave. Well, big investments equal huge payoffs, right? Not so fast. Despite the cash offers, engagement scores overall haven't budged much across most organizations.

WHAT DOESN'T WORK

The reason that these and other efforts at employee engagement don't work is simple: They have very little to do with engagement. They range from the well intentioned and clueless to the cynical and destructive, but they don't come close to the core qualities that help employees be personally engaged in their work.

When senior executives talk about engagement, they're usually thinking of "perks" like on-site gyms and health spas, nap pods, soda pop in the break room, Taco Tuesdays, dog-sitting and laundry services, and so on. These are typically costly investments. So, why do we continue spending money with little engagement to show for it?

First, most managers don't understand the difference between engagement and satisfaction. Second, we're taught in management school that every return requires an investment, and that investment always has a dollar (or euro, or yen, or . . .) figure attached to it. We're taught to throw money at problems. Third, and perhaps most pervasive (and dangerous), it's simpler to build an on-site gym than it is to help an employee find meaning in his or her work. Bringing in a few treadmills is more tangible and easier to get our arms around than building a sense of purpose in one's work.

Simply put, while some managers may know how to bring in lunch for the team, or even how to have a productive conversation with employees about sales targets, few are comfortable with helping an employee find purpose and a sense of fulfillment in his or her work. This isn't something we're taught to do, at least not in business settings.

The environment and culture, not the bells and whistles, set the tone for how engaged, fulfilled, and challenged we feel at the office. Compensation and perks matter, but they're far from the only factors. To put it another way, it's the soil, not the flowers.

Think of this in terms of your own experience (we'll dive into this in more depth a little later). Have you felt the energy that comes with doing something you feel is worthwhile, something that really floats your boat? How did it feel? What did it cause you to do?

When our consultants conduct workshops or facilitate team sessions, we often ask the question "What does a good day look like at work?" Responses vary. Participants may relate a good day to having accomplished something important. Or they may focus on solving a customer issue, making a significant discovery, healing a patient, or rewiring a machine on the assembly line that nobody else could fix. "Whenever my boss is gone, it's a good day!" inevitably shows up somewhere in each session. But that's a separate discussion.

Two important points emerge from these discussions. First, responses rarely relate to perks or compensation. Second, employees intuitively know how engagement feels—and when it's not present. They get it.

WHAT IS ENGAGEMENT?

Here's the definition we will refer to throughout this book:

> Employee engagement is an emotional state where we feel passionate, energetic, and committed toward our work. In turn, we fully invest our best selves—our hearts, spirits, minds, and hands—in the work we do.

When you see engagement, you know it. For example, in 2001, Douglas Conant took over as CEO of Campbell's Soup and called it a "bad" company. Its products were bleeding market share, and research showed that 62 percent of the company's managers did not consider themselves actively engaged in their jobs. Yet by 2009, 68 percent of the company's employees said they were actively engaged, while just 3 percent considered themselves actively disengaged. More important, Campbell's increased its earnings by up to 4 percent per year over those eight years.[6]

How did Conant do it? He made a commitment to his people, embodied in the phrase "Campbell valuing people, people valuing Campbell." He took down the prison-style barbed-wire fence surrounding the corporate HQ. He launched programs to get managers communicating with direct reports, and had direct reports evaluate managers. The top criterion that managers were expected to show: the ability to inspire trust. Those who didn't measure up were replaced from within. Conant also instituted programs to celebrate individual success, from sending personal thank-you notes to having lunch with employees.

That's a *culture* of engagement. It had nothing to do with air-hockey tables in break rooms or on-site clinics. People engage with people, and they give more when they feel heard, empowered, and appreciated.

What about Google? They're the perennial champ of the best-places-to-work lists, and the role model for companies trying to create an environment that makes the best and brightest feel totally engaged. But to believe that the secret is the awesome organic cafeteria food or the famous personal-project policy is to ignore the brilliance of what Google does.

The company has a "people analytics team" that asks, "What makes our employees happy now versus in the future?" As economic conditions, business focus, and individual employees change, so does the research. Google uses the results to create evolving programs congruent with employees' concerns, needs, and tastes.

MYTHS VERSUS FACTS

Engagement, done right, yields results. Then why is there so much fear and loathing surrounding the topic? In part, it's a result of persistent myths propagated by polling companies and the news media. For example, if you're in a leadership or human resources position at a company, you've almost certainly come across this alarming statistic (or something similar): "78 percent of your employees are disengaged and looking for new jobs!"

Those "scare quotes" are designed to do exactly that: scare you into hiring a consultant to help prevent all your employees from bolting. But that 78 percent figure is misleading. Polling companies arrive at it because they make engagement a binary equation: You're either fully engaged or fully disengaged. They might gauge employee engagement on a 1–5 scale, with five being full engagement. If 22 percent of your workers score fives, the polling company will take the other 78 percent who score 1–4 and say they're disengaged! Voilà—scary numbers.

Furthermore, many of the questions asked are not true engagement questions; they're satisfaction questions (I'll get into this in more depth later). But let's apply some common sense here. Do you really think that over three-quarters of your workforce couldn't care less about what happens at work? That goes against basic human nature.

Engagement isn't binary. It's a continuum, a spectrum. There are many levels, and they change over time. In our engagement surveys, we break down the results into four categories:

Fully Engaged (32 percent of respondents to our surveys)	These are the most enthusiastic champions of the organization, whose excitement is palpable and contagious. They are constantly learning and taking calculated risks; feel that they are able to stretch beyond their comfort zone; take personal gratification in the quality of their work; feel that while work can be stressful, it can also be fun; and love their jobs.
Key Contributors (48 percent)	They meet performance expectations, do what they know well without taking many risks, respond well to leadership, don't often feel challenged, and while they don't necessarily love all aspects of their jobs, are actively contributing and involved in the day-to-day. We call these people the "strong-and-steady." They make up the bulk of the workforce, and they generally perform. But much of their work is transactional, rather than transformational. They get things done, but they typically invest limited time in innovating, improving processes, or breaking from the status quo. It goes back to the old joke about the difference between the chicken and the pig in a bacon-and-egg breakfast: The chicken is involved; the pig is committed. These employees are involved, but they're not putting their all into their work.
Opportunity Group (16 percent)	They generally feel underutilized, spend a lot of work time taking care of personal needs, do enough to get by and not get in trouble, seldom speak up, work mainly for the pay, and are basically marking time. In our interviews and focus groups with these individuals, we have found that many in the Opportunity Group are actually potential top performers who are burned out. It's often difficult to identify these individuals, as they disengage and suffer in silence, checking out mentally and emotionally. They don't make noise, but their contributions are limited. They are the "undecided vote." As the name implies, there is a huge opportunity to sway this group to a higher level of engagement. However, if nothing is done, they leave the organization, either physically or psychologically.
Disengaged (4 percent)	They are bored and frustrated; say negative things about the work, the company, and its leadership; tend to blame others for their failures; and rather than quit, tend to stay on and, consciously or unconsciously, sabotage things. They are often the most vocal and negatively contagious group within the organization. They can be cancerous and toxic. Many leaders discount this group because of their small numbers. Yet having even one of these individuals on a team can have a significant negative impact. On the other hand, because these individuals tend to be quite vocal about their dissatisfaction and disengagement, management teams often spend a great deal of unproductive time addressing their demands.

People tend to move in and out of these four categories of engagement depending on the environment, incentives, and where they are in their careers and lives. It's a complex, fluid, true-to-life model that more closely resembles the makeup of a team or organization than the alarming (and inaccurate) statistics being thrown out as scare tactics. It also means that any claim that 78 or 80 percent of your employees are job hunting is a myth. Our research shows that, in fact, even during the employment challenges across the world from 2010 to 2015, less than 11 percent of employees were actively seeking new employment. Why? A tough global economy over the past decade may be a factor, but more important is the reality that under-engagement does not mean destructive disengagement. Jobs evolve. Opportunities change. People advance. But we've now entered a new era, one which I like to call the "Age of the Employee." Now, the employee has choices that he or she might not have had in any previous era.

The polling company Gallup, in its *State of the Global Workplace* report, states that:

> Only 13% of employees worldwide are engaged at work . . . In other words, about one in eight workers—roughly 180 million employees in the countries studied—are psychologically committed to their jobs and likely to be making positive contributions to their organizations.[7]

Wow. Scary. But are we really to believe that seven of the eight people you work with aren't making positive contributions to the organization because they aren't psychologically committed? Quick! Lock the doors. Keep the employees away from your customers.

Not so fast. It's easy to get caught up in bad interpretations of the data, and plenty of organizations do. But don't make critical business decisions based on faulty assumptions about what's going on with your team.

A CULTURE OF CYNICISM

So, on one hand, we have employers certain that their people are either running for the exits or sabotaging their businesses from within. On the other, we have employees who've become jaded in the wake of "engagement" projects that are insulting, inauthentic, inept, or all of the above.

When that happens, you get *Dilbert*, the famous comic strip by Scott Adams. In the *Dilbert* universe, bosses are all incompetent and self-serving, employees are all arch-cynics manipulating a nonsensical bureaucracy, and nothing much gets done. The dialogue from this cartoon that ran on November 25, 2009, pretty much says it all:

> **The Pointy-Haired Boss:** "We need more of what the management experts call 'employee engagement.' I don't know the details, but it has something to do with you idiots working harder for the same pay."
>
> **Dilbert:** "Is anything different on your end?"
>
> **The Pointy-Haired Boss:** "I think I'm supposed to be happier."

Our employee surveys tell us that when these conditions are present, employees become certain that regardless of what's said, nothing is going to change. Typically, when we survey a company for the first time, 50 percent of the respondents to our global benchmark survey say they are not confident that the engagement survey will lead to any changes being made. For these employees, the pattern has always been consistent; when changes do occur, they're usually at the top and don't filter down to the rank and file. Employees can't connect changes in the organization with their feedback or input. This leads to further cynicism and eroded trust.

In contrast, when companies give more data to frontline managers and empower them to share the survey data with their teams, create their own action plans, and take the initiative, employees become confident that surveys will lead to changes. Empower individuals, and cynicism retreats.

Unfortunately, for many companies the survey *is* their engagement campaign. That's where it ends, and that doesn't work. An engagement program has to be integral to every part of your organization. A survey is just your opening move, like cutting down the trees in order to build the house.

It's no surprise that when senior executives perceive employee apathy and read that three-quarters of their people are looking for new jobs, despite $1.5 billion spent on engagement, they become cynics. Some may even begin to suspect that employees are claiming to be disengaged only so they can get new perks.

But engagement works. The key to success is knowing what engagement is, how it differs from satisfaction, and how to cultivate it on an organization-wide scale. Let's take a look at the first two issues.

SATISFACTION VERSUS ENGAGEMENT

Many managers mistakenly think that increasing employee satisfaction will increase employee motivation and engagement. But satisfaction is a complex system in itself, so let's break it down before we get too far into engagement.

Egghead Alert!

American psychologist Frederick Herzberg's Motivation-Hygiene Theory proposes that job satisfaction is influenced by two factors: motivation factors and basic "hygiene factors." Motivation factors include challenging work, recognition, and responsibility. Hygiene factors consist of pay and benefits, supervision, working conditions, and job security (among others). Herzberg suggests that while the presence of hygiene factors does not create motivation, the lack of them creates demotivation.

Hygiene factors play a big role in determining a person's level of satisfaction with their job, and strongly influence employee retention. If they aren't met, they lead to job dissatisfaction and cause employees to look for better opportunities elsewhere.

Let's look at an example. A number of years ago, a large automobile manufacturer contacted our firm with a concern that had tremendous impact on their levels of employee morale. Several employees had reported being robbed in the parking lot while leaving the assembly plant at night. The final straw prompting the call was that an employee was assaulted, leaving the employee bruised and in poor shape. The manufacturer had reached out to us to help them understand what, specifically, they needed to do in order to restore levels of employee confidence in their safety and well-being.

For these employees (and employees anywhere, for that matter), safety was not something that motivated them or got them excited to come to work. It was a hygiene factor. Being safe did not cause satisfaction, but taking away their safety (robberies, assault, etc.) quickly caused them to become dissatisfied and demotivated in their jobs. While safety is certainly not a perk, it illustrates an important reality: Constantly introducing more and better hygiene factors doesn't increase job satisfaction or performance. But the lack of these factors could cause huge declines in satisfaction.

Blame the *adaptation principle*. Psychology research says that when someone jumps to a higher level of income or a new standard of living, they quickly adapt and become dissatisfied again. If you try to buy employee satisfaction by upgrading perks and hygiene factors, the price always goes up. Give employees a bonus, and they want a bigger bonus. Build them a gym, and they'll expect a gym with a pool. Taco Tuesdays? Great! But the company down the street also gets Fajita Fridays. That's not greed; it's human nature.

The notion of the adaptation principle is highlighted in a classic psychological study involving lottery winners, a control group, and accident victims. The researchers observed 22 major lottery winners, 29 paralyzed accident victims, and 22 control group participants (those who neither won the lottery nor were involved in a serious accident), asking them to rate their levels of happiness both before and after these life-changing events. Not surprisingly, the lottery winners rated winning as a highly positive event, while the paraplegic victims rated their accident as a highly negative event.

The findings were fascinating, however. Lottery winners and the control group showed no significant differences in their ratings as to how happy they were at present, how happy they were before winning, or how happy they anticipated being in the future. Did you catch that? No significant difference between lottery winners and non-winners, even after hitting it big with the lottery!

As would be expected, accident victims and those in the control group were significantly different in their ratings of present happiness (actually, accident victims tended to see their past happiness as significantly better than did their control counterparts). However, there was no significant difference between these groups in terms of their anticipated *future* happiness.

It doesn't stop there. Perhaps even more interesting was the fact that the lottery winners derived less pleasure from mundane events than did the control group. In other words, they no longer found as much joy in ordinary, day-to-day pleasures.[8]

The fact is that while employees may find short-term satisfaction in a raise, free lunch, a bonus, or a new laptop, that will soon become the new baseline, and employees will adapt to that new reality. These factors now become the new standard; we adapt to the current status. These new factors don't create engagement when we become accustomed to or adapt to them, but take them away and dissatisfaction is the result.

Here's the rub: While you must have employee satisfaction in order to have employee engagement (and you can't have lasting engagement without it), satisfaction factors on their own don't *create* engagement. Satisfaction is just the price of admission.

You've created a transactional experience when . . .

- The main goal is maximum productivity; employees operate according to guidelines so thoughtless that activity seems automated.
- Employees are commodities who can easily be replaced, and they know it.
- It emphasizes management, rather than leadership.
- Conformity is valued over creativity.
- A "what's-in-it-for-me" entitlement mentality is pervasive.
- The culture is a give-and-take of negotiated compromises. When something is given, a commensurate reward is always expected.
- Reciprocal trust is low between individuals and leaders.
- The same issues and mistakes are continually repeated. Effort is not dedicated to creating an environment in which people are learning, nor are they motivated to improve or correct past mistakes.
- Focus is on working longer and harder, rather than smarter.
- People are motivated to work just hard enough not to get fired. There is little or no discretionary effort. It's about the paycheck. You get exactly what you pay for—and employees often remind you of that fact.

Satisfaction is transactional and contractual. In return for their work, you promise to provide employees with the basics: compensation, tools and resources, physical safety, dignity, and respect, to name a few. Both the organization and the employee must continue to make constant deposits in the relationship "bank account," and both sides continually monitor the account activity. For every withdrawal on either side, a deposit must be made. When there's an imbalance on either side, a deposit must be made or a deficit—employee apathy or employer resentment—results.

Satisfied employees will put out as much effort as they are compensated for, and no more. They deliver on what is asked of them, as long as you deliver on your part of the deal. They show up and do their work, but that doesn't necessarily mean they are going to say no when the phone rings and it's a headhunter on the other end.

For the most part, the organization owns satisfaction. They cut the checks, deliver the benefits, and pay for the perks. There's no sense of "we're in this together" on the part of the company or the employee. It's truly contractual.

Engagement is very different:

- Satisfaction is transactional; engagement is transformational.
- The organization owns and controls satisfaction; employer and employee have a 50-50 responsibility for engagement.
- Satisfaction and motivation involve only feelings; engagement involves feelings but requires action.
- Satisfaction is about temporary happiness; engagement is long-term.
- Satisfaction is imposed on employees from without; employees *choose* to be engaged.
- Satisfaction occurs when hygiene factors are met; engagement occurs when employees have the capacity, reason, freedom, and know-how to engage.[9]
- Satisfaction is about hygiene factors, which do not necessarily motivate people but when taken away can cause them to be demotivated. Engagement is about hearts, spirits, hands, and minds (I'll cover this in more depth later on).
- With satisfaction, you get out exactly what you put in; with engagement, you get a multiple of what you put in.
- Satisfaction is a zero-sum game in which employers and employees do the minimum in order to fulfill the contract; engagement contributes to "peak experiences" that make employees eager to give extra, discretionary effort.
- Satisfaction is expensive. Raises, perks, and office extras cost a lot of money. Engagement can cost nothing but requires a conscious effort.

• Satisfaction is about surviving; engagement is about thriving.

CREATING SABOTEURS

Another critical difference is that the absence of satisfaction can be far more damaging than disengagement. Engagement isn't continuous. On some days we might be disengaged and have to slog through our jobs. We've all been there, right? But overall, we remain engaged as long as the organization continues creating fertile soil for engagement. Over time, the big picture matters, even if we're temporarily unhappy or have the occasional day when we're just glad to leave the building.

But when people become dissatisfied, it's usually because they feel that something they were entitled to isn't there, or has been taken away. That breeds the kind of bitterness and resentment that can lead to sabotage.

The origins of the word *sabotage* are murky, but it has a connection to a French word for shoe, *sabot*. One version has it that the word derives from the fifteenth century, when disgruntled Dutch workers would supposedly throw their wooden shoes into the wooden workings of mills or textile looms in order to break them and bring automated textile manufacturing to a standstill. Another story suggests that *sabotage* comes from nineteenth-century French slang for an unskilled laborer who did poor-quality work, because such laborers often wore wooden shoes.

In any case, the basic meaning of the word hasn't changed: deliberate action aimed at harming an organization, government body, or other entity, usually in secret. Sabotage has long been viewed as both noble and justified: The *Simple Sabotage Field Manual*,[10] produced in 1944 by the U.S. Office of Strategic Services (the precursor to the CIA), instructed U.S. citizens in ways to sabotage domestic factories and other industries should America fall under the control of either Nazi Germany or the Soviet Union. It's fascinating reading and quite a primer on the many small ways that ordinary people can gum up the works in order to, in theory, bring down an enemy.

Though written over seven decades ago, instructions from the *Simple Sabotage Field Manual* appear to be strangely applicable to modern organizations:

- **Managers and Supervisors**: To lower morale and production, be pleasant to inefficient workers; give them undeserved promotions. Discriminate against efficient workers; complain unjustly about their work.
- **Employees**: Work slowly. Think of ways to increase the number of movements needed to do your job: use a light hammer instead of a heavy one; try to make a small wrench do, instead of a big one.
- **Organizations and Conferences**: When possible, refer all matters to committees for "further study and consideration." Attempt to make the committees as large and bureaucratic as possible. Hold conferences when there is more critical work to be done.
- **Telephone**: At office, hotel, and local telephone switchboards, delay putting calls through, give out wrong numbers, cut people off "accidentally," or forget to disconnect them so that the line cannot be used again.
- **Transportation**: Make train travel as inconvenient as possible for enemy personnel. Issue two tickets for the same seat on a train in order to set up an "interesting" argument.

While engaged employees actively contribute to the success of an organization, disengaged employees can actively sabotage the organization's progress. However, this is fairly uncommon: According to our research, fewer than 4 percent of employees are *actively* disengaged.

Far more common is the employee who commits "passive sabotage." These employees may refuse to go the extra mile for the customer, balk at training the new guy, be inattentive in meetings, or not report a quality concern when it's noticed. They may be the people who simply don't seem to care about anything beyond doing what's required and then clocking out. Our research has found that roughly 16 percent of employees—the Opportunity Group—fit into this category. Even though their intention may not be to harm or hamper (the dictionary definition of *sabotage*), the outcome of their indifference is often the same as if they were actively trying to cause harm.

Dissatisfaction can have the same result. Employees who feel that the organization is not fulfilling its contract can become saboteurs by doing subtle things like criticizing colleagues and missing important deadlines, or by taking drastic actions like stealing files or revealing trade secrets to competitors.

ENGAGEMENT ≠ HAPPINESS

Now, here's where many organizations get confused. Thanks to the growing field of positive psychology, it's become trendy to study what makes us happy. As a result, we've found out that happiness is important in the workplace: Research reported by the *Wall Street Journal* shows that happier workers help their colleagues 33 percent more often than unhappy employees, and are 36 percent more motivated in their work.[11]

However, happiness isn't the same as engagement, and it's important that we do not confuse these two concepts. It's an *outcome* of engagement. Part of happiness is being engaged at work. We talk to a lot of people about work–life balance, and we've found that true engagement promotes happiness at home, not just at work. When you're engaged at your workplace, you feel better about your life. You feel appreciated, recognized, and connected to the people with whom you spend the lion's share of your day.

We often pursue what we think will make us happy—money, security, status—but find that those things actually make us unhappy. In fact, happiness may not be something that we can even aspire to. A study conducted at the University of Denver found that the more study participants valued happiness for its own sake, the more they felt disappointed and unhappy when confronted with even minor life stresses or setbacks. The researchers concluded, "Paradoxically, therefore, valuing happiness may lead people to be less happy just when happiness is within reach."[12]

Researchers from Florida State University, the University of Minnesota, and Stanford University dug deeper into the importance of happiness in a study published in the *Journal of Positive Psychology*. In surveys of 397 adults about happiness and meaning (spoiler alert for the chapter on meaning!), several eyebrow-raising results emerged:

- The factors that predicted a person would be happy were different from those that predicted the same person would find meaning.
- Satisfying one's needs and wants increased happiness but was irrelevant to meaningfulness.
- Happiness was based largely in the present, while meaningfulness was linked to thinking that integrated past, present, and future.
- Taking, not giving, increased happiness, while giving rather than taking increased meaningfulness.[13]

The clear conclusion is that happiness, while important, has little to do with meaning or engagement. Aid workers toiling in sub-Saharan Africa under harsh conditions may be temporarily unhappy with the heat, mosquitoes, and poor sanitation, but these same people inevitably find their work deeply meaningful and engaging.

WHAT DOES AN ENGAGED ORGANIZATION LOOK LIKE?

Satisfaction, motivation, and happiness are like seeds, soil, and water. Without them, you can't grow engagement. But on their own, they don't *create* engagement. To grow crops, you need one more thing: the sun's energy. To grow engagement, you need the energy of employer and employees communicating, collaborating, building trust, and promoting shared values. That's when magic happens.

This is what an engaged organization looks like compared to a disengaged one:

Engaged Organization	Disengaged Organization
Employees take primary responsibility for their own engagement.	Employees leave engagement up to the organization.
Employees are the strongest advocates for their company and their brand; our research shows that in these companies, more than 80 percent feel that an insult to the company is also a personal insult.	Employees don't care about the organization, and talk negatively about their jobs and superiors.
Employees remain committed, even during hard times.	During difficult times, employees complain, blame, shirk duties, or leave (psychologically or physically).
Employees eagerly bring quality and safety issues to management's attention.	Employees have little commitment to safety or quality, beyond required compliance.
Employees create energy in others that can be felt—it's almost palpable.	Employees drain energy from others. The organization feels lethargic.

There is appreciation, gratitude, and willingness to contribute.	Employees feel entitled and become resentful when they don't receive what they feel entitled to.
Employees engage customers, vendors, and each other.	Employees are apathetic.
Employees can engage whether at the office, telecommuting, or traveling.	Employees won't put forth discretionary effort away from the supervision of bosses.
Collaboration is active and enthusiastic.	Sabotage is occurring, whether active or passive.
There is a "we" mentality.	There is a "me" mentality.
The organization is self-led, empowered, and determined.	The organization is over-managed and under-led.
Feelings of engagement and love for the job are genuine.	Enthusiasm for the job is blatantly artificial.

What does your organization look like? What impact is your level of engagement having on performance, retention, and the bottom line?

CHANGING OUR MINDS ABOUT ENGAGEMENT

When it comes to the all-important bottom line, employee engagement (not satisfaction or happiness) matters. It's a powerful engine for growth and profit—a next-level competitive tool.

That's long been a tough sell. In the minds of many executives, engagement is "soft"—something that real, in-the-trenches businesspeople don't need. Business culture is bursting with war metaphors, and the command-and-control structure of traditional organizations has its roots in the military. According to the stereotype, the work environment is macho, unemotional, and impersonal. Nobody cares if you have work–life balance or feel fulfilled. Many leaders still believe that engagement is about being happy and holding hands.

Another reason for skepticism is manager denial. If you convince yourself that the reason your people aren't performing is that they're underpaid, you offload your personal responsibility for the problem. But if you admit that the problem is lack of engagement, you're also admitting to a failure of leadership. That's why businesses waste millions of dollars a year trying to buy their way to an engaged workforce. Money does matter; it's hard to be engaged when you feel underpaid. But money isn't why people love their jobs.

Finally, from a personal standpoint, we may feel that engagement is the responsibility of the organization, and not ours as individuals. Unfortunately, many employees with this belief operate under the "Engage me, I dare you!" mentality. It's easier to believe that our lack of engagement is something created externally, and that we have limited responsibility for our own levels of engagement. For managers accustomed to controlling all aspects of the business, this is a difficult concept to grasp. One's personal level of engagement is only partially influenced by the organization and the manager; it's not fully within the circle of control of the organization or the manager. Engagement is a two-way street, and an individual must *choose* to be engaged.

TOBIN'S Q

As evidenced by the huge jump in spending on engagement, the skepticism about engagement is beginning to break down. One reason is the concept known as Tobin's q. Since the Industrial Revolution, entrepreneurs have assessed the value of a business based solely on its physical assets: assembly lines, materials, buildings, machinery, and so on. But in 1969, economists James Tobin and William Brainard introduced Tobin's q, which quantified the differences between a company's market value and the replacement value of that business or assets.

One of the key findings associated with Tobin's q was that there were two factors of value that accountants weren't typically measuring: *market hype* and *intellectual capital*. Market hype is speculation about what a company may do. Is it poised for growth (think Amazon.com, Facebook, and Instagram)? Is there a merger in the future?

Intellectual capital is complex and has three components:

- *Organizational capital,* also known as structural capital, contains the supportive infrastructure that allows the human capital to succeed. This includes such essentials as databases, patents, networks, strategies, and processes.
- *Customer capital* is about the relationships a company has with its customers. The stronger the connection with prominent key customers, the higher the value of the entity.
- *Human capital* comes from the skills and knowledge of the individuals within the organization. It's the "people" component of Tobin's equation. However, it extends beyond what employees know and can do; it requires action.

Because of increased awareness of such important factors as those defined by Tobin's *q*, organizations are learning that engagement is a measurable factor that increases the value of a business. They know they must create the experience in which employees choose to actively contribute to intellectual capital. This is why employee engagement has moved from a "nice-to-have" to a "must-have" factor. By the way, Tobin was later awarded the Nobel Prize in Economics, and his theory has become a basic concept of business valuation.

Egghead Alert!

Another factor in the acceptance of engagement involves two competing motivation theories: Theory X and Theory Y. Until recently, most businesses (American businesses in particular) have been operating in a Theory X world. Someone operating under Theory X assumes that employees are naturally lazy, will avoid work at all costs, and need authority and threats to perform. It's management by the stick. Theory Y is about the carrot. It insists that employees can be ambitious and self-motivated, and given the right conditions, will not only perform admirably but also innovate.

Initech, the company in *Office Space,* is a Theory X workplace—a nine-to-five purgatory where people hate their jobs. A fully engaged company like

CHG Healthcare is a Theory Y organization. Appalled by the high cost of employee attrition, CHG's leaders accepted their responsibility to help their people be their best and wound up reducing attrition, saving millions of dollars and making the company far more competitive.

"I think that almost all of our employee engagement can be attributed to our efforts to have an engaged, motivated, and satisfied workforce," says Mike Weinholtz, former CEO of CHG Healthcare. "We measure satisfaction as well as engagement, because they run parallel. We know that when we have engaged people, they see more value in the work, feel more appreciated because they're enabled, bring their best selves to work, and do a good job for themselves and the company.

"We have an open, transparent and trustful culture," Weinholtz continues. "The defining, core value of our culture is 'Putting People First.' Every decision that I make with my team has to be held up against that core value. If it doesn't put our people first, it doesn't happen. All of our leaders follow that same core value. Putting people first has helped us achieve high engagement levels and low turnover, and build a workforce of committed, engaged people. That has translated into great financial performance that has allowed us to outcompete everyone else."

This "Putting People First" philosophy has continued with CHG's new CEO, Scott Beck. Beck makes it clear that the company's emphasis on its people is at the core of CHG's success: "Taking care of people, adding meaning and value beyond the job, making it clear that the company is going to be doing work to give back to the world beyond the commercial value we produce—that's how we've undertaken building a company that's great for our employees first." He continues by saying, "CHG is family. We start by asking, 'How do you treat the members of your family or the people who are closest to you?' That's how we treat our employees. They reward us by staying and contributing, and we reward them by helping them achieve what they want to achieve in their lives."[14]

ENGAGEMENT IMPROVES PROFITS

For all the talk about self-actualization and intellectual capital, business is still business. If employee engagement didn't boost profitability, it would be in the dustbin of history. Fortunately, engagement turns out to be a robust tool for improving the bottom line. That, above all else, has made it a hot commodity.

For example, researchers doing work for the UK government found the following correlations to employee engagement:

- Companies with low engagement scores earn an operating income 32.7 percent lower than companies with more engaged employees.
- Similarly, companies with a highly engaged workforce experience a 19.2 percent growth in operating income over a twelve-month period.[15]

There's more. The Corporate Leadership Council studied the engagement level of fifty thousand employees around the world to determine the direct impact on employee performance and retention. Two of their critical findings:

- Engaged companies grow profits as much as 300 percent faster than their competitors.
- Highly engaged employees are 87 percent less likely to leave the organization.[16]

According to HR consulting firm Towers Perrin, 66 percent of highly engaged employees reported that they had no plans to leave their company, and only 3 percent were actively looking for new jobs. Among disengaged employees, only 12 percent had no plans to leave, and 32 percent were sending out resumes.[17] Meanwhile, McLean & Company found in its research that a disengaged employee costs an organization approximately $3,400 for every $10,000 in annual salary.[18]

More? Sure:

- Organizations with engaged employees get seven times greater five-year shareholder return than those with less engaged employees.[19]
- Engaged companies increase their profits at a rate as much as 300 percent faster than non-engaged companies.[20]

These statistics all paint a similar picture: The connection between engagement and profitability is not something we've created out of thin air to support our own beliefs. The data add additional credibility to what we've found through our 30 million survey responses, which is:

Employee engagement substantially improves organizations' revenue, profitability, open market value, employee retention, and customer satisfaction.

IT'S AN ENGAGED WORLD

As the reams of pro-engagement research have piled up, business and government are catching on. Apart from anecdotal accounts of increased media coverage, a look at data from Google Trends reveals that engagement is a hot topic. Specifically, searches of the term "employee engagement" increased by 122 percent during the period from 2011 to 2013 versus the period from 2005 to 2007. Data from 2015 to 2018 shows a continued increase, with the number of searches for related terms growing by nearly 25 percent each year. The trend line is striking: a steady, dramatic climb in interest around employee engagement.

But it's not just financial benefits and competitive advantage driving the interest in engagement. Since engagement factors impact corporate value (and thus share price), laws such as Sarbanes-Oxley now require that those factors be measured to a greater degree, particularly in the health-care and financial industries.

Employees not only represent the company; for many customers, they *are* the company. As Robert Haas, CEO of Levi Strauss, says, "We must . . . create an environment where every employee feels like a representative of the firm."[21] For most organizations, employees not only represent the brand, they *are* the brand. They're on the front lines. They interact directly with the customer and the product. That's why the Employee Experience (EX) dictates the Customer Experience (CX). Or, as we say, EX = CX.

Retention has also become more challenging. Today's workers have more choices of where and how to work, and technology has made pay and benefits more transparent. What's more, 91 percent of Millennials will remain at a job for fewer than three years.[22] With economic conditions slowly improving, the supply–demand equation has tilted toward job seekers again, especially for those firms that covet younger workers. In this environment, employers who want to retain their best people are paying more attention to more ephemeral qualities like trust, creativity, and meaning—issues that more and more workers are saying matter to them.

Globalization is changing conditions as well. In a global marketplace, people need to build trust and respect with people who may be half a world away, speak a different language, or come from an alien culture. Engagement fosters those kinds of personal connections.

Finally, employers are starting to understand that cultivating employee engagement is a wise, ethical policy. Simply put, it's the right thing to do. Engaged workplaces are less stressed, are more enjoyable to work at, and have lower rates of absenteeism. Engaged organizations treat their people holistically, as human beings rather than cogs in a machine. As a result, their employees make those organizations more prosperous. Engagement is the "killer app" for twenty-first-century competitiveness.

HEARTS, SPIRITS, MINDS, AND HANDS

Culture and the employee experience are critically important for online retailer Zappos.com, a business renowned for its exemplary customer experience. It's so vital that a new Zappos hire be comfortable with the company's culture that Zappos maintains a policy of paying disaffected new hires $2,000 if they choose to leave the company after completing their four-week introductory training period.[23]

Of course, Zappos seems to have made that policy moot. CEO Tony Hsieh has engaged his entire workforce by hiring a full-time life coach and relocating the company to Las Vegas, spending $350 million to create a Zappos neighborhood called the Downtown Project. The idea: to give employees fun, affordable, stimulating places to live and socialize.[24] And let's not forget about Amazon, the company that purchased Zappos in 2009, which also got into the act by offering its associates—full-time and part-time—up to $5,000 if they choose to quit.[25] Amazon and Zappos both have understood the power of engagement and the importance of having team members who *choose* to be a part of the organization.

Engagement doesn't work wonders only in business. Consider the Netherlands, a country that lies mostly below sea level. In 1953, this nation experienced a massive flood that killed 1,836 people. Afterward, the entire nation banded together to launch an unprecedented program of designing and constructing flood-control systems. The engineering efforts took decades and are built to withstand a one-in-10,000-years storm—the strictest standard in the world.

But the Dutch didn't work wonders just with engineering. They also managed to engage an entire country around the effort. As journalist Sarah Goodyear writes in the *Atlantic*:

> For the Dutch, coordination is a simple necessity. It's only coordination that has enabled the Dutch to hold their ground against a rising tide for the last few centuries—and to market their expertise around the world. Yes, they have built dikes and levees and barriers. Yes, they have drained inland seas and reinforced beaches. They have piloted programs that allow water to flow rather than just trying to push it back, such as the "Room for the River" initiative.
>
> But the Dutch approach is about much more than engineering. It's about governance, openness to new ideas, flexibility, and a willingness to realize that sometimes, when the common good is threatened, stubborn individualism is useless.[26]

The ability for the Dutch to unite in engaging an entire nation in solving a problem is just one example of how engaging hearts and spirits can lead minds and hands to accomplish some pretty amazing things.

We live in a knowledge, information, and creative economy. The old reality, in which we bring in workers, pay them, and give them benefits, and they shut up, do their jobs, and go home, is becoming obsolete. The new reality will leverage employees' hearts, spirits, minds, and hands. To be effective, leaders must bridge the gap between the old workplace built on authority and the new one built on engagement.

Leaders who want their organizations to thrive in this new world must continue to focus on factors like employee satisfaction—the essential precursor of engagement—but must also refocus their organizations and themselves on creating fertile soil where engagement culture can grow and employees can choose to become fully engaged.

Now, let's dig more deeply into what makes engagement work.

RECAP

- Employee engagement is an emotional state where we feel passionate, energetic, and committed toward our work. In turn, we fully invest our best selves—our hearts, spirits, minds, and hands—in the work we do.
- Engagement is not the same as employee satisfaction, though satisfaction is necessary for engagement to occur.
- Both the organization and the employee share the responsibility for engagement equally.
- The factors that produce happiness and those that produce engagement are often incongruent.
- EX = CX
- Engagement yields tangible bottom-line benefits, such as increased profitability and reduced turnover.

CHAPTER TWO
The Power of Engagement:
How and Why Engagement Works

"The real damper on employee engagement is the soggy, cold blanket of centralized authority. In most companies, power cascades downwards from the CEO. Not only are employees disenfranchised from most policy decisions, they lack even the power to rebel against egocentric and tyrannical supervisors."
—*Gary Hamel, author of* What Matters Now

RECENTLY, A FRIEND DESCRIBED his adventure at a Four Seasons location. He had requested a wake-up call so he could make an important meeting that had been on his calendar for months. At the Four Seasons, wake-up calls are not automated; a staff member calls your room. But in this case, no one made the call. The guest was late for his meeting—a customer service nightmare and an easy target for throwing one's colleagues under the bus in a blame game.

How would most employees and hotel chains respond? A free orange juice, perhaps? Not at the Four Seasons. The transgression required a more personal apology. The guest was delivered a gourmet breakfast that morning by the staff, and a gift basket awaited him on his return, along with a hand-written note of apology from the manager. It was clear that the hotel staff felt terrible about the oversight, owned up to the lapse, and salvaged the guest's experience. It was also clear that those directly responsible for the mishap took ownership for the problem. In their minds, it was *their* concern, not just the hotel's problem. What started out as a negative customer experience quickly turned positive. Needless to say, that wasn't the last time this guest stayed at a Four Seasons property.

A simple example of how individual engagement can have a big impact comes from a U.S.-based warehouse grocery chain. We were consulting with them in one of their huge distribution centers, where we interviewed a number of their employees. One of these employees, we learned, had been loading pallets and driving forklifts on the night shift for more than ten years. Despite the repetitive nature of his work, it quickly became apparent that he was in it for more than just a paycheck, and others knew it. He went beyond his job description—which, if we were to boil it down, amounted to moving boxes from one shelf to another, day after day after day. Yet this individual was so engaged in his role that he enlarged the scope of his responsibilities to go beyond that of soup-can mover.

This amazing employee showed us that he had created a manual listing all the things he did to perform his job better. From driving techniques to forklift maintenance to box stacking, this guy was a fork operator extraordinaire. This gentleman even explained to us how he calculated his efficiency so he could have the least wasted effort possible. He was the most productive employee in the distribution facility and had become a mentor to a lot of the younger employees. Remember, this was a *warehouse* job—picking items off high shelves, moving pallets, work that many people would find mind numbing. But not this guy. Even more extraordinary? Nobody had asked him to do anything but drive the forklift. He did everything else by his own initiative.

That's the power of engagement. Again and again, we've seen people in jobs that would be considered mundane, repetitive, even unpleasant, and watched them turn those jobs into meaningful, fulfilling occupations because they chose to be engaged in what they were doing. *Choice.* That's what makes engagement the secret sauce behind a productive, inspired workforce and a more profitable enterprise: Employees choose to become engaged, and they can do it even if their employer doesn't create an environment that's conducive to engagement.

Some time ago, I was on a plane when I noticed I was sitting next to a man wearing a shirt that read "I'm Building the World's Biggest Indoor Coliseum." Well, who wouldn't ask about that—especially someone trying to learn more about engagement? I did just that, and the man, beaming with pride, said he was working on the Philippine Arena in Ciudad de Victoria, the Philippines. But what was his job? Architect, perhaps? Designer of the audio entertainment system? Surely his role was something glamorous, to be so proud to sport the T-shirt.

No. He screwed on the switch plates for all the light switches in the huge structure. It's hard to think of a more routine job than spending eight hours a day installing switch plates in every room in a structure designed to seat more than fifty thousand people. Yet this guy had found meaning in being part of something bigger—albeit a small part—that was doing something unprecedented. He had chosen to become engaged in a job through which others might have sleepwalked.

We don't know if the Four Seasons, the warehouse grocery chain, and the contractor working on the Philippine Arena did something that encouraged these people to become engaged, or if they simply did it on their own. The point is, whether you run a company or manage a team, you don't have to wait for people to engage on their own, "accidentally." You can consciously create an environment that unlocks the power of engagement that already exists within individuals and rewards them when engaged. As you've already seen, one employee can change the path of a company. Imagine what ten thousand engaged employees can do.

Of course, before you can begin building that sort of environment, you must have an understanding of what engagement really is, how it works, and why it works. So, let's have a look at the man behind the curtain.

PERKS ON THE PATH TO ENGAGEMENT

To discuss why engagement is such a powerful force, we need to look first at companies that do it well. As you know, each year *Fortune* publishes its "100 Best Companies to Work For" list. Our research teams looked at the companies on these lists and asked ourselves what made these companies different. After some late-night number crunching and a few heated disagreements, we identified just a few of the factors that set some of these companies apart from the rest:

- **Promoting fitness and wellness.** Google and CHG set the tone for corporate wellness by offering fully equipped fitness facilities and subsidized gym memberships to their employees. Healthy employees are happy employees, right?

- **Telecommuting.** Many of the top companies offer telecommuting as an option to employees. According to Telework Research Network, a telecommuting resource website, 72 percent of employees surveyed say flexible work arrangements would cause them to choose one job over another. And allowing employees to work in their jammies is also good for the bottom line. "Even half-time telecommuting can save a company $10,000 per employee per year," says Telework cofounder Kate Lister.

- **Paid sabbaticals.** Paid sabbaticals don't just give employees the time and space to recharge their batteries. They also give them the freedom to cultivate concepts, ideas, and skills that can become added value when they return to the workplace. Boston Consulting Group even goes so far as to manage its employees' workweeks, offering sabbaticals or short respites at the best possible moment.

- **Creative bonuses.** Have you ever considered offering every employee in your company a $100,000 check if the company meets a lofty five-year goal? Hilcorp Energy Company did.[27] Do you think its employees were incentivized to meet that goal? You bet they were. In 2015, Hilcorp doubled its production . . . and paid out nearly 1,400 bonuses.

- **Support for family and loved ones.** An overwhelming majority of these companies offer health-care benefits for all of their employees' spouses and families. They also offer unique programs that involve not only the employee, but those important to the employee as well.

The intent here isn't to draw up a list of the "Five Most Important Perks That Will Engage Your Employees." It's to reiterate an important point about perks. In talking about some of these factors common to many of the best companies, it may seem like a contradiction. Aren't those all just very cushy perks, extras that lead to satisfaction but not engagement? On the surface, yes. But look deeper and it becomes clear that each is as much a harbinger of an engaged culture as it is an outcome of that culture. It's not the perk that leads to engagement; that's a contributor to satisfaction. It's what the perk *represents*.

Consider a simple example to illustrate this point. It's completely unrelated, but stay with us.

Let's suppose you find a person attractive. After several weeks, you finally get up the nerve to ask this person out to dinner and a concert. You say, "I think you're cute and have a great sense of humor, and I would like to get to know you better. Would you consider joining me this Friday night for dinner and the [insert your favorite artist here] concert?" (Okay, not the smoothest line, but I've thankfully been out of the dating scene for a while.) You might stand a decent chance of getting a yes.

Now, consider this alternative conversation and the likely result: "I find you attractive. I'll pay you $350 if you'll go out with me on Friday evening." Ouch! Not only is this approach more likely to get you a slap in the face than a date, you had also better hope the person you are asking out isn't an undercover police officer. You may find yourself in handcuffs with some serious explaining to do. At the very least, you sound desperate, and the object of your affection is likely to be deeply insulted.

It's a bit of a stretch, but you get the point. While both scenarios may end with the inviter spending $350 on the invitee, the first implies a relationship in which the invitee feels valued. The second scenario creates a quid-pro-quo expectation: "I'm forking out money, so you owe me."

Perks are important, but they are often misused to create a transactional, this-for-that relationship. At the very least, they are often perceived that way. It's important to focus on what perks really represent. Health and wellness extras are typical of organizations where employees are encouraged to be their best and reach their full potential. Telecommuting and sabbaticals not only encourage a "whole person" view of the employee, they also promote autonomy, a key driver of engagement. Bonuses may be transactional, but they are also signals of respect and appreciation. Showing that a company understands and appreciates an employee's home life is more likely than ever before to lead to an open, trusting, engaged culture.

Perks don't unlock power; they create implicit and explicit contracts. If an employee feels that she is tied to the organization because of certain perks, she will feel that some of her choices are being taken away. If she feels that the perk is transactional, and is there only as a carrot, she will not appreciate the perk. She may, in fact, see it as coercive. It's critical to recognize, then:

> Perks are important, but it's what they represent that engages an employee, not the perks themselves.

What the most desirable workplaces are really doing—in some cases, probably without being aware of it—is creating employee experiences that meet the requirements of something called *Self-Determination Theory*, which says that human beings will usually choose to be our best if put in a setting that evokes our best.

According to Self-Determination Theory, most people are naturally proactive and naturally inclined toward growth and self-actualization . . . if their innate needs for autonomy, competence, and relatedness are met. Self-Determination Theory is universal. In other words, the power is within most individuals. The surroundings aren't critical; you can have autonomy, extra effort, and emotional engagement on an assembly line where workers are empowered to stop production if they see a safety or quality problem.

Egghead Alert!

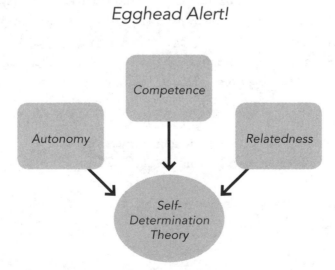

Self-Determination Theory, which was introduced in the 1980s,[28] is the study of the motivation behind the choices that people make without outside influence. The theory says that if you meet three basic human needs—*autonomy* (the need to be in charge of one's life and choices), *competence* (the ability to excel and experience mastery of a task or skill), and *relatedness* (the desire to connect with and care for other people)—you activate inherently positive emotions. These three components allow us to best determine our own destiny, rather than feeling we have little control over our path. Those emotions translate into discretionary effort and self-motivation—the qualities that lead to engagement.

The ultimate objective is to create an environment that can unlock that power, and individuals will choose to be engaged. Successful organizations enact policies and create ecosystems that meet those deep-seated human needs for autonomy, competence, and relatedness. Organizations that fail to meet those needs—or worse, pretend they don't exist—risk creating a phenomenon called *reactive autonomy*. That's when people still have a powerful drive to choose their own path, but since the company won't allow them to do so, they choose what's best for themselves, often to spite the company that (in their minds) is disrespecting their needs. It's what we refer to around our office as the "to heck with you" phenomenon.

HOW WE KNOW ALL THIS

If you said that engagement is what companies wish they meant when their HR departments rolled out lame employee satisfaction programs with cheap T-shirts and mouse pads and slogans like "We're All Part of the Same Family," you win the prize. How do we know that? Because for the past decade, we have had a team of researchers analyzing more than 30 million survey responses from employees of for-profit corporations, not-for-profit organizations, and government agencies all over the world.

Using painstakingly designed surveys and analysis, we've developed a massive benchmark database of employee responses to engagement-centric questions. The surveys we design and implement in organizations are relevant and actionable, based on the areas most critical to employee engagement and the overall success of the organization. Because of this, it's important that the employee is able to respond positively ("Agree" or "Strongly Agree") to each of the questions on the survey. A neutral response, then, would indicate an area of opportunity—the employee simply did not feel strongly enough to agree.

Based on our 2013–2018 survey responses, for example, we discovered that a majority of employees feel they are not fairly compensated for their work (a "satisfaction" element). That's hardly surprisingly, really. Who doesn't feel that they're worth more than they're paid? But other findings raise eyebrows:

- In surveys from 2012 to 2017, nearly 50 percent of employee responses to some sets of questions were "Neutral," or a three on our 1–5 scale. This indicates that in those areas, employees were either reticent to share what they think or had no firm commitment to a response (positive or negative).
- Only 57 percent of employees responded favorably to questions related to growth and development opportunities within their organizations.
- Only 47 percent felt there were opportunities for upward mobility or promotion.
- While 90 percent feel they make a valuable contribution to the organization, 34 percent do not feel their work is valued, and 40 percent do not feel valued as employees. That's troubling.

Perhaps even more troubling was this result. When asked to rate the statement "I am confident that we have the right people in senior leadership positions in this organization" from one to five—with five indicating "Strongly Agree"—nearly one-third of employees responded negatively. Another 24 percent responded neutrally. In other words, more than half of employees surveyed lack confidence in their leaders. And, referring back to the statistics I opened the book with, 34 percent don't even feel like they can raise these concerns without fear of negative consequences.

Ghosts in Aisle One

Our employee surveys have yielded some responses that were hilarious, painful, and downright puzzling. Our favorite answers to the question "What could this company do to become more effective?":

- "Give me the weekends off so that I can go to parties and dances."
- "We used to be a family; now no one trusts anyone anymore. My team members steal jobs, and one impersonated me on the phone."
- "Don't be friends during work hours."
- "It would help if a few managers took a chill pill."
- "I would like to talk to the managers just to see where I am in the company. And let me dye my hair green."
- "Four words: music in the bathrooms. Please. I read it in an email once, and it's true: 'When you hear those kinds of noises coming out of your coworker, you can leave that place and pretend that things are still the same. But they never will be.' Music would help us all at least FEEL like we're alone in there."
- "Everything is all good in the hood."
- "Fire half the staff and replace them with trained monkeys."
- "I would love some little straws for hot chocolate on the third-floor break room."
- "There is a sighting of ghosts in aisle one. It is really freaking us out."

Those results support a harsh conclusion: While many organizations may have read about the power of engagement and pay lip service to it, most misunderstand it and lack the tools or know-how to cultivate it. It's faster and easier—and the optics are better—to create a splashy program with a name like "All Pulling on the Same Oar" (yes, that would send your boat in circles, but bear with me), throw wads of cash at things like on-site pet sitting, and hand out fat bonuses. Over the long term, nothing changes.

If leaders had a better grasp of the harm that disengaged employees can do to an organization, they might approach things differently. Hallmarks of disengaged organizations include lack of support, lowered performance, inability to change, employee attrition, decreased quality and output, and employee burnout.

THE MOUNT EREBUS DISASTER

Most of all, disengaged employees simply don't care. They don't turn off lights. They don't back up data. It's that passive (or even active) sabotage we talked about earlier. They don't do more than the minimum. That can have catastrophic consequences. An extreme example is the Mount Erebus disaster—the 1979 crash in which an Air New Zealand DC-10 flew into the side of Mount Erebus on Ross Island in Antarctica, killing all 257 people on board.

An investigation concluded that the root cause of the crash was that the people at Air New Zealand who laid out the flight plan for the sightseeing trip had altered a computer file so that the flight's "waypoint" (a coordinate that the pilots would check en route to ensure that they were on course) would match up with an electronic navigational beacon. The change would lead the aircraft from a clear route over the wide McMurdo Sound to a flight path dangerously close to Mount Erebus . . . but no one informed the pilots of the change. As a result, in snowy whiteout conditions that made it difficult for them to gauge their altitude, the pilots lost track of their location and flew directly into the side of the mountain at 1,500 feet, killing everyone aboard instantly.

Why didn't anyone at Air New Zealand bother to inform the crew of Flight 901 that their navigation information had changed? It's impossible to know for sure, but the evidence points to a simple answer: Nobody cared, at least not enough to act. And to make it even worse, at multiple points in the process someone should (and could) have stopped the disastrous outcome. While we don't have evidence to support our claim, we can't help but wonder if there weren't people who would have spoken up had they felt safe to do so.

Engagement is about emotion, and if you care about your work, you remember important things and anticipate potential outcomes. You both feel and create a sense of urgency. You act. No one did. Nobody was engaged enough to make the extra effort to give the crew its new course information, a simple bit of discretionary effort that would have saved 257 lives.[29]

ENGAGEMENT (AND DISENGAGEMENT) IS INFECTIOUS

The great philosopher Calvin (not John Calvin, but the kid from the *Calvin & Hobbes* comic) once said, "Nothing helps a bad mood like spreading it around." Ever work in a place with somebody who constantly complained and moaned, who had a talent for sucking the air out of the room? Sure, we all have. What you probably noticed is that disengagement spreads like the common cold. One person starts saying nasty things about management, and before you know it half the people in the office think the boss is an idiot.

Several years ago, I worked with the senior officers of a government institution. In facilitating conversations with a group of 120 key people, our team learned some appalling things. Most notable was the fact that it was, according to the people in the room, difficult to fire people because they were public employees. Instead, troublesome staffers were "transferred to the boneyard"—sent to remote departments where they wouldn't interface with the public and couldn't impact other people's attitudes or work.

Nice theory. Too bad it's bogus. Engagement and disengagement are even more contagious than a virus. If you have someone with the flu, you can isolate them and prevent it from spreading. But how do you isolate a worker who's infected with disengagement? You can't. You either help them engage or fire them. In this agency, they did neither. As a result, the people who had been sent to the boneyard continued to send email, talk to coworkers, and negatively impact their colleagues with their cynicism, criticism, and apathy.

Some organizations, however, are acutely aware of the infectious nature of disengagement and enact policies designed to prevent it from inflicting damage. One such organization is the UMC Health System, the primary teaching hospital for the Texas Tech University Health Sciences Center in Lubbock, Texas. UMC attaches a great deal of importance to its leaders' ability to maximize engagement. When it is noted that a particular department or leader has low scores on the annual survey, they receive extensive support—up to a point.

"Employee satisfaction and well-being have been extremely important to the growth of UMC's culture over the past ten to twelve years, and it's landed us in the top ten percent of all hospitals in the nation for patient satisfaction," says UMC Chief Executive Officer Mark Funderburk. "It is also a significantly weighted measure of a leader's performance at UMC. Leaders with lower than expected satisfaction scores are offered additional education and support from leaders with higher scores. The goal is to help them improve.

"It's more art than science," Funderburk continues. "The art part comes in looking at the department. What are they up against? Did they deal with a layoff, a rate increase, or an influx of new physicians? Is there something that accounts for a drop in engagement in a particular year? If someone is doing well in other aspects of an evaluation, we'll be patient. We'll wait to see if a trend exists. Eventually, if the leader is not able to improve, we'll make a move toward finding a new leader in an aggressive and timely fashion."

MYTH BUSTING

With more organizations becoming aware of the importance of engagement, the media coverage of the topic has become widespread and more scholarly. This, however, can be a double-edged sword. In a *New York Times* opinion piece titled "Do Happy People Work Harder?" Harvard professor Teresa Amabile and researcher Steven Kramer shared some of the results from a project in which they collected more than twelve thousand diary entries from 238 employees at seven companies.

They found that about a third of the time, the workers were unhappy, unmotivated, or both—but that on the days that they were happy, they were more apt to have new ideas. Amabile and Kramer write:

> Managers can help ensure that people are happily engaged at work. Doing so isn't expensive. Workers' well-being depends, in large part, on managers' ability and willingness to facilitate workers' accomplishments—by removing obstacles, providing help, and acknowledging strong effort. A clear pattern emerged when we analyzed the 64,000 specific workday events reported in the diaries: Of all the events that engage people at work, the single most important—by far—is simply making progress in meaningful work.[30]

Articles like this create a compelling and data-driven case for the importance of engagement and the role that engagement plays in performance. However, they can also confuse readers who don't understand the concept of engagement. For many, words and phrases like *happiness* and *work harder* create confusion and fuel misconceptions about what engagement is and isn't. Is engagement about feeling happy? Is it about simply getting work done? Not quite. So, before we get under engagement's hood and dirty our fingernails in its inner workings, let's take a look at some of the myths surrounding engagement and the facts behind them:

Myth: Engagement is about people working harder.

Fact: Engagement is about people being inspired and working smarter, more creatively, more mindfully, and more efficiently. Although for some this may mean working longer hours, the true result of engagement is greater overall contribution.

Myth: Engagement is about happy employees.

Fact: Happiness doesn't equal engagement. Happiness and satisfaction are transitory because they're dependent on external factors: how much you're paid, if you like the people on your team, and so on. Engagement is about feeling that your work matters, makes a difference, and is respected. Those feelings persist even if you're having a rotten day or get a nastygram in your inbox from a miffed customer.

Myth: Engagement is about extracting more from workers.

Fact: Employees are not a strip mine. Engagement is about empowering and inspiring employees to give more of their own accord. It's a departure from the traditional command-and-control structure, which is why so many managers find it difficult to implement.

Myth: The same factors or experiences will engage everyone.

Fact: People (and organizations) engage differently based on the things that matter to them. That's why it's a fool's errand to create engagement programs based on specific incentives or activities. The best engagement initiatives create the conditions in which employees can find and express what matters to them.

Example: Our engagement teams worked with two restaurant companies, one a 400-location fast-food chain and the other a 110-location upscale chain. The fast-food employees turned out to be most engaged by flexible schedules (which allowed them to meet family, school, and social obligations), the ability to associate with friends while on the job, and getting 50 percent off lunches (a perk that cost about 78 cents per week per employee). The upscale restaurant workers were engaged by completely different factors: opportunities for growth, development, and advancement; the trust of their managers; and satisfied customers.

Myth: Everyone wants to engage.

Fact: Most healthy human beings *want* and *need* to engage. However, some people will always refuse. Engagement is a choice, and in every organization there will always be people who choose to remain disengaged. Regardless of the environment created by the organization, some will simply choose not to engage.

Myth: Disengaged employees will leave.

Fact: Many disengaged employees will stay but experience *burnout*. Burnout is a prime symptom of disengagement. It's not just working hard and feeling overwhelmed. It's where you actually feel detached and depersonalized from your work. You're on automatic pilot most of the time, emotionally spent, and your anxiety level is off the charts. Burnout is debilitating. You're like an engine whose tachometer needle is constantly redlining. Eventually, you overheat and blow a gasket.

Burned-out employees may sleepwalk through their duties, decline to share information (they're responsible for most of the "Neutral" answers on our surveys), and passively sabotage everyone around them.

Keep in mind that true engagement does *not* lead to burnout. You can be exhausted from putting in great effort on a project, but if you're engaged you won't lose your enthusiasm for your work. Once you're rested, you'll be right back on the job.

Myth: Engagement makes leaders obsolete.

Fact: Engagement requires less management but *more* leadership. Engaged employees are self-starters who don't need coercion or managers looking over their shoulders in order to produce excellent work. In an engaged workplace, effective leaders are custodians of the shared narrative and sense of purpose that drives engagement.

Myth: You can always engage a workforce with a compelling end goal.

Fact: Compelling goals are critical to engagement, but what you think of as a compelling goal may not be my idea of a compelling goal. The organization's stated goal could be to increase revenue by 20 percent, but that's not likely to inspire the individual employee. An engaged organization is one that makes it possible for individuals to pursue the goals that are uniquely important to them *in the context* of the organization's larger goal.

So, what does engagement look like? It involves bringing hearts, spirits, hands, and minds to one's work. It looks something like this:

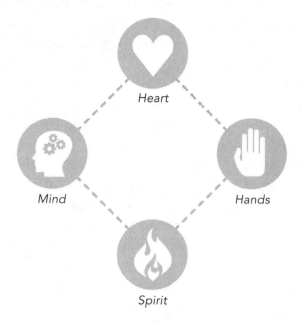

The *heart* is about meaning, passion, and fulfillment, even finding joy in what you do. *Spirit* is about attitude, energy, and excitement. It's something that can be felt when you walk into a room or work with a highly engaged team. Heart and spirit imply that we must *feel* the work that we do. Unfortunately, that's where most engagement models stop, and that's a mistake. There is more to engagement than just "feeling something."

The *mind* is about intellect, interests, curiosity, and creativity. The *hands* are about effort, productivity, and self-determination—using your skills and sweat to produce something of value. Mind and hands imply that we must *do* something. In order to be fully engaged, we must *act*. To put it simply:

HEART AND SPIRIT = FEELING

MIND AND HANDS = ACTION

Don't believe that factors like heart matter in an organization? Ask David Smyth, coach of the NCAA multi-championship-winning Brigham Young University men's rugby team, about the importance of heart. It's key to his ability to take gifted athletes with little or no rugby experience and turn them into dominant squads.

"When students come for tryouts, we can see the desire to be a high performer," he says. "Even if he doesn't have a lot of experience, we will put in the effort and time to help that young man become a player. You can tell in two weeks if a young man has the heart to get himself to a point where he can be a positive contributor to what we're trying to do." Many of Smyth's athletes may have had little or no rugby experience prior to their first semester at BYU. Yet they have become a recognized force in rugby. Smyth attributes much of this to heart.

"The player who has heart won't quit and won't accept second best," Smyth continues. "He's someone who is continually looking for pride in his performance. He's someone who's looking at himself after the effort is made and saying, 'Should I expect more?' Heart is an inherent desire to do the best you can. You can help nurture that in a player, but you can't transplant it." While there are likely many factors contributing to their success, with heart being near the top of the list, it's clear that it's working.

Engagement requires that we bring both our emotions and our actions to the table—our hearts, spirits, minds, and hands. To be engaged, we must feel something and take action on what we feel. Take one away and you don't have engagement. You can think of feelings and action as two oars in a rowboat. They are complementary opposites. Both are necessary. Row with just one and you'll travel in circles. You might work up a sweat and feel as though you should be getting somewhere, but you won't. Pull on both at the same time and you'll make progress.

YOU CAN'T HAVE ONE WITHOUT THE OTHER

This kind of wasted effort is inherent in a majority of so-called engagement initiatives within organizations. While well intentioned, most of these initiatives row with only one oar. Some target the heart and spirit, while others involve the mind and hands, but few encompass them all simultaneously. The results? A lot of energy spent, little distance traveled.

Sometimes leaders mistakenly feel that if their people row hard enough with one oar, the other will come along with it. Our team worked with a large technology company that had just acquired its formidable competitor. To the employees of both companies, the acquiring company effectively communicated the steps of the acquisition, the reason behind it, and the actions that would need to take place over the subsequent months. Employees clearly understood that their minds and hands would be required to make the integration process a smooth one, and they knew that it was financially beneficial for the company overall. On paper, everything looked solid. Yet the integration was failing miserably.

It quickly became apparent that, while minds and hands were active, hearts and spirits were stagnant. When we surveyed employees, we learned that although they were *acting*, they were not *feeling*. In short, the company had failed to gain buy-in. Though the process was very solid and clearly outlined, the acquiring company had failed to see that nearly a quarter of its people felt that the integration process would most likely result in the loss of their jobs (although this proved not to be the case).

Even more damaging was the feeling we found in employees of the acquiring company that the company they had purchased was built around a "culture of cutthroats." Talk about toxic. They had made little effort to bring hearts and spirits along for the ride, and so the acquisition was doomed from the start.

On the other extreme, we have worked with a number of organizations that worked hard to attend to hearts and spirits but failed to engage minds and hands. These companies made great strides in energizing the workforce and even instilling a sense of passion. But while the employees felt great, they weren't required to act. These companies invested a great deal of effort and money in creating what they thought was an engaged culture when, in reality, it was only a company that felt good about itself.

When you involve hearts, spirits, minds, and hands, your organization is both feeling and acting. You have an engaged workforce that produces its own bottom-line improvements in retention, quality, customer service, and profitability. You don't have to design those outcomes into engagement; they are inevitable.

Zookeepers are an interesting example. Researchers studying zoo-keepers found that they are uniquely engaged in their work (something any four-year-old could have told you). The most interesting part of the research centered on why the zookeepers were so engaged in what is by any standard a demanding occupation. The researchers discovered that while much of the work is decidedly unglamorous (cleaning up animal poop) and some is downright dangerous (working with injured or agitated animals), the zookeepers also felt their work had a greater purpose: caring for the welfare of amazing creatures that were often endangered. So, while not every aspect of their jobs was engaging, their jobs as a whole engaged them deeply. They not only brought their hearts and spirits to their work, they did something significant with their minds and hands because of their feelings. They created their own engagement.[31]

THE THREE TYPES OF ENGAGEMENT

As these examples show, engagement is much more than a matter of replacing the traditional management stick with a warm-and-fuzzy carrot (and anyway, fuzzy carrots are disgusting). But while it does feature as much art as it does science, there is solid behavioral science behind engagement. Understanding this science gives well-led organizations an advantage in developing engaged workforces.

Organizational psychologists and personality theory have broken down engagement into three discrete types:

1. **Trait engagement.** Trait engagement is based on inherent qualities (they are born with these or develop them over time) that cause some people to engage in almost any environment. That's a rare quality; a small percentage of the population is "wired to engage" in this way.

People who engage based on inherent traits tend to be positive forces in the workplace. They're fully present no matter what job, industry, or organizational environment they're in. They'll often become your superstars, your Employees of the Year.

It's hard to predict who will be a trait-engaged employee, but they do have some predictable characteristics:

- optimism
- conscientiousness
- positive affect (those who are naturally energetic, confident, positive, and can make the most of nearly any situation)
- initiative
- autotelic personality (when presented with a problem, they see it as a challenge rather than as a debilitating event)

Because trait engagement is unpredictable, hiring for it isn't easy. Apart from looking for the qualities in the above list, it's also smart to determine the traits that your organization appeals to. Are you a place for edgy, creative types with green hair and body piercings? Are you all about sustainability and wellness? Or is your culture built on order, precision, and efficiency? A clear understanding of your organization's character can make it easier to recruit people whose personal character is a good match.

You can't do a blood scan to determine if someone's creative DNA or emotional intelligence makes them a good match for your company (though wouldn't it be cool if you could?). However, you can cultivate conditions that optimize trait engagement and improve your odds of attracting and keeping people who are disposed to engage in what they do.

In conducting research for our 2017 book, *The Employee Experience*, my co-author, Matthew Wride, and I discovered an interesting phenomenon related to employee engagement. In most cases, the conditions (work environment, compensation, cleanliness, noise, etc.) in which an individual worked had less impact on an individual's engagement than did whether her expectations of that environment were aligned with what she experienced. One of the key factors in this was whether the employee's perception of the company's employer brand (what the company claimed or suggested would be the experience of the employee) aligned with the actual experience once the employee began work. Those for whom the work conditions and environment aligned with what the employee experienced tended to be highly engaged. Those whose anticipated experience and on-the-job experience were misaligned (their experience turned out to be different than promised or anticipated) quickly disengaged. This was the primary cause of attrition for employees during the first year of employment. Organizations that succeeded in retaining employees past the one-year mark were those that carefully aligned the work with those employees most likely to engage in that environment.

2. **State engagement.** Unlike trait engagement, state engagement ebbs and flows, varying over time. People who are state-engaged put themselves into an emotional state based on the job they're doing, and that state changes.

   In our survey database, state engagement is reflected in survey items like "I find enjoyment in the work I perform" and "Most days I look forward to coming to work." The levels of qualities like satisfaction, involvement, commitment, and empowerment may go up and down over time, but what matters is the employee's *engagement trajectory*, the big-picture direction of their engagement. In a healthy, engaged organization, employees will find ways to create engagement around those most critical parts of their jobs. It's their long-term performance—not any short-term ups and downs—that matters, just as a baseball player's periodic slumps during the season are unimportant as long as he winds up batting .300.

   Think of it this way. Most of us have been in positions (whether at work or outside) where we would say we've been highly engaged in what we do. Does that mean that if we were to strap an "engagement-ometer" on your wrist (they don't exist today, but who knows . . .) that 100 percent of the time it would read "fully engaged"? Or would there be times—perhaps when you fail to save the document you've been working on for the past four hours, or the supervisor informs you that you'll need to work on the weekend—that engagement levels slip for a short period? State engagement varies. It's the long-term engagement outlook that matters.

   State engagement also differs from trait engagement in that it's often within the organization's control, or at least its influence. You can create an environment where employees can love their work and enjoy coming to the workplace, even if their engagement needle isn't pegged 24/7/365.

3. **Behavioral engagement.** This final type of engagement is all about how people behave on the job and what they do. It's where the "act" components of engagement—hands and minds—come into play. Are people

fully present in what they're doing? Are they using all their senses? Are they bringing their full selves to the role or are they on automatic pilot?

Behaviorally engaged employees are also *psychologically present* on the job (hearts and spirits). Not only are they acting, they are feeling as well. They express their thoughts and feelings, question existing assumptions and conventional wisdom, develop innovative ideas, and are attentive, connected, integrated, and focused.[32] They bring their full selves to their roles no matter what role they are filling on a given day.

One important indicator of behavioral engagement is that it's instinctive. Think about a great Formula One race-car driver like Fernando Alonso. When he gets behind the wheel, he's not thinking about steering, braking, and the other mechanics of a race. If he's fully present and using all his senses, muscle memory and thousands of hours of repetition will take care of the mechanics of guiding a Ferrari around a racecourse at 200 mph. He can focus on the subtle nuances of driving that separate the good drivers from the great ones. He can act without conscious thought and produce excellence.

Behaviorally engaged employees, like great athletes, don't need to think through each stage of their jobs. They are fully present; bring their heads, hands, and hearts to their work; and leave the rest to training, education, and skill.

As with state engagement, organizations can influence behavioral engagement by doing things like reducing workplace distractions or regularly matching employees with new challenges that require them to be fully present.

ENGAGEMENT MIGRATION

Another critical thing to know about state and behavioral engagement is that employees often migrate to different levels of engagement over time. Our research has established that employees fall into one of four categories:

- Fully Engaged
- Key Contributors
- Opportunity Group
- Fully Disengaged

Through assessments such as surveys, we are able to categorize employees within one of these four groups. But when we come back a year later for another round of surveys, we notice that some have moved into a different engagement group compared to the previous year. Some go from being in the Opportunity Group to being Key Contributors, while others go from being Key Contributors to Fully Disengaged . . . or leave the organization.

The Fully Engaged group, we have found, is fairly consistent. People who are fully engaged typically remain so unless circumstances significantly change within the organization. They engage primarily based on their innate traits and the fact that they've found their place in their work and the organization; they and the company are a perfect fit. It generally takes a major negative event or series of events in someone's work experience to force them from full engagement to full disengagement.

Key Contributors, the "strong and steady" performers who make up the largest percentage of any organization, are also quite stable. Given effective leadership, fair policies, clear direction, and the right tools and training, they will continue to perform well. But don't expect that they will automatically join the Fully Engaged. While in the right environment they can, it's not a given that they will. Remember, they must choose to engage.

The heaviest *engagement migration* happens in the Opportunity Group. Their situation is volatile. While they are not fully engaged, they are not fully disengaged, either. They're on the fence. When we ask them if they enjoy their jobs, they'll respond neutrally. There are things they like and things they don't like. They're not really excited, but not ready to leave, either.

As the name suggests, people in the Opportunity Group represent an organization's greatest opportunity for increasing the engagement of its workforce. We've found that they are often an organization's key talent and can be its most productive workers. Discover the factors that keep them on the fence, and change them for the better, and you can not only keep these employees but empower them to migrate toward full engagement.

The X factor here is that by making changes aimed at keeping your Opportunity Group from heading for the exits, you might just increase your all-important trait engagement, too. In other words, you could evolve into an organization that engages your current employees based on traits you didn't even know they had. If you find people whose inherent traits suddenly mesh with your adapting culture, do whatever it takes to keep these employees in the Fully Engaged category. They are potentially important contributors to your future success.

What about the Fully Disengaged? Our humanistic side says, "But we have to help them engage!" Unfortunately, our research shows that these wishes seldom come true. As we track disengaged individuals from one year to the next, we have found that less than 5 percent ever migrate from full disengagement to any of the other engagement categories, regardless of what changes are made to the individual's environment. The bottom line is that (and this is hard to hear) fully disengaged employees rarely engage over the long term.

Now, keep in mind we're not talking about people who have an occasional bad day or don't like certain aspects of the job. We've all been there, and might even be there more often than we'd care to admit. Instead, these are employees who are truly disengaged. Most organizations find that by not helping these individuals move on, they postpone the inevitable, and often with a good deal of damage to both the organization and the disengaged individual. It's generally better to make the tough call now, and move that individual out of the organization, than to postpone the inevitable, risking infecting others throughout the organization (as well as your customers!) in the meantime. And, if you are this individual, it's time to think about moving on. It's highly likely that your disengagement is rubbing off on others, both inside and outside the walls of the workplace.

PUT THE EMPLOYEES IN CHARGE

Given that, with the exception of the Fully Disengaged, employees can (and often do) migrate across the four categories depending on the work environment, how do you bring about all these engagement-friendly changes in a way that doesn't reboot your organization or throw it into chaos? Try turning the process over to your employees.

Relax. Before you panic, hear me out. In the past, management has largely ignored the individual's ownership of engagement. Most organizations approach the subject from a top-down perspective exclusively. The results from employee surveys are often addressed at the top levels of the organization, when it should be the employees who read the results, determine what they mean, and come up with solutions. But instead of a survey being an organizational report card, it's treated as a senior management report card

Well, C-suite, it's not all about you. Why not get your employees involved in creating the solution? We understand that this is a mind shift. The traditional command-and-control structure keeps us placating employees instead of trusting them to solve problems. But this is in the best spirit of self-determination, the psychological theory that underpins engagement.

While you may not be comfortable asking your people to develop specific policies, this isn't about policies. Since different people and organizations will find engagement in different things, we're not in the business of prescribing specific actions. That doesn't work. Instead, creating engagement is about creating the conditions under which it can flourish and then letting people *choose* to engage. Well, who better to create those conditions than the people who will work in them?

There are precedents for this. For example, when a San Diego advertising technology company called Zeeto Media wanted to renovate its twelve thousand-square-foot HQ, CEO Stephan Goss put the employees in the driver's seat. With little involvement from architects (all architectural drawings had to be okayed by a licensed architect), staffers revamped the space in the mold of a hip office in San Francisco's South of Market (SoMa) district. They ripped out cubicles, turned carpeted floors into gleaming concrete, designed new furnishings, and created a collaborative space that increased productivity. Everyone, from employees to owners, was thrilled.[33]

Many of the organizations we work with create teams of "engagement ambassadors." As the heads of these organizations come to understand that one of the best places to address engagement concerns is through the employees that identify these concerns, they have selected representatives. Their roles are to address engagement issues, possibilities, and concerns at the employee level. These companies generally find that these ambassadors not only have most of the answers but, given the resources and support, can address the majority of the engagement issues. Not to mention, these ambassadors become more even more engaged themselves through the process of creating an engaging environment.

The formula is actually pretty simple:

- **Step 1:** Determine the needs that must be met to increase your levels of state and behavioral engagement (remember, you can't control trait engagement). A comprehensive survey or focus groups are often a good start.
- **Step 2:** Determine the job conditions or aspects of your culture that need to change in order to meet those psychological needs.
- **Step 3:** Create programs that bring about those changes, creating an environment where people can choose to be engaged.
- **Step 4:** Let your people choose to engage based on their personalities, needs, and other unique traits.

See, that wasn't so bad. You're not ceding control of your organization. You're acknowledging that you can't control how or why people engage, because it's not about PlayStations in the break rooms or free yoga classes. You're tilling the soil and planting the seeds of employee engagement, and then letting your employees do the harvesting. Each man or woman will decide how he or she will respond to the new environment—or not respond. That's empowering your people to play a profound role in transforming the organization that forms such a vital part of their lives.

There are many examples of this, but few on the scale of some of the initiatives that have been taking root around the United Kingdom. Faced with massive budget shortfalls, community councils throughout the UK began implementing employee engagement programs to enable them to reduce head count while still operating efficiently and serving their constituents. The County Council of Somerset has done this particularly well, using methods that include:

- Creating a consumer led council to direct the delivery of services.
- Moving away from a command-and-control hierarchy, and having managers take more ownership of decision making and become more empowered.
- Aligning organizational culture with the council's core values.
- Communicating openly and frequently with employees using a variety of tools.

The result? Somerset County trimmed head count by 10 percent in eighteen months, yet employee relations remain positive and public services have improved.[34] A straightforward process with tremendous returns.

BRING THE MAGIC

So far, this may seem like a lot to take in. I've thrown out a lot of theory and statistics. But how do we move from theory to action?

There is a mechanism for turning the employee engagement formula into a reality. These are the Five Keys to Unlock the Power of Engagement: the elements of the organizational ecosystem that our extensive research has shown us are the most powerful for increasing positive emotions, energy, and commitment on the job. They are:

- Meaning
- Autonomy
- Growth
- Impact
- Connection

Yes, line them up and these five keys form the acronym MAGIC. That was a convenient accident from our development process, but our team took it as a sign that we were on the right track. Over and over again, we have watched companies take steps to focus on these five keys, and watched most of their personnel choose to more completely engage their hearts, spirits, minds, and hands in their work.

MAGIC is about changing the growing conditions of engagement, not telling employees how to engage. For that reason, it's a highly successful tool for creating what author Seth Godin calls "linchpins." Those are employees who eagerly take their careers in their hands—who take pride in shaping and improving things.

On an individual level, becoming a linchpin means becoming more in demand. People who are fully engaged have a knack for producing excellence, and this tends to be reflected in their compensation, advancement, and income. In simple terms, if you want to prosper professionally, engage. From the manager's perspective, you want your employees to be linchpins. Perhaps they won't be as easy to manage (at least from the command-and-control perspective), but the outcome will be far better for your organization.

Do you want more engaged people in your organization? Do you think they would help you become more competitive and profitable and make your company a better place to work? Odds are, the answers are yes and yes. Then turn the page and let's dig into the five keys that unlock the power of engagement—MAGIC.

RECAP

- Organizations can create an environment that unlocks the power of engagement that already resides within employees.
- Most organizations misunderstand engagement, leading to ham-handed attempts to impose it.
- Perks are important, but they don't engage.
- Both engagement and disengagement are infectious and can easily spread throughout an organization.
- Engagement requires the involvement of the heart and spirit (feelings) and the mind and hands (action).
- There are three types of engagement: trait (based on innate qualities), state (based on the emotions present in a situation), and behavioral (based on actions and mindful presence).
- People can and do migrate over time from one level of engagement to another.
- Fully disengaged individuals rarely, if ever, become engaged.
- The five keys to engagement are Meaning, Autonomy, Growth, Impact, and Connection—MAGIC.

PART TWO

Keys to Unlocking Engagement

CHAPTER THREE
MEANING

"It is impossible to have a great life unless it is a meaningful life. And it is very difficult to have a meaningful life without meaningful work."
—*Jim Collins*

ON FEBRUARY 10, 2013, a fire broke out in the engine room of the 893-foot Carnival cruise ship *Triumph*, leaving it without power and propulsion—adrift in the Gulf of Mexico 150 miles off the Yucatán Peninsula. During the five days that followed, a dream cruise became a nightmare for the four thousand passengers. Most of the food spoiled, forcing passengers to wait in four-hour lines for stale vegetables. Without its thrusters to counter the action of wind and waves, *Triumph* heeled onto its side with every swell, causing toilets to spill human waste onto floors and into hallways. When tugboats finally towed the crippled liner into port in Mobile, Alabama, some relieved passengers kissed the ground after disembarking.

But it's not the squalor and hardship that make the Carnival *Triumph* story so interesting. It's the actions of her crew. According to accounts from passengers (none of whom would have been blamed for bad-mouthing everything about their experience), the crew was "amazing." One passenger after another praised the crew's professionalism and care. They continually checked on passengers, and handled with aplomb the red biohazard bags that passengers had to use in lieu of toilets. They made an unbearable situation more bearable. As one passenger remarked, "They did the dirtiest work, doing things I wouldn't do."

For their part, the crew members seemed unimpressed with their own gallantry. One crew member said of the crew's heroic work, "It's very simple because we are used to it. That's why we make the best effort for them . . . it's a part of the job."[35]

WHEN WORK MAKES A DIFFERENCE

"Part of the job"? Sorry, not quite. It would have been so easy for the *Triumph*'s crew to say "every man for himself" and leave the passengers to survive while they hoarded food, water, and comforts. On many ships, that's what would have happened.

Contrast this event with the 2012 wreck of the Italian cruise ship *Costa Concordia*. Traveling with more than 4,200 passengers, the ship ran aground in Tuscany, resulting in the deaths of 32 passengers. Rather than alerting authorities on land, the ship's officers and crew insisted that passengers were not in danger, and that the pending partial sinking of the ship was no more than a minor electrical issue. With the officers refusing to report the condition of the sinking vessel, panicked passengers were left to contact the shore on their own. Reports by crew and passengers during the trial of the ship's captain indicated that the captain didn't seem to care if the crew and passengers died.

Yet on the *Triumph*, crew members—many of them poorly paid and exhausted—stepped up to do the extraordinary. Why?

Meaning. Somehow, the Carnival culture or the leadership aboard the *Triumph* herself managed to lend the floating community a sense of mission and purpose that animated the crew. For some reason, those men and women—porters and bartenders, housekeepers and waitresses—felt that their work was about more than serving drinks and cleaning up the messes of a shipload of spoiled, drunken tourists. It was about caring for the welfare of fellow human beings and making their time aboard as relaxing and enjoyable as possible. When things went downhill fast, that care became a deep, selfless protectiveness—the perception that the passengers were their charges, their responsibility, and that it was each crew member's job to do whatever it took to keep them safe and as comfortable as possible until help arrived.

The work became *meaningful*. Meaning transforms the mundane into the transcendent. The definition of meaning:

Your work has purpose beyond the work itself.

When was the last time you felt that the work you were doing was about more than just making money? Have you *ever* felt that way? When was the last time you took bone-deep pride in knowing that your work made a positive difference in a million people's lives, or even just your own? Have you ever done something that filled you up so completely that you could work nonstop for hours without realizing it, and not even feel tired when you're done?

If you have, then you know what we mean by meaning. Meaning is how we go from job to career to calling. It's when you know that your work makes a difference that you care about personally. Meaning is *why* we work beyond the obvious reason of getting a paycheck. It's also critical because it's the factor that sustains us during times of difficulty, stress, or challenge. It helps us see past the issues and focus on the reasons we're working in the first place. It's where the heart really kicks in.

So many things may create meaning for an employee or an individual. This list contains only a tiny fraction of them:

- mentoring younger employees
- earning enough money to pay for their kids to be the first in their family to attend college
- helping create products that clean the environment
- preventing crime or abuse
- improving people's health
- giving people a voice
- assembling an awesome product
- designing beautiful things
- keeping people safe

Take commercial airline pilots, for instance. They work long hours, sometimes flying as many as sixteen hours in a day. The work is complex and demanding. Yet most pilots will tell you they still can't believe they get paid for flying. Why? Because the work is meaningful. A heart surgeon has one life in her hands at a given time; a commercial pilot might have as many as three hundred lives depending on him, including his own. There's nothing like being entrusted with the safety of people's lives and families to make you care passionately about what you do.

Engagement is about employees putting forth discretionary effort to improve quality or provide an incredible customer experience. And nothing breeds engagement like a culture that suggests work is deeply, powerfully meaningful.

QUESTIONING WHY

The need for meaning is a fundamentally human one. At some point, everyone questions why they're doing what they're doing. If a leader or an organization is not able to provide a sufficient answer, or if you can't find an answer yourself, work becomes mundane. You detach, becoming disengaged. Abe Akroff illustrates what happens in *The Illuminated Life*:

> Imagine a happy group of morons who are engaged in work. They are carrying bricks in an open field. As soon as they have stacked all the bricks at one end of the field, they proceed to transport them to the opposite end. This continues without stop and every day of the year they are busy doing the same thing. One day one of the morons stops long enough to ask himself what he is doing. He wonders what purpose there is in carrying the bricks. And from that instant on he is not quite as content with his occupation as he had been before.[36]

After a time of searching for meaning and purpose in your work, you are likely to become cynical and skeptical, inflicted with a "chronic, lingering dissatisfaction; an absence of inner peace and a sense of not being in synch with your inner self."[37] A study of social exclusion published in the *Journal of Experimental Social Psychology* provides a telling example. In this study, individuals who were deliberately excluded from their social group suffered an impaired sense of purpose—the ability to connect current activities to future outcomes. This made those individuals less likely to pursue fulfillment in their lives and more likely to perceive their lives as futile.[38]

At the opposite extreme, we have the story of the late Nelson Mandela and his Mercedes-Benz. Back in 1990, when Mandela was released from South Africa's Victor Verster Prison after twenty-seven years behind bars, many in the country saw fit to give their hero a gift. The workers at Mercedes-Benz South Africa's East London plant thought it would be appropriate to give Mandela a custom-built, top-of-the-line 500SE.

Up to that time, the Mercedes plant had been plagued with errors, slow production, and unhappy workers. But when presented with the chance to build a car for their national freedom fighter, the workers were energized. In just four days, working mostly unpaid overtime hours, they built Mandela's red Mercedes by hand, dancing and singing in celebration as they worked. It was an astonishing example of the power of purpose and meaning to instantly transform an organization. The car was presented to Mandela on July 22, 1990.[39]

MEANING AND THE MISSION STATEMENT

Try this experiment: Describe a piece of music without singing or humming it. Even if you have a doctorate in musicology and can use terms like *chromatic scale* and *hemiola* without sounding pretentious or ridiculous, it's nearly impossible to convey what a piece of music is *like* with words alone.

Meaning is the same way. It's a feeling that is unique to each individual, which is why meaning rarely comes from where an organization's leadership thinks it should. That's not to say management doesn't try to transmit meaning to the organization as a whole; on the contrary, that's the purpose of the much-maligned (and most of the time, justifiably so) mission statement. Companies spend months and sometimes years crafting the perfect mission statement that will inspire employees to give their all. Some even hire advertising agencies or consultants to help them massage a few dozen words that will convey the company's soul.

So it's amazing that so many of them are so *bad* at it. Here are some of the most uninspiring mission statements our consultants have run across in our travels:

- "The Company's primary objective is to maximize long-term stock-holder value, while adhering to the laws of the jurisdictions in which it operates and at all times observing the highest ethical standards."[40]

Wow. Did Dean Foods basically just say they plan to make a profit while not breaking the law? I feel more inspired; how about you? But lest you think that was the low-hanging fruit, here are some other gems:

- **Sony Europe:** "Sony is committed to developing a wide range of innovative products and multimedia services that challenge the way consumers access and enjoy digital entertainment. By ensuring synergy between businesses within the organisation, Sony is constantly striving to create exciting new worlds of entertainment that can be experienced on a variety of different products."[41]
- **Volvo:** "By creating value for our customers, we create value for our shareholders. We use our expertise to create transport-related products and services of superior quality, safety, and environmental care for demanding customers in selected segments. We work with energy, passion, and respect for the individual."[42]
- **ExxonMobil:** "We are committed to being the world's premier petroleum and petrochemical company. To that end, we must continuously achieve superior financial and operating results while adhering to the highest standards of business conduct. These unwavering expectations provide the foundation for our commitments to those with whom we interact."[43]

An old saying goes, "You can't bore people into doing business with you." You also can't bore them into being inspired to give you their best work. Yet these mission statements are boring, rambling, cliché-ridden, trite collections of corporate-speak fluff cobbled together by committees. They say nothing. They don't touch the emotions—the heart. They don't communicate a sense of why people should want to come to work every day . . . other than to not be fired.

With employee engagement being such a powerful competitive force, a leader's most important big-picture task may be to create a culture that imbues the work of the organization with meaning and mission. It can do this by being the caretaker of the company narrative—the CEO as Chief

Storytelling Officer: "This is what we do, why we do it, and the impact we hope to have on the world." It can do this by making sure employees always have a clear perspective on what they do—what the work is for, what values it reflects, who it affects and why, and so on. And it can do this by writing a mission statement that actually conveys a mission in a way that human beings care about. Two great examples:

- "Our mission: to inspire and nurture the human spirit—one person, one cup, and one neighborhood at a time."
- "Build the best product, cause no unnecessary harm, use business to inspire, and implement solutions to the environmental crisis."

You've probably got the first one nailed: Starbucks. No matter what you think of their coffee, that statement captures the company's fierce activism as well as the personal nature of connecting with people over coffee. The second is a little tougher. It's the clothing company Patagonia. That phrase perfectly reflects its famously progressive, eco-conscious ethos—it's what you'd expect from a granola-crunchy, "we're a family" corporation that actually *shuts down early* when the surf is up in its Ventura, California, hometown.

WHEN MEANING IS MISSING . . .

When meaning is present, even mundane, repetitive work becomes much more than that. Take the story of medical-device maker Medtronic. CEO Bill George regularly brought patients in to meet with the company's employees so they would see how their work was making a difference in the lives of real people. The effect was to clarify the company's mission—not to make money but to give the gift of health—and make it resonate with everyone from assembly plants to accounting.

"Bringing Medtronic customers in to meet our team was the most important day of the year," George said in an interview with Daniel Goleman, author of *Focus: The Hidden Driver of Excellence.* "We brought in six patients—one of them my mentor, Warren Bennis, who got a Medtronic defibrillator. He went out and met all the people on the production line. What did he do? He thanked them for the quality of their work that was helping keep him alive, and then he came in front of three thousand people on our atrium, but also at that time another 20,000 watching on webcasting, telling his story."[44]

That kind of broader perspective on purpose and gratitude is vital for everyone from the production-line employee who's putting together electronic components to the administrative assistant making photocopies. Work can give us tunnel vision. We can start to feel hermetically sealed in a cubicle or office, cut off from the bigger reality that our work makes possible. We can forget *why* we're doing what we're doing. Meeting with customers, seeing the good that comes from the whole of which we're a part—that's how organizations create fertile soil for meaning to grow.

The opposite of meaning is apathy. When an organization is indifferent or even hostile to the idea of asking "why" about work, apathy is the result. Rather than taking ownership of their work and treating it as a matter of personal pride—one of the hallmarks of meaningful work—employees just stop caring. They stand around talking. They mark calendars with lots of colorful blocks to look busier than they are. They take more sick days. They plod through work, doing the minimum. They remain detached from coworkers. They spend time at the office on non-work activities, like surfing the Internet, catching up on email, and making personal calls. The discretionary effort that's the heart and soul of engagement? Gone, replaced by an attitude best illustrated by a classic speech from our favorite movie, *Office Space*:

> **Peter:** I generally come in at least fifteen minutes late. Uh, I use the side door, that way Lumbergh can't see me. And, uh, after that I just sorta space out for about an hour.
>
> **Bob:** Space out?
>
> **Peter:** Yeah, I just stare at my desk but it looks like I'm working. I do that for uh, probably another hour after lunch, too. I'd say in a given week I probably only do about fifteen minutes of real, actual work . . . The thing is, Bob, it's not that I'm lazy, it's that I just don't care.
>
> **Bob:** Don't . . . don't care?
>
> **Peter:** It's a problem of motivation, all right? Now if I work my [tail] off and Initech ships a few extra units, I don't see another

dime, so where's the motivation? And here's something else, Bob. I have eight different bosses right now.

Bob: Eight?

Peter: Eight, Bob. So that means that when I make a mistake, I have eight different people coming by to tell me about it. That's my only real motivation is not to be hassled, that and the fear of losing my job. But you know, Bob, that will only make someone work just hard enough not to get fired.[45]

It's a funny scene, but it would be funnier if it weren't so accurate. In fact, we see this time and time again in the staggering number of employee comments we receive each time we conduct an employee survey.

"Yeah, every time my manager yells at me in her shrill voice, telling me 'do this . . . do that,' it really motivates me to want to work harder" is just one example of a recent survey comment that suggests the scene from *Office Space* isn't all that fictional. Being directed from one task to the next, with no purpose beyond complying with a series of instructions, doesn't answer the all-important "why" of what we are doing.

When meaning is lacking, employees quickly come to feel that their leaders don't care about them. That feeling quickly turns into resentment and the certainty of being exploited. It's not far from there to becoming a saboteur, inadvertent or otherwise. That's why most corporations, when they terminate someone, lock them out of their computers and have security escort them off the property. When meaning goes, the bridge burns.

EMPLOYEES CREATE THEIR MEANING

Meaning is one of the five keys that engaged people have that others don't, and it may be the most powerful. One reason for that power is that meaning is self-determined.

But, meaning rarely comes from where senior management thinks it should. Engagement is a 50-50 proposition; neither management nor employees own it completely. The same holds especially true for meaning.

The leadership team of an organization can create an environment where meaning can flourish—sharing the corporate narrative, having a clear organizational mission, giving everyone from the C-suite on down the broad "this is *why* we do what we do" perspective of their work, and so on. Those are vital strategies in promoting meaning. They allow the employee to connect organizational meaning to personal meaning. But nobody can tell you what's meaningful to *you*.

It's up to each individual employee to find his or her own meaning in the work he or she is doing. No one can attach meaning or mission for you; that's a do-it-yourself project. Each of us translates our effort, sacrifice, and accomplishments into meaning based on our background, upbringing, beliefs, morality, and a host of other factors that are private, personal, and unique to us. If you're lucky enough to be part of an organization that gives you the freedom to find meaning in what you do, it's on you to do the heavy lifting.

Consider Vic Firth. At his factory in the north woods of Maine, Firth's company turns out eighty-five thousand drumsticks a day. Not the fried kind of drumsticks, or the ice-cream kind. The musical kind. It's hard to imagine a humbler product for a legend to be passionate about. Firth passed away in 2015, but his passion for making the perfect tool for playing any kind of drum resonated across the company throughout his tenure at the helm. Back in 2009, his company had 62 percent market share in the drumstick market, where such qualities as density, weight, moisture content, and natural pitch separate a professional-quality pair of sticks from tools fit for a garage band.

For Firth, turning pieces of Tennessee hickory into something that helps musicians be their best is meaningful. "The key word for me is *persistence*," he says. "Whatever you set out to do, you have to have a magnum passion for it, and you've got to work beyond what you ever dreamed you're gonna work to succeed at the level that you want to succeed at."[46] Passion pays off: In 2010, Vic Firth merged with the world's leading maker of cymbals, Zildjian, a music titan with roots stretching back to Constantinople in 1623.

Meaning transforms the mundane into a life's pursuit, something that gets you out of bed every morning excited to go to work.

WHAT MAKES MEANING?

The things that make meaning may be highly individual, but we can state clearly what does *not* make meaning in an organization: satisfaction factors (turn back to chapter one for a refresher, if this term doesn't ring a bell). Compensation, espresso machines, and certainly "creating shareholder value" have zero power in giving people a sense of mission and purpose. They're the bare minimum requirements for engagement, but that's all. Executives who don't understand the importance of meaning in the workplace might try to force-feed meaning to their employees, but without an understanding of what meaning is, such efforts are doomed from the start.

We've seen some examples of how employees find meaning in unlikely places—in seemingly routine, even distasteful work. Well, the opposite is also true: Employees working in seemingly engaging, challenging, fulfilling jobs can become disengaged if they cannot find meaning in them.

There must be something inherent in the workplace that enables the employee to serve a purpose uniquely important to him or her. It's up to the organization to till the soil and lay down the nutrients that allow people to create their own meaning out of what may be mundane or exhausting, then stand back and let that meaning find its own form.

While facilitating a training session on meaning with a number of managers, I heard a story that perfectly illustrates this point. As we were discussing how people can find meaning in even the mundane, one of the women attending the session raised her hand and told the story of her grandfather. The company she worked for was a medical-staffing company; this woman spent a large part of her day placing physicians and other medical personnel in health-care facilities. She admitted to reaching a place in her career where she was "simply going through the motions," as she put it. It was about filling orders by placing people in positions. A good job, but the meaning wasn't there.

That changed when her grandfather fell ill and was placed in a facility in order to receive extended care. The family was delighted at the care he received, and it was at that point that she realized the people who were lovingly and professionally caring for a beloved family member were the very medical professionals that she had placed in those positions just a few months prior. From that time forward, she was no longer "simply going through the motions" or "filling positions." She was finding health-care professionals who could provide critical care needed by real people—like her grandfather. She had discovered her own meaning.

Other lessons we've learned about meaning:

- It's inner directed, impacting only the individual. Meaning by itself won't change a thing at the office unless the employee has a way to *express* that meaning on the job. This is the "act" element that follows "feel." In fact, if an employee finds meaning in work but isn't able to express it at the workplace, he or she can become resentful and unhappy.
- Some people get meaning in other ways and don't need to find it at work. An employee who volunteers at a homeless shelter on the weekends might show up for work every Monday feeling emotionally and mentally recharged and not *need* her work to be a source of meaning.
- Meaningful work doesn't have to be sexy. Look at some of the people this book has already talked about. They're not taking naps in sleep pods at Google. They're scheduling temporary workers or screwing in switch plates. Conversely, there are probably a lot of people at some of these "coolest places to work on the planet" who don't find much meaning in what they do. They're there to make money or pad their resumes.

INHERENT AND ASSOCIATED MEANING

But the most important truth is that while employers are charged with creating an environment where employees can feel empowered to seek meaning in what they do, the employees themselves are responsible for choosing to find that meaning. Meaning is a matter of perspective—choosing to see something a certain way.

Two types of meaning can be found in any organization: *inherent* and *associated* meaning. With *inherent* meaning, the work itself produces the meaning that the individual feels. A heart surgeon saving lives, a teacher helping illiterate children learn to read, a loan officer assisting a young family in purchasing its first home—for these people, their work is the direct cause of the meaning they experience.

Associated meaning is not found in the work but in what the work enables you to do away from the work environment. Imagine two workers at a factory that makes the air pressure sensors for modern automobile tires. The work is tedious and uninspiring. One man chooses to see the work as nothing more than a miserable job that he must suffer through in order to earn a paycheck. The other, however, chooses to see himself and his work as one small piece in a larger system designed to help keep people safe. His job helps protect families, he reasons. Therefore, his job is far more meaningful than that of the man next to him who does the exact same thing. Further, he sees his work as a way to put his daughter through college—the first in his family line to ever get a college education.

Inherent and associated meaning need not be mutually exclusive. In fact, both are commonly present in an organization with a healthy engagement culture. In such an organization, employees both find the work itself meaningful and also express their hunger for meaning in non-work ways. Some enlightened employers may even encourage their people to pursue such extra-organizational meaning with initiatives that promote community volunteerism, charitable giving, and so on. CHG, for example, will give $500 to employee groups or clubs started by the employees of the organization. These clubs have ranged from neighborhood cleanup to brewing beer in a bathtub.

The most striking difference between inherent and associated meaning is in who "owns" them. Inherent meaning is the shared property of the organization and the employee. While the employee must choose to find and embrace meaning in the work, the organization must also create an environment that highlights and values that meaning.

However, the individual has 100 percent ownership of associated meaning. Even in the most grim, sullen organizations, where management couldn't care less about engagement, there will always be some employees who manage to look beyond meaningless tasks and find a larger sense of purpose behind what they're doing. It could be saving for a home or retirement. It could be paying down debt or sending money to family overseas. This embrace of meaning, even in an "engagement desert," is the exclusive purview of the individual—and often a source of our most inspiring stories of engagement against seemingly impossible odds.

"Employees should not demand that companies imbue their lives with meaning," writes E. L. Kersten, Ph.D., a former professor of organizational communication at the University of Southern California. "Employers and employees have something the other needs. One of the keys to a mutually beneficial relationship is a realistic understanding of what that something is."[47]

Egghead Alert!

Positive psychology, essentially the study of happiness and how it affects people, has been trendy since the 1990s. However, the trend isn't without merit. Published, peer-reviewed research has shown that people with positive mental attitudes (also called "positive affect") are more efficient decision makers,[48] are more motivated to strive to reach their primary career goals,[49] and are more likely to experience overall success at work independent of other causes of positive workplace outcomes.[50] This, and extensive additional research, suggests that a positive outlook may make people more likely to become engaged in their work and thus experience greater satisfaction and success.

"WE WILL HAVE MEANING IN THE BREAK ROOM AT THREE"

Meaning may ultimately be in the eye of the beholder, but that doesn't mean employers are powerless to influence their people's search for meaning. There are four factors that, when propagated throughout a company's culture, strongly encourage workers to find mission, purpose, and meaning in what they do:

1. **Congruent Values.** Your employees should be able to say, "This company has a clear and compelling vision for the work I do. My talents, role, and values are aligned with the organization's values." People want to know that what is important to them is important to the company. They need to understand that the organization shares their values, and it's up to the organization to communicate its values clearly and consistently. Interestingly enough, our survey data show that, in some companies, fewer

than half of all employees indicate they know what the company's vision or direction is, let alone how it applies to the work they do.

Vision is one of the things that Apple has done so well. They disrupted half a dozen industries, but they never talked about being disruptive. They just did it. They lived their values: incredible design, incredible user experience, incredible technology. That's *authenticity*, a key aspect of values. Don't talk about your values; demonstrate them. Shut up about your mission statement and just do great work. Nobody outside the company cares about your mission statement—and there is a good chance that nobody inside cares, either. Unless, that is, they can see the connection to what matters to them.

Values must reflect the truth of how the people in the company see their place in the world. If they're not authentic and grounded in reality, they become nothing more than manipulative slogans that breed cynicism.

I was working with a group of student volunteers in a remote village in the mountains of Guatemala. This village had suffered from a plague of malnutrition for the past decade that, unfortunately, had caused a number of recent child deaths. Surprisingly, it was found that the children often had plenty of food, as they lived in a mountainous region in which fruits and vegetables, and even meat, were in abundance. The problem was in the soil. It was crawling with parasites. These parasites, along with the bacteria in the soil where crops were grown and animals fed, were making it impossible for the children to digest and pull life-sustaining nutrients from the available food sources. The children were starving to death, surrounded by food.

The volunteers, along with the villagers, were taught how to clear the soil and rid the impacted area of contamination. Under several small fields, makeshift concrete beds were poured and soil was brought in from outside the village to cover the concrete. Piglets and other livestock were then brought from the city. Children were provided with needed medical care. After several months, the children were found to be healthy. The village began to thrive, so much that not only could they support their own families, but they could also sell food in the local marketplace.

The enterprising young volunteers, many of them business students from the United States, got an idea. If the villagers could devote a little more time and effort to the project, they could sell their excess produce and pork at the market in the cities down in the valley, about an hour from the village by truck.

Excited about the possibilities for the village, the volunteers approached the villagers in a community meeting and presented their plan. But when the teams talked with the farmers about taking their crops into cities to sell them, one asked, "Will this take time from our families?" When the volunteers admitted that going to market would reduce family time, a number of the villagers stood up and left. The village officials quickly ended the meeting. Family, not commerce, was at the heart of their values system. Their values— the "why"—were different from the values of the well-meaning volunteers.

2. **Giving.** Work that makes employees feel that they are making the world a better place is inherently meaningful, but it certainly doesn't hurt if an employer overtly communicates that meaning to its people. Paramount Citrus Company, a huge citrus grower, is one of the most meaning-rich companies we've worked with, despite the fact that its people are engaged in work—picking, packing, and shipping fruit—that some people would describe as tedious. Instead, the culture encourages older workers to mentor younger workers, and the company reminds its employees that their work helps millions of people eat and live healthier. It's a culture filled with a sense of giving and sharing. This is part of the "why" behind what they do.

Giving also transformed investment firm Cantor Fitzgerald, which lost two-thirds of its employees in the September 11, 2001, attacks on the World Trade Center. In the wake of that tragedy, CEO Howard Lutnick vowed to distribute 25 percent of the company's profits over the next five years to help the 658 families affected by the attack, and ended up giving more than $180 million to those families. The company also founded the Cantor Fitzgerald Relief Fund, which has raised and distributed another $180 million to over 800 families as well as to victims of Hurricane Katrina, the 2004 tsunami, the Haiti earthquake, and other disasters. Each year on September 11, the firm also holds Charity Day, when 100 percent of revenues go to charitable causes.

Ironically, Lutnick was a villain before he was a hero, becoming infamous and nationally reviled for cutting off payroll to dead or missing employees immediately after the disaster. That could have cost him everything, but the charitable efforts transformed Cantor Fitzgerald into a model for corporate charity. Lutnick himself received the highest honor granted by the U.S.

Navy to nonmilitary personnel, the Department of the Navy's Distinguished Public Service Award.[51, 52]

3. **Impact.** There's an entire chapter devoted to impact as part of MAGIC, but it's important to discuss its relationship to meaning. Simply put, it's essential for members of a team to know how their work is affecting the people and community that they're trying to serve. No one wants to feel their efforts are futile. It's the job of leaders to make sure that people are able to see the organization's higher purpose, so they're not laboring in a vacuum.

One of our client partners, Accellent, is a wonderful example of this. They make small parts for catheters and surgical instruments for heart transplants, among other things. Much of the company is a manufacturing environment where many employees were having a hard time connecting with the good that the company is doing. While they saw their individual piece of the puzzle (adding part B to part C, or soldering the tip of a piece of wire), many employees were unaware of the "why" behind what they did. They failed to see the importance of their role in the big picture.

To address this, Accellent interviewed patients who had used some of their products, created posters that featured the patient's face and personal story, and put them up in all of their offices. The effect has been amazing. Overall engagement has continued to increase year after year, due in part to the fact that people truly understand the good their work is doing. *That's* creating a sense of meaning.

4. **Story.** Narrative and story can give employees a strong sense of "why we do what we do," connecting them with the past, a higher purpose, or a legacy. Leaders are in charge of the overarching story and need to both share and safeguard it.

Printing giant RR Donnelley can trace its roots back to 1864 and founder Richard Robert Donnelley. While it's a Fortune 500 firm, the company still maintains a strong sense of family, tradition, and, literally, story. Found throughout the company are generations of proud printers who pass down both an art and a science, along with the story, across generations. In fact, it's not uncommon to see two or three generations of printers or press-men working together in some of these plants.

This "story" is also reflected in its Lakeside Classics series of books. These beautiful hardcover, gold-embossed books, which tend to focus on American history, are printed annually during the Christmas season. But Lakeside Classics are never sold. Instead, they are given to RR Donnelley employees, clients, and others, continuing a tradition started in 1903 by then-president Thomas E. Donnelley.[53] Those receiving these books are not only presented with an impressive keepsake, they are presented with a piece of an ongoing story. It's a tangible, palpable object reminding them of RR Donnelley's rich history, the quality products each employee helps print and bind, and the joy found by millions in the books they produce each year.

MEANING AND HAPPINESS

Early on, I mentioned that engagement and happiness are two different things, although many confuse the two terms. Meaning is one of those areas where this difference comes to light.

The *Journal of Positive Psychology* article titled "Some Key Differences Between a Happy Life and a Meaningful Life," which was cited earlier, sheds some light on this. First, the researchers found that satisfying one's needs did lead to happiness. This makes sense, as was pointed out earlier when I highlighted differences between satisfaction and engagement. However, they found that satisfying one's needs and wants was largely irrelevant to mean-ingfulness. In other words, meaning found in one's work had nothing to do with whether or not people's basic desires for satisfaction had been met. So, it is quite possible that an individual could be working in trying circum-stances yet still find a great deal of meaning in what he or she is doing.[54]

"Meaning comes from proximity to your mission, engagement with your mission, from being able to do something about a calamity that's not an abstraction," says Chip Lyons, president and CEO of the Elizabeth Glaser Pediatric AIDS Foundation. EGPAF, as the organization is commonly known, has thousands of people working around the world—85 percent of them in Africa—often under difficult conditions. Yet they consistently score high on measures of meaning. "Our colleagues are working against something that is the leading public health crisis in the countries we work in. We are part of the community. We don't blow in and set up our own tents. We work through the public health systems in places like Kenya, Namibia, and Mozambique.

"Let's say we have 100 colleagues in a country," Lyons continues. "A substantial number of them will be out of the office one, two, three days a week. They're providing supervision at health-care sites, training providers on providing care for children and pregnant women; they are working with communities to come up with strategies to get more men to go to clinics and get tested. They have a connection to an exquisitely focused mission: to end AIDS deaths in children.

"I don't know anybody who hasn't lost a family member, colleague, or part of the community to AIDS," Lyons says. "They are part of the response to a crisis and part of the solution. Getting up every day, they feel that they are part of a mission. They are helping their community and their country. That isn't to say we don't have organizational issues, because we do. We're an organization of human beings, but there are some unusual and remarkable factors that connect us to the meaning of our work."

HOW TO CULTIVATE MEANING

Steve Jobs said that he wanted to "put a ding in the universe." This "ding" told a story about Jobs's vision. The importance of vision has been known since the beginning of human civilization. In fact, the Old Testament states, "Where there is no vision, the people perish." Employer and employee share the responsibility for imbuing the workplace with meaning, and that often begins with a shared vision. If you want to create fertile ground in which meaning can grow on an individual basis, start by articulating a clear vision of why your organization does what it does and invite each employee to shape that vision.

A great example of this comes from one of our client partners, International Market Centers, L.P. (IMC), the world's largest operator of showroom space for the furnishings, home decor, and gift industries. In analyzing their survey results, it became clear that IMC is doing an exceptional job of communicating its leaders' vision and making sure that employees feel that vision is meaningful to them. When we looked at fully engaged IMC employees, they had several things in common. On a 1–5 scale, with five being "Strongly Agree":

- Ninety-four percent marked a five when asked to rate "Our CEO is a trustworthy leader and inspires confidence."
- Eighty-nine percent marked a five when asked to rate "I believe IMC has a successful future."
- Eighty-nine percent marked a five when asked to rate "The vision and goals of IMC are important to me personally."
- Eighty-five percent marked a five when asked to rate "I understand how my work contributes to the overall success of IMC."

The fully engaged people at the company are fully engaged because they believe in the vision articulated by their leaders, see the vision as meaning something personal to them, and understand how what they do contributes to the fulfillment of that vision.

In cultivating meaning, communication is everything, and it's a two-way circuit. Not only does the organization need to talk sincerely about vision and purpose, but employees at all levels need both the tools and the encouragement to speak up when they feel that work is becoming bereft of its sense of meaning.

Another step that organizations can take is to help their people connect with organizational outcomes that are non-monetary. Although there is nothing inherently more meaningful in a non-monetary outcome, culturally we tend to think of monetary outcomes as shallow and less meaningful. Connecting employees with company charitable efforts, volunteer opportunities, or human impacts in the community can help them see that the company is "walking its talk" and backing up its stated values with real action.

Meaning comes from understanding motivations and concerns. Most employees in large organizations don't see the people at the top of the company (and, in some cases, even their own bosses) as "people." If employees cannot connect with the top of the organization, they won't connect with their vision. But if employees can internalize that the people at the top of the company food chain are real people who care about real things, they become much more likely to care about the things that leadership teams care about, or at least feel empathy for them.

Finally, keep it real. If your organization isn't warm and fuzzy, don't pretend that it is. If you're not oriented toward public service, don't create a public service program just to win employees' hearts and minds. It will ring inauthentic, and inauthenticity will doom engagement. There are many ways to make work more meaningful. They range from sharing the story of how products impact real customers, to creating a college savings plan, to printing books each Christmas (as in the case of RR Donnelley). The possibilities here are nearly endless. The key here is to help people find meaning, purpose, and mission in what they do. Help them see the "why" in their work.

Do what feels real within the culture of the organization. Back up your stated mission and values with action. Give employees the freedom and opportunity to find their own meaning, and those who can, will.

As the authors of the positive psychology study mentioned earlier write: "Humans may resemble many other creatures in their striving for happiness, but the quest for meaning is a key part of what makes us human, and uniquely so."[55]

FIVE QUESTIONS

1. How does my job support what's important to me? Where does my job detract from what's important to me?
2. Where are the values of the organization where I work congruent (or incongruent) with my own personal values?
3. How could I better align my work with what's most important to me?
4. What about my work provides me with a sense of purpose, and where do I feel I am making a difference because of my work?
5. What about my work brings me joy?

RECAP

- Meaning is about work having a greater purpose than the work.
- People create their own meaning. What isn't meaningful to one individual may be highly meaningful to another.
- Inherent meaning comes from the work itself; associated meaning comes from what the work allows you to do, such as earn money to support a family.

- Mission and vision statements are useful tools for communicating an organization's values and purpose to employees . . . provided they say something true that addresses the heart and not just the mind.
- Lack of meaning leads to cynicism, a sense of futility and, possibly, sabotage.
- Aligned values and authenticity are critical if an organization is to create a meaningful work environment.

CHAPTER FOUR

AUTONOMY

"Control leads to compliance; autonomy leads to engagement."
—*Daniel Pink*

A MOVIE SCREENPLAY is one of the most tightly structured forms of writing around. To even be considered for production, a screenplay must follow a strict form: three acts, "plot points" around which the story suddenly changes, a "dark night of the soul" where the main character feels that all is lost, and so on. If you want to have a prayer of having your script produced by Hollywood's mainstream, you have to follow the rules and check in with each critical story point.

However, once you've built that narrowly defined framework, you as the screenwriter have limitless freedom *within* it to create scenes, characters, dialogue, gunfights, car chases, Jedi knights, you name it. The exterior structure is defined by outside forces that are beyond your control; within that structure, you're in control of the results.

That's a terrific analogue for *autonomy*, the second key to engagement in our MAGIC formula. Autonomy is:

The power to shape your work and environment in ways that allow you to perform at your best.

Despite this clear definition, there are a lot of misconceptions about autonomy, so before diving into what it is, let's take a detour through some of the things that autonomy most definitely is *not*:

- Autonomy does not mean working in isolation. Being autonomous doesn't give a person the right to work without supervision or collaborators. Just because someone telecommutes doesn't mean he or she is autonomous.
- It's not doing whatever you like whenever you like. In an organization with high levels of autonomy, the employer defines the boundaries of the employee's control and decision-making power, creating the environment in which the employee can choose how autonomous he or she wishes to be.
- It's not working without a net. In a well-run organization, autonomous employees receive strong, clear guidance from supervisors, established procedures, manuals, and so on. It's only in dysfunctional organizations that employees are left to figure out their jobs with little or no input from management. That's not autonomy; that's lack of leadership.

Autonomy is not about leaving people alone. In fact, in my experience people actually don't want to be left alone. They want clear direction and to understand the rules and expectations under which they are performing. Are they permitted to make direct contact with key clients? Is it okay to deviate from the strategic plan? If they have an idea, can they go right to the head of the division or do they have to follow the chain of command? Such questions must be answered. Once they are, employees are free to complete their work in whatever way they choose.

At the same time, too much supervision can wreck productivity. University of Chicago researchers found that people who are being monitored too closely—supervisor peering over their shoulder closely—generally underperform. In other words, when there's too much pressure, people are more apt to buckle beneath it. The sweet spot appears to be just enough freedom with just the right mix of checking in and offering help when needed.[56]

Meaning "Hands-off" or "Let things ride," *laissez-faire leadership* describes the type of leadership or, better stated, lack of leadership, where the leader abdicates responsibility for leading to his or her subordinates. This manager provides little or no direction or feedback, and decisions are pushed to the subordinate. While appropriate in some cases, such as when employees are skilled and focused, subordinate needs are generally not addressed. Some managers, under the guise of "empowerment," claim that they are allowing their subordinates to exercise autonomy, but laissez-faire leaders often leave their employees to fail.

In an autonomous organization, it's *what* gets done that matters, with less concern for *how* it gets done. As long as the results are there and the methods are appropriate, it doesn't matter how employees deliver them. In some organizations, that even extends to letting people design their own flexible schedules or work from remote locations. What really matters is that the work gets done on time according to agreed-upon standards of quality and costs. There is a definite bottom-line benefit: Research shows that workers who are free to make more choices are likely to be happier, more committed to their jobs, more productive, and less likely to leave.[57]

HOW AUTONOMY LEADS TO ENGAGEMENT

William L. McKnight, chairman of the board of 3M Corporation from 1949 to 1966, was an early champion of employee autonomy, even in an era when employees were more often viewed as machines than as valuable, autonomous assets. He famously said:

> As our business grows, it becomes increasingly necessary to delegate responsibility and to encourage men and women to exercise their initiative. This requires considerable tolerance. Those men and women, to whom we delegate authority and responsibility, if they are good people, are going to want to do their jobs in their own way.

Mistakes will be made. But if a person is essentially right, the mistakes he or she makes are not as serious in the long run as the mistakes management will make if it undertakes to tell those in authority exactly how they must do their jobs.

Management that is destructively critical when mistakes are made kills initiative. And it's essential that we have many people with initiative if we are to continue to grow.[58]

In other words, hire good people, give them what they need to do their jobs well, and get out of their way. Doing so encourages employees to take risks, try new ideas, and innovate. 3M's most lucrative product came out of its program that allows employees to spend 15 percent of their work time on personal projects. Free to experiment with the adhesive invention of colleague Spencer Silver, 3M chemist Art Fry invented a little thing called the Post-it Note in 1974.[59]

Airline JetBlue has relied on autonomy to create its unique, award-winning customer service experience. Since 1999, the company has "home-shored" its telephone service agents, letting them work from home and using a third-party company to manage their activities. The practice has earned the airline ongoing J. D. Power and Associates awards for customer satisfaction,[60] but that's far from the only benefit of this autonomy-friendly policy. According to a report by Frost & Sullivan report, homeshoring draws from a wider range of potential applicants (including students, parents, retirees, and the disabled), and approximately 80 percent of homeshored telephone service agents have college degrees.[61]

A policy like homeshoring demands that the organization trust employees to perform without someone physically looking over their shoulders at all times. That's something that many (I would even dare say "most") managers have trouble with. Most managers still feel a need to "run the machine." We see it everywhere. For example, not long ago, members of our coaching team were consulting with a manager at a European grocery chain. He told us that he required his employees to copy him on every email they sent. When asked why he did this, he replied, "Well, I want to catch them when they do something really well and reward them for that."

We hadn't just tumbled off the turnip truck that morning. Our lead consultant, sensing that something was up and willing to confront the manager about this, said, "That's not why you're doing this. You don't trust them."

He replied, "I do trust my employees."

"No, you don't."

He grimaced, caught with his hand in the cookie jar, and said, "Yeah. It doesn't work, does it?"

Without trust, autonomy is impossible. However, when trust is present, it sends employees the message that they are in command of their time, effort, and reward. Because of this, it's an incredibly powerful factor in reducing workplace stress.

Stress? Some managers would claim that leaving employees to their own devices causes even more stress, and not only for the manager. Some managers we have coached over the years have felt that making decisions is the responsibility of the supervisor, not the rank and file. Removing the weight and responsibility from the employee (so the manager would say) also removes the burden for the consequence of that decision. However, Dr. Steven F. Maier of the University of Colorado suggests that the degree of control that someone has over a potentially stressful situation may be the most powerful factor in modulating or reducing the negative impact of that stressor.[62]

Trusting competent employees with the autonomy to act provides a degree of control that can greatly reduce levels of stress. Additionally, because the employee is closest to the situation, he or she often has a better understanding of how to address a potentially stressful condition.

Autonomy makes you feel respected, valued, and in possession of some degree of self-determination. Leadership values your ideas and your methods and gives you the ability to choose the best way to make something happen. It's management of adults by adults, rather than the parent–child model put into practice by most organizations until fairly recently.

While some organizations are making progress in this area, it's still not a common strength. We took a look at results from organizations that provided 71,205 survey responses to the following statements:

1. I have the authority I need to make decisions affecting my work.
2. I am satisfied with my level of involvement in decisions that affect me.

Egghead Alert!
Transactional Analysis

In the 1950s, psychiatrist and author of the best-selling book *Games People Play*, Eric Berne, developed a model he referred to as Transactional Analysis (TA). This model is commonly used today when counselors and psychologists look at interpersonal interactions—particularly abusive relationships. TA analyzes three ego states: *parental, child,* and *adult.* When an individual operates from the parental state, he could be nurturing and caring, or autocratic, disciplined, and critical, much like a parent. When operating in a child state, the individual may act playful, or could rebel. Those of us who have children can certainly understand this! TA claims that when one individual takes on either a child state or a parental state, the other person responds by *cathecting*, meaning that they match their response to the state of the other person. For example, if a leader takes on a parental state, the subordinate *cathects*, acting from a child state. This applies to leaders and followers in a business setting as well. The ideal relationship, then, is where both leader and follower move to an adult state. An adult-to-adult relationship involves a process of interaction and discussion, where both are involved in the decision.[63]

The results were not surprising. To the first statement, 75 percent of employees answered positively, meaning they felt they had the authority to make important decisions on their own. To the second, just 65 percent provided a positive response. Now, consider the inverse of these responses: One-fourth did not feel that they were given decision-making authority, and more than one-third felt they were not involved in decisions that affected them.

We decided to put a little twist on these questions in order to see where the hang-ups might be. Did employees simply not feel comfortable making decisions? Did management not provide them with opportunities to participate in the decision-making process? We asked employees to rate the following statement:

1. This company's leadership involves people in decisions that affect their jobs or work environment.

This time, only 61 percent responded positively. Problem identified.

When was the last time you felt like your superior turned you loose to do your best work, trusting you to deliver excellence? Did you feel flattered? Trusted? Respected? Did you want to repay that trust, respect, and regard with your very best effort and results? If so, then you've experienced the power of autonomy. If you haven't ever experienced this, then you may feel disrespected, distrusted, and uninvolved.

CHOICE, BOUNDARIES, AND JAZZ

Barry Schwartz writes in his book *The Paradox of Choice*: "Autonomy and freedom of choice are critical to our well-being, and choice is critical to freedom and autonomy. Nonetheless, though modern Americans have more choice than any group of people ever has before, and thus, presumably, more freedom and autonomy, we don't seem to be benefiting from it psychologically."[64]

Schwartz was writing about consumer behavior, but the principle applies to employee behavior as well. Too much choice can be detrimental. That's why those who think that autonomy means there are no boundaries are in error. In fact, firm boundaries—and a system to hold people accountable for results—are essential for autonomy to flourish. Within clear boundaries, people are empowered to determine how they will accomplish the tasks they are given. So, a simple autonomy formula might look like this:

BOUNDARIES + FREEDOM + ACCOUNTABILITY = AUTONOMY

Of course, it's trickier than that. Acceptable types of boundaries, freedom, and accountability vary by the individual. For example, some employees will not settle for anything less than the freedom to work from home, totally flexible hours, and minimal supervision. For others, autonomy will mean the ability to choose their own team members. Still others may simply want flexible schedules with lots of status reports to superiors. That's exactly why this is a 50-50 proposition.

Many people want and need tangible boundaries affecting space, time, or behavior: Work *here*, work during *this time*, or achieve *this goal*. Too much autonomy—too much choice—can paralyze, especially in organizations that don't have a "fail forward" culture where bold failures are welcomed.

Think about jazz music. Some people hear chaos when they listen to jazz, but that's because it's an improvisational art form, with free-form solos orbiting around a structured center. Boundaries are like jazz, allowing improvisation and creativity within the underlying structure of the melody and key. Applied with precision, they create safety and security for both employer and employee. Ambiguity is lethal to autonomy, but when deliverables, expectations, deadlines, and acceptable procedures are clear and accepted in advance, everyone is more likely to relax and get the job done.

EXTRINSIC AND INTRINSIC MOTIVATORS

Of course, if you give someone freedom of choice, you first have to give them the motivation to choose. Autonomy carries with it the risk—sometimes overt, sometimes implied—of failure and even punishment. People unaccustomed to freedom in the workplace can be reluctant to choose autonomy, even when it's to their advantage. Employers overcome this by tapping into employees' *extrinsic* and *intrinsic* motivators.

In his book *Drive*, author Daniel Pink draws the differences between these two types of motivators. Extrinsic motivators are things like bonuses and the threat of being fired. This is the typical carrot-and-stick, reward-and-punish business model. The trouble is not only that it often doesn't work, but that it may do more harm than good. Once an employee receives a promised bonus for reaching a goal, where's the motivation to keep working long hours?

Another way to view the motivation question is to look at *satiation* versus *saturation*. Satiation is the satisfying of hunger, a positive state where no more is *needed*. Saturation is the state of overabundance, where so much is provided that no more is *wanted*. It's the difference between sitting back after a terrific meal and feeling a sense of well-being, and overeating and feeling that if someone shows you another morsel of food, you'll be sick.

When organizations rely on extrinsic motivators, they saturate employees with perk after perk in the hopes that employees will keep performing. Eventually, it all becomes too much—and, at the same time, not enough. Too much abundance, and abundance loses all meaning. After you've had six bonuses, does a seventh motivate you, or have you simply come to expect it? Intrinsic motivators like autonomy, on the other hand, satiate each individual's hunger for self-determination, meaning, and impact without filling them up. After you've had a fantastic meal at a restaurant, you can't wait to go back and try something else. You're excited, intrigued, motivated to act.

Scientific research shows us that lasting motivation comes from autonomy, mastery, and purpose.[65] These are intrinsic motivators—pride, the desire to do something well, making a meaningful impact on people—that differ from person to person in type and intensity. However, while these intrinsic motivators may have a longer shelf life, Pink's rejection of extrinsic motivators is a bit idealistic. The same task may have extrinsic and intrinsic motivators, so the smartest organizations tend to be those with a culture that lets employees gravitate to whichever motivator fuels the best performance.

If *what* is more important than *how*, does it really matter if your people surpass their goals because they feel inspired, or because they want a $500 bonus? From what we've seen, the organizations that are the best motivators are those who say, "We don't care how you motivate yourself as long as you do."

This is where the heart and spirit give way to the mind and hands. This is where we move from feeling to acting. If you give your best because your dad did the same job fifty years ago and you tear up when you think about him, great. If you give your best because you want to make more money, great. Find what moves you, and let's get to work.

THE FOUR TYPES OF AUTONOMY

Clearly, autonomy isn't as cut-and-dried as saying, "Work from home." In fact, along with all the other variables, there are four types of autonomy that an organization can grant to its employees:

1. **Spatial autonomy:** The power to control the environment (or space) in which you work. The most obvious example of this is homeshoring or telecommuting, but we also see spatial autonomy when employees customize their work spaces. When French e-commerce software company PrestaShop opened its first U.S. location in Miami back in 2011, the offices were start-up barren—not exactly the kind of surroundings to attract the young tech geniuses the company had become known

for. However, for its office redesign PrestaShop turned not to an interior design firm but to its employees. They planned, organized, painted, decorated, and brought in perks like giant flat-screen TVs, aquariums, and game tables, creating a rich, colorful, youthful environment.[66]

2. **Social autonomy:** The power to control who you work with. Rather than have managers assign people to a team or work group, some organizations allow teams to choose their own members and manage themselves. Research shows that these "self-selected teams" actually outperform traditional teams.[67] In working with students in university courses, I have found that those teams allowed to self-select work better together and provide better final outcomes than those forced to work together due to some arbitrary assignment system, such as alphabetical order or seating charts. The same applies for work groups.

3. **Temporal autonomy:** The power to control when you work. We no longer work in a nine-to-five world. People have access to email and information at all hours of the day and night (both a blessing and a curse). Because of this, many employers have not only accepted revised work schedules, but have embraced them as a recruiting advantage.

A number of our food-services clients have implemented systems in which employees can log into a scheduling app from home and input shifts they desire most, as well as those for which they are available. As long as all shifts are covered, employees typically work the shifts and number of hours they have chosen. Rather than fighting about shifts and hours, as was the suspected outcome of the managers when implementing these systems, miraculously all shifts are covered, and with very little noise.

4. **Task autonomy:** The power to control how you approach and complete your work and to set your own milestones. For many managers, this is the tough one. It's where they must truly be willing to let go of some of that power they've been holding on to. When suggesting this concept to managers, we often hear rants such as "If we let them decide the end goal, as well as how to go about getting there, their targets will be sure-hit targets, not something they need to stretch for." However, notice this doesn't mean having employees set the end goal. In fact, that's part of the idea of setting parameters, discussed earlier. The organization sets

the parameters and guidelines. But employees are given the latitude to accomplish the task in the way that will best use their skills and available resources in bringing about the best result for the organization.

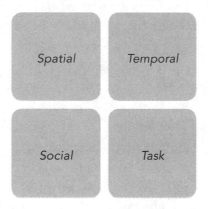

The ability to control some (or all) of these four determines each person's perceived level of autonomy. However, different individuals will place different value on each type of autonomy. One employee may not care about working in a bare cubicle as long as she can set her own hours; another might be happy to work any schedule but needs a space full of light, plants, and art in order to deliver her best work.

In most organizations, managing task autonomy is one of the greatest challenges. For one thing, it goes contrary to what we've been taught about management for most of the past century—and beyond. When considering temporal autonomy, for example, both the emergency-room nurse and the table busser must work a designated shift. Others are depending on them to be where they are supposed to be when they are supposed to be there.

Of course, there are some situations where different types of autonomy are simply not an option. Many industries are highly regulated, which compromises the degree to which some types of autonomy may be allowable. If you work in a nuclear plant, task autonomy may not be possible or even desirable. However, that doesn't mean leaders and employees don't have at least some ability to control certain aspects of their jobs. For example, perhaps the assembly-line employee has the power to choose his shifts or the responsibility to start a new line in whatever fashion he thinks best.

Furthermore, we rarely have all types of autonomy available to us at a given time. Working at home (spatial) may not be an option for me at my job, but if it's something I value highly enough, then I must choose an environment where this type of autonomy is available. Autonomy takes many forms, and finding it is often a matter of looking outside the box.

Allowing people to determine where, when, how, and with whom they will work are largely matters of setting policy; either your workplace allows telecommuting and flexible hours, or it doesn't. But there may be an unlimited number of ways that an employee can achieve a given task or reach a given goal. Keep in mind as well that to many people, especially those unaccustomed to creative and procedural liberty at work, the idea of creating their own process and setting their own milestones can be terrifying.

So, while it's critical for leadership to determine the right balance of all four types of autonomy, finding the right type and level of autonomy takes special time and patience. The engaged workplace should provide opportunities for autonomy that help employees feel empowered to be their best, rather than feeling intimidated or confused.

Autonomy and Goal Setting

Allowing employees to set their own project milestones is not the same as letting them set broad goals that impact the organization as a whole. While it's fine for an employee to create his own series of goals and deadlines for a given project, management must be responsible for setting the larger goals, such as customer satisfaction, sales revenue, or product shipped, especially when bonuses are involved. It's difficult for an employee to be objective about his own ability and compensation, and rank-and-file personnel may not have the organization's "big picture" in mind.

PICK UP A PIG AND WALK

The desire for autonomy is not a recent development. In fact, it's been an issue in human relations since the dawn of civilization. Wars have been fought over the right to self-determination and independence, including one precipitated by some gents named Jefferson, Washington, and Franklin, and another led by one Mohandas K. Gandhi. The Civil War, one of the most cataclysmic events ever to befall the United States, came about in great part because a large segment of the population wanted to end the ultimate insult to autonomy, the institution of slavery. From apartheid in South Africa to Black Friday strikes against Walmart, humankind has proven that we will expend energy and shed blood in order to be free to decide our own fates.

In the modern world, the drama of more-or-less autonomy plays out in the environment where we spend a great deal of our time: the workplace. Before the Industrial Revolution, work was largely small scale and individual. From blacksmiths and weavers to artisans and farmers, most individuals worked on their own, subject only to their own supervision (and, in some cases, the rules of professional guilds). It might be a stretch to call preindustrial craftspeople entrepreneurs, but they were definitely autonomous.

That changed with the rise of heavy industry, factories, assembly lines, and mass production. Suddenly, individual initiative was not only useless, it was actually an impediment to performing the single repetitive task that each worker was assigned. In the primitive, dangerous factories of the nineteenth century, if you decided to do things your own way not only might you stop production, you could be injured or killed.

Assembly lines required little thinking, creativity, or change, only labor and exactness. Innovation wasn't important. This type of organization endured for a century because it gave the people at the top more of the Three Cs: command, control, and compensation. Owners and senior executives had more people reporting to them, enjoyed greater control over their work and career paths, and took home the lion's share of the money. Managers captured the initiative of the rank and file by enforcing a uniform, inflexible code of workplace behavior. Workers were interchangeable parts who needed to be ruled with an iron fist to keep them from misbehaving.

Frederick Taylor, the father of Scientific Management Theory and the assembly-line mentality, had a memorable phrase for this sort of corporate culture: "Pick up a pig and walk." Dating back to the era of the Spanish-American War, when massive amounts of pig iron were piling up on the loading docks at the legendary Bethlehem Steel Company, the saying means that as an employee, you're here to do what the boss tells you. As Taylor said of the manager, "When he tells you to pick up a pig and walk, you pick it up and walk, and when he tells you to sit down and rest, you sit down. You do that right through the day. And what's more, no back talk." Your value comes from your ability to follow orders without question. Nothing more.[68]

Egghead Alert!

In 1957, future Nobel laureate Herbert Simon's Rational Man Theory debunked scientific management. Simon argued that workers are not mindless cogs who need to be treated like children. Instead, Simon argued that if the consequences of their actions could be predicted and evaluated, and if they had relevant knowledge and an organized and stable system of preferred actions and outcomes, employees would tend to act more rationally than not (though their behavior could never be fully predicted). In other words, give people boundaries, accountability, and resources and they should effectively manage themselves.[69]

Jump to today's economy. Now, even many assembly-line jobs demand independent thought and personal initiative. Rigidity and uniformity may have worked before, but now we have quality-obsessed companies like Toyota giving factory workers the freedom to halt all production if they see a quality problem—a policy called *jidoka*.[70]

We've come full circle, though our command-and-control structure hasn't figured it out yet. Executives and managers weaned on scientific management still act like benevolent parents and treat their employees like errant children . . . but that's a management style that is slowing dying out, at least in many parts of the world.

In an age when intellectual capital, not manufacturing prowess, creates wealth, autonomy makes good business sense. We *want* our people to take the initiative, disrupt hidebound business models, and innovate. For an extreme example, take the Seattle video-game developer Valve Corporation. This company has no bosses or hierarchy. Employees interact with and direct one another, a committee hires people, and each person can move freely among any of the company's many projects (this is task autonomy at its finest). Discipline and bonuses are determined by peer review. It's workplace socialism . . . or anarchy, depending on your point of view. But based on the company's growth—a value of about $4.1 billion as of 2017—it's working.[71]

WHEN AUTONOMY GOES

Dr. David Rock, founding president of the NeuroLeadership Institute, writes in *Strategy + Business*:

> A perception of reduced autonomy—for example, because of being micromanaged—can easily generate a threat response. When an employee experiences a lack of control, or agency, his or her perception of uncertainty is also aroused, further raising stress levels. By contrast, the perception of greater autonomy increases the feeling of certainty and reduces stress.[72]

You're familiar with claustrophobia, the fear of enclosed spaces? Well, lack of autonomy can make employees feel claustrophobic. Lacking options or control, they can have the sense of being trapped in their situations, unable to move or escape. Such a situation can lead to desperation or panic.

Put simply, when you take away autonomy, you don't just take away the capacity and capability to do something. You take away the individual's choice. Instead of just tying people's hands, you tie their minds. Hearts and spirits are not far behind. A lack of autonomy can bring about active rebellion on one hand or apathy on the other. Either way, employees distance themselves from the organization. In other cases, the absence of autonomy leads to dependency. Employees don't take the initiative on projects, for fear of being punished by their superiors. Without self-starters, getting anything done requires a lot more management resources. Innovation suffers. Overall engagement drops. Stress worsens. No one takes unnecessary risks or speaks up, leading to missed opportunities and increased dysfunction. We may even see the reactive autonomy that we discussed earlier, in which people reflexively act on their own without guidance or restriction, often producing negative consequences.

RESIGNATION AND LEARNED HELPLESSNESS

Often, autonomy vanishes when the *locus of control* shifts from the individual to the authority figure. This concept, developed by psychologist Julian B. Rotter in 1954, refers to the two concepts of personal control over one's life.[73] An internal locus of control implies the belief that your life is largely determined by your actions and decisions; an external locus of control implies that life is controlled by external factors that you cannot influence.

When employees in an organization who are used to a high degree of autonomy (i.e., an internal locus of control) suddenly lose their autonomy to a controlling manager (an external locus of control), problems tend to manifest in two ways:

1. **Resignation**—You accept what comes and do the best you can, but absolve yourself of responsibility and follow authority figures blindly. Resignation can be useful in high-stress situations where individuals need to decouple themselves from the results of their work—trauma wards, military campaigns, and so forth. Otherwise, it's a short step to apathy and indifference to suffering.
2. **Learned helplessness**—In this well-known mental state, first described by psychologist Martin Seligman, individuals learn through repeated episodes of failure that they are powerless to change or improve their current conditions. Eventually, they perceive that this inability to effect change is permanent and accept a total lack of control over their circumstances.[74] We see this in organizations where managers exert continual high levels of authority, taking choice or control out of employees' hands. Then, when circumstances require employees to think for themselves, they lack the capacity to do so.

Take the example of Hewlett-Packard (HP) in the interval before the hiring of Meg Whitman as the new CEO. Starting with the ill-advised merger with Compaq in 2002, one of Silicon Valley's greatest companies careened from one disaster to another. Bottom may have come during the five-year tenure of CEO Mark Hurd, when:

> HP was traumatized, its employees disengaged. Internal "voice of the company" surveys revealed that morale had cratered. One top executive told (new CEO Leo) Apotheker she felt "maimed" by Hurd's hard-charging style. A company hailed for its vaunted "HP way"—which emphasized employee autonomy—had stifled creativity to the point where workers now had a rueful phrase to describe the way they tuned out and pretended to be clueless when executives asked them to do something: "flipping the bozo bit."

In the new, autonomy-poor HP, innovation stopped. Employees had to run a bureaucratic obstacle course in order to buy new software. Buildings began to fall apart. By the time Whitman addressed employees in early 2012 after taking the helm in September 2011, employees were miserable and openly hostile.[75]

Under CEO Marissa Mayer, Yahoo! conducted a real-time experiment on the effects of taking away autonomy in favor of connection. In February 2013, the newly installed Mayer stunned the company by announcing that employees who had been working full time from home would henceforth be required to come into the office. "To become the absolute best place to work, communication and collaboration will be important, so we need to be working side-by-side," the memo announcing the change read. "That is why it is critical that we are all present in our offices."[76]

The controversy over this change in policy has since somewhat died down, but has also provoked some important insights. One is self-evident: Sometimes an organization must choose to emphasize one driver of engagement over another. In this case, Mayer decided that connection (I'll address this in its own chapter later) was more important to Yahoo!'s comeback than autonomy.

Choosing to emphasize one driver of engagement over others is one of the real-world choices that leaders must make. In fact, in mid-2017, IBM issued a similar edict: "Leave your home workspaces and relocate to a regional office—or leave the company."[77] We'll see how this all plays out. Workers in offices can still provide high levels of autonomy, even though in many employees' minds much of their spatial autonomy has been compromised. Companies like Google, Skullcandy, Facebook, and Apple encourage (or even require) employees to devote part of their time to working on a personal, self-directed project. (On August 16, 2013, business news website Quartz reported that Google had killed its famous 20 percent time policy, but this turned out not to be true.[78]) This stipulation clearly promotes autonomy while still maintaining connection between employees.

Working at home or according to one's idiosyncratic personal rules doesn't necessarily lead to autonomy, and being compelled to work in the corporate environment doesn't by definition lead to the loss of all autonomy. Autonomy is an unpredictable thing, and we'll watch the goings-on at IBM with great interest to see how this choice of connection over autonomy works out.

CHOICE AND AGENCY

In the end, autonomy is about *choice* and *agency*. The ability to consciously choose what we do and how we do it is central to our concept of personal independence. It is the core of something deeper, our sense of agency. Agency is the idea that we can make conscious decisions that will lead to a hoped-for outcome—essentially, that we can determine our fate. We are not pawns of a deterministic system, powerless to decide where we end up.

Employees will express their need for choice and agency in a wide variety of ways:

- choosing where to work
- choosing how to complete a task
- choosing how to dress at work
- choosing who to work with
- choosing how to communicate

This list is nowhere near complete, but you get the picture. Organizational leaders would be well advised to allow employees as much freedom of choice as possible. Even allowing choice in small areas, while maintaining tighter top-down control in big ones, can bolster people's sense of agency and autonomy.

HOW AUTONOMY CREATES VALUE

Back to Google. The Internet titan wasn't the first company to give its people a chunk of their on-site time to dedicate to personal projects, but it's probably been the most successful. After all, intellectual property created by employees using company resources belongs to the company; that's where Gmail and AdSense (the advertising algorithm that produces about 25 percent of Google's $50 billion in annual revenue[79]) came from. Business is filled with stories of empowered employees, allowed by management to do their own thing, who've worked wonders.

It's human nature to be self directed and curious. People who are given autonomy and recognition want to use their skills to impact their organization in a positive way. If we compare companies known for their high levels of autonomy with similar companies known for lower levels of autonomy, we can see that autonomous employees tend to make their organizations more competitive, profitable, and customer friendly. Here are a couple of examples:

- **Delta Airlines versus Southwest Airlines.** Delta is a traditional airline with a conventional corporate culture. If you read their "Rules of the Road" manual, under Core Values you'll find things like "Always tell the truth," "Always keep your deals," "Don't hurt anyone," "Try harder than all our competitors," and "Care for our customers, our community, and each other." It's like flying Boy Scout Airlines.

  Southwest, on the other hand, is notorious for empowering its employees and allowing behavior that's the antithesis of the staid, buttoned-up Delta. (Flight attendants, for instance, have rapped the safety instructions and appeared out of the overhead bins.) Which airline do you think is more successful? Well, in 2017 Southwest celebrated 45 successive profitable years—which included the years after 9/11 when many airlines folded—and has continued to lead the way in customer loyalty ratings for two decades.

  One reason for this is that Southwest famously has its employees' backs. As former company president Colleen Barrett said in an interview, "The truth of the matter is . . . sometimes the customer is not right. If you really want to have the trust and the love and the support and belief of the employees, then you've got to tell the customer on the few occasions when they have done something that is so outrageous or so disrespectful or so degrading to the employee, you've got to say 'stop.'"[80]

- **Costco versus Walmart.** Walmart may be the world's largest retailer, but while the behemoth of Bentonville, Arkansas, was cutting prices even further to keep same-store sales at a meager 2 percent, Costco was flying high with 5 percent same-store growth in the United States and 7 percent outside the United States.[81] How? For one thing, Costco is renowned as a stand-up corporate citizen, which makes members more willing to pay the minimum $60 annual fee.

  However, autonomy also plays a big role in establishing the sense of community that Costco is famous for. Each Costco location operates with high autonomy, giving each warehouse manager the authority to hire, fire, and manage the people at his or her store with little or no interference from the corporate office. Even more important, the guidelines for managing employees are written (and rewritten) by the employees themselves in focus groups that convene every three years.

  Meanwhile, Walmart is infamous for paying its workers wages so low that they need to ask fellow employees to donate food to help feed them during the holidays,[82] and for the widespread strikes by its employees during the 2013 holiday shopping season. Which company's employees are more likely to deliver the discretionary effort that leads to long-term, sustainable success?

- **Zappos.com.** The Amazon-owned retailer is renowned for its unique employee experience, much of which revolves around autonomy. In fact, with practices such as their recent introduction of "holacracy," which is based on self-management, some would even say they go overboard when it comes to autonomy. Zappos policies includes such practices as "Let employees explore their passions and express creativity.[83]

CREATING AN AUTONOMY CULTURE

Autonomy can be one of the most powerful pro-engagement factors for an organization. Of course, doing so requires getting past the old command-and-control structure to let employees be who they are, all while giving them clear boundaries and accountability structures.

If you're starting from scratch in the kind of company where employees feel compelled to look over their shoulders at all times, begin by figuring out the level and type of autonomy that your people want. Are they most interested in spatial or temporal autonomy, which you can provide by allowing telecommuting or exploring scheduling possibilities? Or are they after something more esoteric, as in the respondents to a Fortinet survey in which more than 50 percent said they viewed using their own mobile devices at work as a right, rather than a privilege?[84] Know what kind of autonomy matters to your workforce before you offer it.

The design and architectural firm Gensler, which has designed work spaces for such clients as the World Bank and Virgin Mobile, has found through internal research that giving employees more control over their physical environment leads to optimal performance. Their 2017 employee survey showed that employees given more control over where, when, and how to work had higher levels of innovation, satisfaction, and job performance.[85]

Having the autonomy to design a physical space—cubicle, office, work van, an area of the plant floor, even a jail cell—engenders in the employee a sense of ownership. He or she immediately does the equivalent of marking his or her territory. It's a way of telling others, "This is my space." Researchers at the University of Exeter School of Psychology studied more than two thousand office workers and found that those who had control over the layout of their work space were 32 percent more productive than counterparts who lacked that control.[86] That's a meaningful difference that impacts the bottom line.

With ownership, one also claims responsibility (and the inherent accountability) for a space, task, role, or assignment. Ownership is a powerful factor in creating engagement.

Make the autonomy you offer meaningful and authentic. The more potential risk a type of autonomy carries for the organization, the more meaningful it is to the employee. In other words, giving employees freedom to decorate their cubicles while directing their team activities with an iron fist means nothing. It's an insult. Meaningful autonomy, at times, may mean that the boss trusts you with something that has the potential to embarrass the organization, or cost it money . . . making you much more likely to handle with care.

Grant employees ownership. Create an environment that offers both extrinsic and intrinsic motivators. Extrinsic motivators can be as straight-forward as performance incentives, an extra afternoon off, or profit sharing. Intrinsic motivators demand more subtlety but can be evoked by measures that attach meaning and purpose to the work, training that fosters the desire for excellence, and other tactics that align work with positive feelings. Effec-tive autonomy empowers employees to tap into the meaning that underlies their work. For instance, allowing an employee with small children to work from home three days a week can connect her to one of the reasons she's working so hard—the welfare of her family—and help her be a more com-mitted, inspired employee.

Next, structure broad goals, desired outcomes, and general boundaries but allow your people to determine everything else about how they reach those goals. Let them do things their way as long as they behave and operate appropriately within the context of key relationships—and as long as they deliver. Also, create clear accountability systems that remind employees they can come and go like the wind, and dye their hair green, only as long as at the end of the quarter they have hit or surpassed their benchmarks.

Provide your people with the tools and resources they need to reach your goals and theirs. Training, technology, new faces, whatever it takes. Again, this is about trust, saying, "I'm willing to invest in you and your ideas because I believe you'll make it worthwhile."

Finally, once you've done all this, get out of the way and let people do their thing. If you hire people who want to give 110 percent and put them in an 85 percent environment, you'll do your organization greater harm than by hiring 85-percenters in the first place. Don't grant autonomy if you as a manager aren't prepared to follow through. Keep in mind that once employ-ees have a taste of true autonomy, they won't want to give it up. We'll watch IBM to see how this real-time experiment in taking away autonomy plays out. For Yahoo!, the experiment has been an interesting ride, and results are still coming in, now that Mayer is no longer at the helm.

FIVE QUESTIONS

1. What type(s) of autonomy—spatial, social, temporal, or task—is/are most important to me? Where do I get this in my job, and where is it missing?
2. How does the level of autonomy I have at work impact my level of autonomy outside work?
3. Where am I unclear about what level of autonomy I might have?
4. In which parts of my job do I feel I have the freedom and power to do my best work? Where do I feel limited?
5. In what aspects of my job are the boundaries (the parameters in which I need to operate) clear, and where are they unclear?

RECAP

- Autonomy is having the freedom to shape your working conditions and environment.
  - It's not about working in isolation, and it's not a total free-for-all.
  - There are several kinds of autonomy—spatial, temporal, social, and task.
- People are motivated by two kinds of factors: extrinsic (money, threats, social pressure) and intrinsic (meaning, emotion, mission, the desire to excel).
  - Trust is essential for employees to be autonomous.
- At the heart of autonomy are choice (the desire to actively choose what, when, and how we do things) and agency (the need to see ourselves as consciously being able to make decisions and take actions that determine our futures).
  - Ownership is a powerful component of autonomy.
- Research shows that employee autonomy reduces stress and increases productivity.
  - Employees need safe boundaries within which to be autonomous.
  - In some situations, autonomy isn't an option.
  - Taking away autonomy once you've granted it is a surefire engagement killer.

CHAPTER FIVE

GROWTH

"The growth and development of people is the highest calling of leadership."
—*Harvey S. Firestone, founder of Firestone Tire & Rubber Company*

A FEW YEARS AGO, our organization worked with a corporate call center that was experiencing a devastating turnover rate. Keep in mind, while turnover rates in customer call centers tend to be pretty high anyway—typically about 33 percent annually, and as high as 51 percent for call-center subcontractors[87]—this business was experiencing even higher turnover. As we worked with the employees, as well as previous employees, our team found that the usual reasons for call-center attrition—low pay and repetitive work—were part of the problem, but not all of it. Employees were also leaving because the job was, well, boring. It was too easy. There was no challenge to engage them.

Our solution was to get the company to create employee teams dedicated to solving problems. These teams met regularly, and many of their ideas were implemented. The effect was remarkable. Introducing opportunities to stretch and grow—to make the work more challenging and less boring—caused annual turnover to drop to nearly half of what it was just six months earlier.

Although the changes were substantial, the financial investment on the part of the call center was minimal. It wasn't a matter of giving promotions and sending people to expensive training courses. Employees were provided more internal training opportunities, some related to responsibilities outside their job descriptions. Some employees were assigned as mentors, which provided growth opportunities to both mentor and mentee. Rather than focusing on a single product, employees were cross-trained on a number of products.

We also found it interesting that these employees were given a choice as to the products for which they wished to handle calls. Some chose to work with technology-focused software clients. Others worked with sporting goods and athletic equipment. Others fielded calls on a variety of different electronic gadgets. Regardless of what they chose, employees saw these changes as opportunities to work with something of interest to them, as well as an opportunity to learn something new.

Even more interesting was the fact that not only did turnover drop, but key performance indicators increased, often dramatically. Employees started feeling better about their work (hearts became involved), the energy level at the call-center locations improved (spirit), and performance increased (minds and hands). By tweaking just one of the MAGIC keys—growth—employees felt the change and acted on the change. They engaged in their work.

Over the past several years, there has been a change in the way call centers recruit. Rather than the typical "Come work for us. We'll pay you, you're guaranteed a job if you have a pulse—and oh, by the way, we have contests where we give away movie tickets," we're beginning to hear a new theme emerge. *Growth*.

Ads recruiting for phone agents now use phrases and words like "career," "tuition reimbursement," and "opportunity to build your resume." They're starting to get it. They've caught on to the real reason employees rarely engage in their stagnant environments, and are attempting to address this—at least on the surface. They're selling (and hopefully delivering on) growth.

The same natural human need for challenge, stimulation, and stretching our personal capacity is what drives most entrepreneurs. Entrepreneurs tend to find the greatest meaning and stimulation from times when they face do-or-die situations in their business, when they must rise to the challenge or perish. That's not to say that all entrepreneurs are reckless risk takers; the successful ones usually take carefully calculated risks. But one thing that the greats have in common is that they thrive on those moments when everything is on the line and they have to step up to a higher level.

Take Ted Myerson and his company, FTEN, a Wall Street trade-execution and risk-management software firm. Myerson incorporated the company on September 10, 2001. You know what happened the next morning. In the wake of the attacks on the World Trade Center, Wall Street froze. It seemed like an insane time to launch a new financial venture. But Myerson persisted. Lack of funds made the company resourceful, and it grew. Then, in 2008, amid the collapse of Bear Stearns and the global financial crisis, FTEN actually went on an aggressive campaign of expansion. As part of this effort, the company placed additional emphasis on becoming a workplace recognized as an employee-focused company. It was able to meet both its operational and cultural targets and, consequently, sold in 2010 to NASDAQ for nine figures.[88]

The September 11 attacks and the onset of the global financial meltdown would probably be enough to make many businesspeople curl into a little whimpering ball. Not entrepreneurs. They're at their best when circumstances afford them the opportunity to try new things, test their ideas and skills, and embrace challenges with the prospect of a satisfying payoff.

Consider Larry Ellison. Ellison had already turned Oracle into a tech titan and made himself wealthy. What challenge could surpass that? Winning the America's Cup, for one thing. After a series of mishaps, Ellison's Team Oracle crew went on to win the coveted cup. Look at Bill Gates and his foundation pushing to cure malaria. Google with commercial space travel and self-driving cars. Wildly successful individuals and organizations tend to be challenge-and-growth junkies. When too much success robs business of its edge-of-disaster adrenaline rush, they find some new impossible thing to tackle—the more audacious, the better. Only when they are moving forward and exploring new frontiers do they feel truly alive and fulfilled.

More? Consider Elon Musk. His goal is to build companies that solve vastly different problems: environmental, social, and economic. His first famous venture was as a cofounder of PayPal during the dot-com bubble, where his marketing campaign became largely responsible for PayPal's initial growth. After a few years at PayPal, he decided he needed to push himself to grow further, so he founded SpaceX, a company with the goal of vastly reducing the costs of space travel and exploration, and ultimately extending human life to other planets. In the beginning, he wasn't able to find a rocket scientist willing to help him in this endeavor, so he simply taught himself rocket science. No big deal. While conquering rocket science and becoming the first private company to launch and dock a spacecraft with the international space station, he continued to push himself to learn and grow by cofounding Tesla Motors. He personally designed many of the key components of these "green" vehicles, teaching himself the steps along the way. His most recent endeavor is the Hyperloop, a conceptual high-speed transportation system that would allow for travel between Los Angeles and San Francisco in about thirty minutes via pressurized capsules within tubes. He has taught himself the necessary physics to provide initial designs for the system. With each of Musk's ideas, he has needed expertise in extremely niche markets, and when he hasn't been able to find that expertise, he has learned it himself. Talk about a desire for growth.

That's a nutshell description (and some pretty strong examples) of growth, the third key in unlocking the power of engagement.

WHAT IS GROWTH?

Growth is simple to define. It's:

Being stretched and challenged in ways that result in personal and professional progress.

When growth is present, employees have the opportunity to be challenged and stretched in their jobs, to use their strengths, and to feel like they are continually learning and developing personally and professionally to benefit themselves and the organization. Words associated with growth include:

1. becoming
2. reach
3. learning
4. expanding
5. goals
6. developing
7. accomplishment
8. innovation

9. improvement
10. progress
11. adapting
12. confidence
13. challenge

Growth is extending yourself. It's getting better. Growing—feeling that we are always improving and expanding into new areas—is a universal human need. So is novelty and variety. We become bored, distracted, and disengaged when we feel that our work is rote, routine, and repetitive. People crave work experiences that challenge their minds and their skills, that are intellectually stimulating, and that offer them the chance to rise to the occasion and excel even in high-stress situations.

This desire for accomplishment, reaching for higher standards, and mastering new skills is also known as the *need for achievement*, a term coined by Harvard psychologist Henry Murray.[89] People with this personality trait tend to have a strong inner drive to take action, compete with others, seek out difficult tasks, and set lofty goals for themselves and their development. But while psychologists suggest that a small subset of the population has this quality to a high degree (entrepreneurs, political leaders, and the like), need for achievement drives almost every individual to some level. Even if we're not driven to change the world, the majority of us want to grow in skill and knowledge and earn the respect of our peers.

What about you? How would you respond to two items that we use on many of our employee engagement surveys?

1. My work offers enough variety and challenge to keep me engaged.
2. Most days, my job provides me with opportunities to stretch beyond my comfort zone.

Based on the responses to these questions, there is a very clear correlation between growth and challenge and overall levels of employee engagement. Cartoons and business sitcoms portray workers that simply "get by," investing as little as possible in their jobs. In fact, movies like *Office Space* and television shows like *The Office* depict most employees as expending more effort to avoid work than they would expend by actually *doing* the work.

Our experience shows just the opposite. People, in general, not only want challenge—they *need* challenge. Think intuitively. Do you get excited to go to work because you know that for the next three days you will have nothing to do but stare out the window? Does that thought engage you? Or do you get excited to work on something that stretches and challenges you? Which causes you to both "feel" and "act"?

We are fortunate to work with numerous organizations where challenge is not a problem. You can actually feel it when you walk into the room. Those are the environments that lead to innovation. Our positive response to challenge is instinctive.

Does your work challenge you? Do you feel that by facing and overcoming those challenges, you're growing as a person? Then you're experiencing one of the powerful keys of engagement.

GROWTH ISN'T (ALWAYS) ABOUT ADVANCEMENT

Calibrating an optimal level of growth and challenge is not always simple. Employee perception of internal opportunities for growth and development is one of the more important predictors of employee engagement. But several years ago, in our engagement research, employee perception of internal opportunities was the lowest it had ever been. Overall levels of engagement had also dropped correspondingly.

When we wrote our first book in 2014, we surveyed more than two hundred organizations, and employees were asked to rate their agreement with the following statement: "This company provides attractive opportunities for growth and development." Only 57 percent of employee responses were favorable. That was as much as twenty points below the overall engagement score average for most organizations.

Consider the environment at that time. Countries across the globe were experiencing their highest levels of unemployment in decades. Budgets for training had been cut across the board. Even more of a factor, however, was the fact that many employees, rather than searching for greater growth opportunities outside their current organization, chose to hunker down where they were—even in a stagnant environment—due to fear of the then-dismal job market. Those that stuck around chose also to play it safe, rather than search internally for challenge and risk.

Now, compare that to the environment four years later. Unemployment in the U.S. during most of 2018 hovered around four percent. While that figure hasn't been duplicated across much of the globe, most countries have experienced a sharp uptick in available jobs. Yet, survey responses to growth opportunities still don't come close to the favorable responses on most other survey items. What does that mean to the organization (and to the employee)? For many, it means, "Thanks for the good times, but I've taken another job."

Growth does not necessarily equal promotion. In fact, when we ask employees about growth, their responses aren't focused on near-term promotions. However, a significant percentage of managers automatically assume that employees equate growth with job promotion and a fancier title. They assume that in order for an employee to feel he or she is growing, a promotion must be available. As a result, in an age when companies are consolidating and reducing bureaucratic layers of management, these managers assume that if the ladder isn't available for climbing, employees will disengage. In reality, that's a cop-out. Growth goes beyond a higher position or a better parking space.

A DELICATE BALANCE

Increased responsibility can be one source of growth, but it's also a delicate balance. You can push a person too far into unknown territory. If you do, instead of stimulating their creativity, you create stress. In a positive growth environment, employees enhance their sense of self-esteem (the evaluation of their own self-worth) and self-efficacy (their belief in their ability to overcome obstacles and achieve goals) by approaching new opportunities with a sense of safety. There's a balance between challenge and autonomy, stimulation and stress.

Egghead Alert!

The zone of proximal development is the difference between what a person can do without help and what they can do with the aid of a teacher, coach, or mentor. When you leave this zone, you cross a threshold where giving someone too great a challenge (or giving them too much autonomy) can lead to diminishing returns. The positive feeling of facing a challenge turns into anxiety. So, the opportunity to try new things can be an opportunity to grow if the employee remains in the zone of proximal development and can receive the assistance and resources to succeed in a new area. If he crosses that threshold into a place where he feels fearful, threatened, or incompetent, then this can actually inhibit personal growth.[90]

Sometimes the push for growth comes at a price: increased levels of negative, harmful stress. Because of factors such as downsizing, job consolidation, and process efficiency initiatives, many employees have found themselves doing jobs that were once done by two or more people. Often, these increased duties are taking people outside their zone of proximal development and into areas where they feel they are in over their heads. Over the past decade, this consolidation has taken its toll on workers' health, motivation, and performance.

We regularly ask questions about stress when we work with teams in focus groups, one-on-one, or through surveys. Two survey items that provide interesting insight into workplace stress levels are:

1. My job requires me to be efficient.
2. The amount of work I am expected to do is reasonable.

We have noticed a steady increase in positive responses to the first question. In the seven-year period from 2010 to 2017, employee scores for this question increased by nearly sixteen percentage points. During the same time period, employee scores for the second question have *decreased* by fourteen percentage points. That's a thirty-point spread. The bottom line? We're asking employees to do more with less.

That's not necessarily a bad thing. According to employees, we are working more efficiently. In fact, according to our 2018 survey database, 81 percent of employees say they regularly feel they are being stretched and challenged in their current roles.

However, this is a double-edged sword. Our findings clearly show that growth is a key to engagement. But can the challenge go too far? Of course. Picture a balloon at a birthday party. In order to keep this balloon inflated, pressure must be applied to expand its elastic boundaries. Exert insufficient pressure and you get a collapsed balloon (and a ticked-off little kid). Put in too much air and BANG! You get a scary pop, flying latex, and a ticked-off mom.

The balloon is the mind of the employee under pressure in the workplace. Growth and challenge cause us to stretch and expand. This expansion can bring with it stress, which can be positive or negative. When we experience stress, the brain instructs the adrenal glands to deliver powerful hormones like cortisol and adrenaline to the bloodstream, causing muscles to tense and heart rate and breathing to increase. But our perception determines whether this reaction becomes healthy or harmful.

When we see the source of stress in a healthy, positive way, blood vessels dilate, which increases blood flow. Researchers from the Department of Psychiatry at the University of California–San Francisco discovered that the effects are similar to those found with aerobic exercise. This increased blood flow allows our brain and muscles to step up to the challenge. We engage.[91]

When we see the cause of stress as negative, our response is more potentially harmful. This kind of stress causes blood vessels to constrict, elevating blood pressure. Scientists with the behavioral chronic pain management program at Duke University Medical Center found that this results in symptoms similar to those you feel when you are angry, such as clouded thinking and an erratic heartbeat. Further, this may result in changed behavior, raised voices, and lapses in judgment.[92]

Beneficial stress challenges us to achieve and deliver. We grow. On the opposite end, unhealthy stress damages interpersonal relationships, impairs logic, and causes us to underachieve. We stagnate. We disengage.

Endocrinologist Hans Selye refined these concepts of healthy and harmful stress when he coined the terms *eustress* and *distress* to differentiate between the two.[93] Eustress describes healthy stress, such as that experienced by an athlete as she approaches the starting line of the 400-meter finals, or a salesperson approaching a new client for the first time. They feel capable, excited, and fully engaged.

On the other hand, employees in constant distress are likely to express it in one of two ways: continual high levels of anxiety, or withdrawal and depression (the slow hiss of air escaping from the balloon). They are more likely to become mentally or physically ill. At the very least, they will disengage.

Research has shown that eustress and distress are not actually a result of the specific stressor or situation, but of how the stressor is *perceived*.[94] One employee may perceive a challenge as a growth opportunity into which he can throw his heart, spirit, mind, and hands. For that employee, the stress is healthy and causes his balloon to inflate. This is eustress. For another employee, that same challenge may cause frustration, anger, and disengagement. The balloon either pops or deflates. This is distress.

Eustress	Distress
Challenge	Anxiety
Excitement	Fear
Stimulation	Embarrassment
Achievement	Doubt
Pride	Tension
Resilience	Blaming
Confidence	Paralysis
Hope	Despair

Eustress/Distress Threshold

For the organizational leader, the challenge of growth is finding that zone where the balloon is perfectly inflated, where each employee feels energized but not overwhelmed by the opportunity to learn new things and develop new skills.

Toxicologists say, "The poison is in the dosage." As explained on the episode of *This American Life* titled "Use Only as Directed," acetaminophen, the pain reliever found in Tylenol, is effective if taken in the appropriate dosage. But take even a little more than recommended and the result can be irreparable liver damage. Growth opportunities follow the same rules. A carefully calibrated amount of challenge and risk can encourage and energize. Too much can frighten and overwhelm.

What explains the huge difference in how people perceive stressful situations? In part, the explanation lies in what psychologists refer to as *framing*.

PICTURES WITHOUT FRAMES

In a study conducted by psychologists Amos Tversky and Daniel Kahneman, participants were asked to make a choice regarding a course of treatment for a population that, hypothetically, had a deadly disease. Six hundred people were expected to die.

A group of 152 participants was asked to choose between two courses of treatment for this population. With Treatment A, two hundred people would live. With Treatment B, there was a one-in-three probability that all victims of the disease would live, but there was a two-in-three probability that all victims would die.

Quick, what would you choose?

The result was intriguing: 72 percent chose Treatment A, and 28 percent chose Treatment B. The thought of two hundred people living was a better option than the unfavorable 33 percent chance of saving everyone.

A second group of 155 participants was then presented with the same story, but asked to choose from two other courses of treatments, C and D. They were told that with Treatment C, four hundred people would die. With Treatment D, there was a one-in-three probability that nobody would die but a two-in-three probability that six hundred people would die.

Only 22 percent of participants chose Treatment C. Treatment D was chosen by 78 percent.[95]

The two problems were, in essence, identical, as were the choices. The only difference was that the first problem (A/B) was framed in terms of number of lives saved, while the second problem (C/D) was framed in terms of lives lost.

The term *framing* or the *framing effect* is used in psychology to describe a bias that occurs when people make different choices depending on how that choice is presented to them. People make different choices, even when faced with identical facts, when those facts are presented with a positive frame versus when those facts are presented through a negative frame. Politicians get this. An incumbent will present employment facts by talking about the number of people employed, while his opponent will discuss the unemployment rate. One advertiser will talk about its product in terms of success rate, while a competitor will use the same information to discuss where that same product is failing.

Think of the old television commercials talking about how "four out of five dentists recommend [a particular brand of gum] for their patients who chew gum." Four out of five doesn't seem too bad, does it? But what if they were to advertise by saying this: "If you do chew gum, 20 percent of dentists wouldn't recommend this brand." Doesn't have the same bite (sorry), does it? Same facts, different framing. Often, different outcome.

Employees facing challenges—or growth opportunities—need positive framing. This doesn't mean simply spinning things in a different way; that can appear manipulative. But it's important to understand that whether an employee sees a challenge as a threat or as an opportunity will often be the difference between eustress or distress.

If an employee sees a challenge as an opportunity to benefit and learn, he or she will see it as positive. This results in eustress. The employee engages in the challenge, and the challenge incites further engagement. If the challenge looks more like an insurmountable task, and there is asymmetry between benefit and risk, he or she will not be engaged. Distress is the result.

Imagine a mid-level employee being offered the opportunity to learn a new and difficult suite of sales management software. If her supervisor frames the opportunity as something that's within her capabilities and makes it clear that there will be resources available to help her, she'll likely see the challenge as an opportunity for growth. But if the project is far beyond her technical abilities or her supervisor gives her no support, she's likely to see it not as an opportunity, but as an occasion full of threat and distress.

WHEN WE RISE TO THE OCCASION

Our conflicted relationship with growth and challenge dates back centuries. Rulers prevented uprisings by not allowing their subjects access to printing materials and learning. For example, in 1536, Englishman William Tyndale was put to death in Belgium for translating the New Testament and parts of the Old Testament, making them available to anyone who could read English.[96]

The reason was elementary: The monarchs and nobles of the age benefited from the inequality of their societies, inequality made possible by the ignorance of the populace. If they didn't know that it was possible to better themselves and grow, the peasants wouldn't be a threat to the power structure.

But today, growth is desirable. It not only gives us a greater sense of satisfaction and engagement with our jobs, it actually leads us to produce better results, both for employee and employer. Research has shown that the highest or most difficult goals consistently produce the highest levels of effort and performance. Additional research has shown that setting lofty goals for employees consistently leads to higher performance than positive verbal encouragement, provided the goals have:

- clarity
- challenge
- commitment
- feedback
- task complexity[97]

When challenging goals are imbued with all five qualities, engaged employees actively seek out opportunities for growth rather than waiting for them to come. They ask their supervisors for challenging tasks, lead teams on the road to difficult goals, and even create their own projects filled with obstacles and challenges. They're the people who consistently receive accolades, rewards, and promotions while others sit back and complain about how unfair it all is.

WHY SOME PEOPLE DON'T GROW

Framing certainly plays an important role in the way we view growth opportunities. But some of us simply don't see the need for growth. The fact is, most of us are just not very good at assessing our own need for growth. To put it another way, we're all a little self-deluded when it comes to looking in the mirror and seeing our shortcomings.

Not surprisingly, there's been quite a substantial body of research dedicated to this topic. These are some of the notable theories about why some of us resolutely refuse to pursue opportunities that will make us better, more skilled, and more successful:

- **The Lake Wobegon effect**: You've got to respect a psychology principle named after a public-radio sketch, don't you? This is the tendency to overrate our own abilities in relation to other people. It draws its name from writer Garrison Keillor's famous radio sign-off on his program *A Prairie Home Companion*: "Where all the women are strong, all the men are good looking, and all the children are above average." Simply put, we think we're better than we are. We don't grow because we already think we've arrived.[98]

- **Positive illusion:** This is the tendency to overestimate one's positive qualities and capabilities while underestimating one's negative qualities. Chip and Dan Heath write about this behavior in their book *Switch: How to Change Things When Change Is Hard*:

  > We've all heard the studies showing that the vast majority of us consider ourselves above-average drivers. In the psychology literature, their belief is known as a positive illusion. Our brains are positive illusion factories: Only 2 percent of high school seniors believe their leadership skills are below average. A full 25 percent of people believe they're in the top 1 percent in their ability to get along with others. Ninety-four percent of college professors report doing above-average work. People think they're at lower risk than their peers for heart attacks, cancer, and even food-related illnesses such as salmonella. Most deliciously self-deceptive of all, people say they are more likely than their peers to provide accurate self-assessments.[99]

- **American (Australian, or Latin American, etc.) Idol syndrome:** We surround ourselves with people who support and reinforce our self-concept. This is a pop culture theory but an interesting one: that we avoid potential criticism by creating a circle of people who tell us only what we want to hear.

- **The Dunning-Kruger effect:** In this cognitive bias that's become much more common thanks to the Narcissus reflecting pool that is the Internet, unskilled individuals mistakenly believe their ability to be much higher than it actually is.[100] One only has to look at the pro-liferation of "mommy bloggers," YouTube videos, and selfies on the Internet to see what some people think of their own talents, knowl-edge, skills, abilities, and looks. If you think you're already a genius (and a good-looking one, at that), why work harder to improve?

Our own research on over-raters supports this. Each year our teams con-duct tens of thousands of 360-degree feedback assessments. With an indi-vidual figuratively in the center of a feedback circle, a 360 process collects feedback from individuals working closely with that individual—supervisor, peers, direct reports, and so forth. The individual is then presented with information about his or her performance and behaviors as seen through the eyes of others. The individual also rates him- or herself on the same criteria, and results are compared. Interestingly, 78 percent of managers score them-selves higher than others score them. In short, we're typically poor at seeing our own areas for growth, but can quickly pick them out in others. Without feedback, we tend to create our own reality.

After years of surveying organizations, we've discovered that often the most competent people are also the most self-critical. They are constantly questioning their abilities (without slipping into the virulent self-criticism that reflects low self-esteem) and seeking ways to improve and grow. They avoid complacency. We have also found that the most effective managers are those who rate themselves closest to how others rate them. That's a sign of high levels of emotional intelligence and self-awareness, both critical to working well with others and being an effective leader.

On the flip side, some of the most incompetent people tend to rate themselves highest. They already know everything; why learn? In the work-place, their misplaced certainty makes them a nuisance at best, a hazard at worst. We call these people "legends in their own minds."

Then we have the employees who are not deluded, just insecure. For rea-sons that could include upbringing, negative experiences, trauma, or anxiety, some people simply have very low levels of self-esteem and self-efficacy. They don't believe that they bring much that is of value to the workplace. They don't believe they are capable of solving problems, mastering new skills, or surmounting obstacles. So, they don't try.

One of the challenges for leaders trying to increase engagement is to help such people find the confidence to choose a path of growth. It's worth the effort: When people build on their strengths and successes, they learn more and enjoy work more. According to Tom Rath and James K. Harter, those who have the opportunity to use their strengths are six times as likely to have an outstanding quality of life and to thrive during a forty-hour workweek. Those whose strengths are not used hit burnout level after just twenty hours.[101]

GROW OR GO

But what about organizations where the employees are not the problem? Where people come in with open minds, and their hands are ready to be put to work on a fresh set of challenges? Where opportunities for growth are either nonexistent or so intimidating and fraught with danger that nobody attempts them?

When growth opportunities are absent, you get stagnation, boredom, and attrition (the deflated balloon). People work on autopilot. They aren't present; their minds are not on their work. Errors happen. Quality drops. Indifference sets in, and the energy associated with heart and spirit is squelched. Work becomes routine. It may still get done—how many times have you driven a familiar route mindlessly, only to end up safely at your destination with no memory of getting there?—but nothing new happens. Innovation grinds to a halt.

Worst of all, turnover rises. Lack of opportunity for personal growth or career development is the number-one reason that employees leave a company. According to a survey by Glassdoor and Harris Interactive, more applicants—52 percent—wanted to hear about growth opportunities when interviewing for a job than about any other "perk." The same survey also found that one-third of employees left a job because of—wait for it—*lack of career growth*—than for any other reason. Only 8 percent left because of their managers.[102]

Our team analyzed survey results from over twenty thousand employees who had left a large biomedical company and its subsidiaries during a period of five years. We compared attrition numbers with engagement scores, and the results were intriguing. Typically, employees enjoyed a high level of growth during the first six months of employment. However, at the nine-month mark, these companies experienced much higher than average levels of attrition, and engagement levels plummeted. What was happening?

Upon further investigation, we learned that during the first six months, these employees were constantly learning. This made sense; the job was new to them. However, at about the nine-month point, employees had learned the basics of the job and were no longer as challenged as they were during the first six months. At that point, their levels of engagement dropped sharply.

What was even more interesting was that once employees hit the fourteen- to eighteen-month mark, engagement and retention increased again until the two-year mark. What was happening at each of these points in time that impacted both engagement and retention? Simple—it was about growth. Employees were learning and growing the first six months, but at about the nine-month mark they stopped. They also had little concept of where to go from there. They couldn't see any growth opportunities awaiting them. They felt stagnant. Those who stuck around for fourteen to eighteen months suddenly began to be presented with further growth opportunities, such as new assignments, promotions, and different team roles. They were, once again, growing. Engagement increased.

This pattern remained constant until the two-year mark, at which time employees began looking outside the organization for new opportunities and challenges. Some of those who remained fell into the same patterns of stagnation and disengagement.

For these companies, the solution was clear: Step up efforts to create growth opportunities at the nine- and twenty-four-month marks. Employees, in turn, had to choose to take advantage of these opportunities (remember, it's a 50-50 proposition). Those who did showed clear levels of engagement. Those who did not generally left the organization. That, reasoned these companies, was "good turnover."

Among some organizational leaders—executives and managers alike—there's a great deal of fear that by helping employees develop professionally, they'll only be preparing them to leave for greener pastures. It's the "help them grow and watch them go" syndrome, and it's simply not valid. As Beverly Kaye and Julie Winkle Giulioni write in *Help Them Grow or Watch Them Go*,[103] career development has become the "killer app" of employee engagement, which in turn leads to higher revenues, greater profitability, increased innovation, and a host of other happy outcomes.

Giving employees an environment where they can elect to develop professionally is very much the lesser of two evils. Is there a risk that by doing so you'll merely train your best people to leave for better jobs? Of course. But consider the alternative. Would you rather have unmotivated, unskilled people, numbed by routine, at the heart of your company, interacting with your customers?

Doesn't it make more sense to help your people develop skills that make them worth keeping—and then hold on to them by creating a culture in which they have the autonomy, respect, and freedom to see how far they can stretch without fear of failing? Based on our research, it's not even a choice: While some growth-minded employees leave, most engage and stick around, and the organization benefits.

A growth-positive workplace is especially important to Millennials, who will form the next-generation workforce. A survey of nearly eight thousand college students conducted by Achievers and Experience, Inc., showed that the most important factor to them in choosing a place to work was career advancement opportunities, beating salary 54 percent to 51 percent. Also, "interesting and challenging work" tied with salary, 51–51, as the most important factor.[104]

Clearly, while pay and other hygiene factors need to be there, employees want growth and development not only to advance their future career prospects but also because it makes work more enjoyable and rewarding. Human beings are curious individuals who want to learn, adapt, and evolve; the circumstances don't matter as much.

Even hourly employees want to be challenged and grow through their jobs. In a study of 2,743 employees in an international manufacturing company, our team found significant differences between the attitudes, beliefs, and values of hourly versus exempt employees. For example, only 51 percent of hourly employees felt that they had a voice in the organization and could speak up without fear of retribution or negative consequences, compared to nearly 70 percent of exempt employees. Only 39 percent of hourly employees reported receiving counseling about career growth, compared to 54 percent of exempt employees. Yet consider how important the role of the typical hourly employee is to a company's well-being:

- Hourly employees often represent the majority of customer-facing roles.
- They are directly involved in production.
- They directly impact quality.
- They are advocates of safety.
- They know where the problems are, and how to resolve them.

When was the last time a manager in your organization worried about training an hourly employee so well that she became too employable to stay? Yet by denying growth opportunities to all workers because of this irrational fear, some managers are preventing some of their most valuable people from getting better at their jobs. It doesn't make sense.

These days, we've noticed a trend we call the "tour of duty." A person comes to an organization, finds tremendous opportunities for professional and personal development, becomes more valuable, and leaves. However, because his supervisors encouraged his growth and gave him what he needed to get better, the relationship remains strong. A few years later, he comes back for a second tour, occupying a higher rung on the corporate ladder and often bringing with him an even better skill set.

That's why the "grow and go" mentality is self-defeating. In the end, growth leads to engagement, and employees who find deep, satisfying engagement in an organization are more likely to form mutually beneficial long-term relationships with that organization . . . even if they're working somewhere else.

MASTERY, NOT MONEY

According to our 2018 employee engagement survey database, employees report that 68 percent of their workplaces offer their people regular opportunities to grow professionally and personally. Still, that leaves about one-third of workplaces that are dropping the ball on a critical component of engagement. Some do this based on a common misconception that growth means spending more on employee training. This is just as false as the idea that money can buy employee satisfaction.

"People have to want to grow, but sometimes they need to be pushed to grow as well," says Tony Bingham, president and CEO of the Association for Talent Development (ATD), the world's largest organizational training and development body. "I think most people naturally want to grow. You're either growing or dying. I think if people don't feel like they're advancing at some level, they're not happy, or engaged.

"However, you can't change behavior unless people want to change it," Bingham continues. "There are people who don't think they need to change. They think they're perfect, and they're defensive about it. In those instances, you have to create what we call a 'disturbance,' some type of catalyst to make them want to change.

"The secret sauce is finding that meaningful reason to try something new. Most individuals, if they see an organization that's willing to invest in them—and all training is an investment—they'll understand that the investment is beneficial to them. If you're helping them be better in their job, more promotable, and have more transferable skills when they leave the organization, they're probably going to embrace growth.

"Take the Millennials," Bingham concludes. "Development is what they really value. Money is not the main driver for them. It's 'How do I make a contribution?' With them, you need to be transparent and link what the individual can do with where the organization is trying to go. If people see how what they do on a daily basis is linked to the organization's success, they will be motivated to be part of that. The trick is that there's no trick."

Engaged organizations create an environment where employees seek out growth opportunities that they find enjoyable and stimulating. This helps defuse the dreaded "don't get involved" reflex, in which employees worry that if they do their jobs too well, they'll be rewarded with more work. But we know that money or advancement alone don't get employees to be passionate about taking on a new challenge. The potential for reward needs to be present, but it's insufficient to spark a growth culture. So, what's the secret sauce?

It's *mastery*, the desire to constantly improve at something that's important to us. In his book *Outliers*, Malcolm Gladwell popularized an idea first posited by psychologists Herbert Simon and William Chase back in 1973: that mastery of anything requires a minimum of ten years or ten thousand hours of dedicated practice.[105] That doesn't necessarily take into account true outliers, like so-called naturals (people of incredible inborn talent), or those who use their practice time with inhuman efficiency, but it's a solid general rule. Well, one of the hallmarks of engaged organizations is that they offer their people numerous ways to have *personal mastery experiences.*

Imposing expensive training programs on employees is not only costly, it presumes that leadership knows what its people care about. Personal mastery experiences may lie outside a person's core job responsibilities but align with their interests and values. By building a culture in which employees are free to explore multiple paths to personally relevant mastery (with minimal concerns about failure), management creates optimal conditions for engagement while allowing workers to choose what matters to them.

This blend of mastery, autonomy, and purpose is the subject of exploration by author Daniel Pink in his book *Drive.* Pink argues that the long-standing reward-or-punishment, carrot-and-stick motivational model doesn't work. The trifecta of intrinsic motivators—autonomy, mastery, and purpose—is the key, he asserts, to motivating people to become engaged and lift companies to new heights. He writes:

> The best use of money as a motivator is to pay people enough to take the issue of money off the table: Pay people enough so that they're not thinking about money and they're thinking about the work. Once you do that, it turns out there are three factors that the science shows lead to better performance, not to mention personal satisfaction: autonomy, mastery, and purpose.[106]

FLOW

Because employees are motivated in great part by the desire to become more proficient at something that matters to them, everyone ultimately aspires to what is referred to as *flow,* the mental state first described by psychology professor Mihaly Csikszentmihalyi. Flow, he says, is the state in which "a person performing an activity is fully immersed in a feeling of energized focus, full involvement, and enjoyment in the process of the activity. In essence, flow is characterized by complete absorption in what one does."[107]

According to Csikszentmihalyi, "The best moments in our lives are not the passive, receptive, relaxing times . . . The best moments usually occur if a person's body or mind is stretched to its limits in a voluntary effort to accomplish something difficult and worthwhile."[108] In other words, we're most engaged not when we're kicking back but when we're kicking butt—testing ourselves, serving others, stretching beyond our ordinary capacity to chase excellence.

Think about a time when work seemed effortless. When the hours flew by without your even realizing. When you finished a time-consuming task and you weren't emotionally drained. When words, notes, or ideas seemed to spring from your mind fully formed. Have you ever felt like that? You probably have, and you probably loved it. That's flow. It's when hard work becomes easy and excellence ceases to be a chore. At times, the end of the day may mean you're exhausted. At the same time, what you do is exciting, renewing, and energizing. You're ready to take on another round.

Even if they don't understand it in this way, most people aspire to some kind of flow, the proficiency to perform a task so well and with such enjoyment that effort is pleasurable and time seems to fly by. To get there, most people follow a predictable path through four states of competence:

1. **Unconscious incompetence**: You don't know what you don't know. You take up a project, hobby, or other pursuit in complete ignorance, unable to see all that you need to work on.

2. **Conscious incompetence**: After a brief honeymoon period, reality sets in: You have a lot of work to do. In a way, unconscious incompetence is merely a "vestibule period," an introductory time before the real effort begins. At this stage, you can see how much you have to learn, and hopefully you have the resources, help, and encouragement to get through it.

3. **Conscious competence**: Now you're learning and getting repetitions, but everything requires thought and conscious effort. You're not fluid or reflexive. Imagine a young baseball player just learning to hit and standing at home plate saying to himself, "Okay, hands back, hip in, stride with the pitch, head down, hands are the last thing through the hitting zone . . ." With all that thinking going on, there's little room for execution, which is why he misses more pitches than he hits. But this is a necessary step toward . . .

4. **Unconscious competence**: This is mastery. This is where flow occurs. After enough hours of practice and repetition, proficiency becomes

automatic, thoughtless. You're able to perform excellently by reflex and use your conscious mind not to work on the basics but to experiment and innovate in real time.[109]

Consider the martial artist who begins as a white belt. She trains and practices for years to learn how to fight and master her art. However, the discipline and self-control needed to undertake years of repetitive practice also change her as a person. By the time she achieves mastery and earns her black belt, capable of winning a fight against almost anyone, she has also become a person who does not need to fight. The transformational nature of mastery is what gives it its powerful appeal.

Want engaged employees? Create the conditions under which all of your employees who wish to can walk the four steps to unconscious competence—to flow—with as much confidence, autonomy, and safety as possible.

The vice president of operations at a major office-supply retailer—we'll call him David—is a perfect example of finding yourself in a supportive environment and using that support to propel yourself upward. David shared with our team his remarkable story of joining the company in 1988 as a night-shift janitor. Asked about the factors that contributed to his advancement, he responded, "I have always had good bosses that believed in me."

Of course, support from superiors is the starting point, not the end point. What made it possible for David to rise from custodian to VP was using the belief of his bosses as a springboard to embrace challenges—to grow and engage. He took responsibility for his growth, and the results have been extraordinary.

None of this is meant to claim that training, raises, and promotions are not important. They matter. However, intrinsic, not extrinsic, motivators are the keys to getting employees to choose growth opportunities. Autonomy is critical in the growth process; each person must be free to choose whether or not to pursue challenge—and what type to pursue. Some other tactics that organizational leaders should consider implementing in the quest for growth, mastery, and flow include:

- **Provide mentors.** Make it clear that experienced people are available and willing to offer their wisdom to employees who wish to undertake learning a new skill, going back to school, or taking the helm of a troublesome project or department.

- **Create a "build the resume" culture.** One of our clients published this objective for its employees: "Help our people add a line to their resume every year." The idea was that ample resources would be made available to employees to develop a wide range of additional skills relevant to their professional lives. In this context, advancement becomes meaningful for some people. If your employer is helping you become more skilled, employable, and valuable, you're probably going to be more engaged.

  Some companies take employee development to an extreme. Shipping giant Maersk sends its people overseas for three years to attend classes and learn more about the world of global shipping. You think those people are fully engaged?

- **Create a "fail forward" culture.** Novelty and challenge carry the risk of failure. Problems occur when the organizational culture has embedded in it the implied or overt threat of punishment for failure. No one will risk stretching and possibly failing when they feel there's a sword hanging over their neck. Instead, imbue the culture with the message that bold failures are not only okay but desirable because they teach important lessons and foster innovation. This isn't to encourage dereliction of duty or sloppy work, but to encourage employees to extend themselves into areas that hold potential benefits for the individual and the organization.

- **People will perform better when they are subject to higher expectations.** This is known as the Pygmalion effect, and it will be covered in more depth in chapter nine. [110]

Believing in your people and demanding their best doesn't cost much. But the payoff can change everything.

FIVE QUESTIONS

1. What level of personal and professional development do I want or expect from my job?
2. In what areas of my work do I feel I have gained mastery? Where do I most regularly feel I'm "dialed in" or experience "flow"?

3. What parts of my job stretch and challenge me to be better? Where do I feel stagnant? Where am I being stretched too far (eustress versus stress)?
4. What am I doing to actively and regularly solicit feedback?
5. What opportunities for growth are available in my organization, and where have I taken advantage of them in the past? What opportunities have I not taken advantage of?

RECAP

- Growth is about challenge and trying new things in order to progress professionally and personally.
- Achievement is a universal human need.
- Growth isn't necessarily linked to advancement or job promotion.
- Organizations must carefully balance challenges that stimulate and excite while not pushing employees into anxiety and apprehension. That balance is called the eustress/distress threshold.
- Whether a situation produces beneficial stress (eustress) or harmful stress (distress) often depends on how we perceive it.
- How employers frame a growth opportunity can determine whether employees see it as inviting or threatening.
- People tend to deliver their best when their best is required.
- Over-raters—people who rate their abilities higher than their peers rate their abilities—tend to resist growth opportunities.
- Given consistent opportunities to grow, along with the support they need, most people will engage. Denied those opportunities, people disengage, become apathetic, and leave.
- Mastery and flow are important elements of growth.

CHAPTER SIX

IMPACT

"A life is not important except in the impact it has on other lives."
—*Jackie Robinson*

FEW IMAGES OF MODERN WORK are more damaging to motivation than that of the cubicle dweller slaving away in a hive of identical cloth-lined squares, accomplishing very little. Instead of working side by side with a group of colleagues in a factory or warehouse setting, this individual is isolated and glued to a computer screen or phone, with little contact with coworkers or the outside world. It's the human equivalent of the worker bee, confined to a honeycomb (most cubicles even resemble the symmetry of the hive), where the bee is expected to produce continuously in his or her area of responsibility, with little line of sight into the end result. That's a depressing, demoralizing state. Fortunately for the bee, it dies after six weeks. The human isn't so lucky. The organization expects to get six years, rather than six weeks, out of the worker.

Don't get me wrong here. It's not a statement on those of us who work in cubicles (which is a good portion of the office population). Rather, it's a comment on the dangers of being isolated from seeing results of the work one does. When people feel that their work is repetitive and lack any connection to the impact of their efforts, it becomes easy to conclude that the work is meaningless. We saw this in both the chapter on meaning and the chapter on growth. Indifference, sloppiness, and neglect often follow.

Here's an example that should make your hair stand on end. In April 2013, the U.S. Air Force stripped seventeen officers based in Minot, North Dakota, of their ability to control and launch nuclear missiles after the group miserably failed a test of its missile launch procedures. Air Force spokespeople said that the officers in question had "more of an attitude problem than a proficiency problem," and that a culture of indifference had settled over the unit, including at least one intentional violation of missile safety rules and a widespread reluctance to report rule violations to superiors.[111]

That was bad enough. Worse came in October 2013 when the Associated Press broke a story about Air Force officers napping while leaving open a blast door intended to prevent intruder access to the underground missile command post.[112] And this terrible story doesn't even end there: In January 2014, thirty-four officers were found to have cheated on their ICBM launch officer proficiency tests.[113] The thought of completely disengaged men in control of hundreds of nuclear-tipped missiles can certainly send shivers down the spine.

Later in 2014, key members, including mid-ranking officers, in the U.S. Air Force's nuclear missile force were reported to have been experiencing burnout from what was seen as exhausting, unrewarding, and stressful work. Associated Press reported that there were also heightened levels of misconduct, such as increased court-martial rates, spousal abuse, drunkenness, drug abuse, and even spending time in Russia with "suspect" women.[114]

How do we know this was an engagement problem? Read the comments of Bruce Blair, a former ICBM launch control officer who's now a researcher at Princeton University: "The nuclear air force is suffering from a deep malaise caused by the declining relevance of their mission since the Cold War's end over 20 years ago. Minuteman launch crews have long been marginalized and demoralized by the fact that the Air Force's culture and fast-track careers revolve around flying planes, not sitting in underground bunkers baby-sitting nuclear-armed missiles."[115]

In other words, without the internal concept that they were frontline fighters in the fight against communism, these missile officers lost any sense that their work was relevant or meaningful. They became detached from the—you should pardon the expression in the context of talking about nuclear missiles—*impact* of their duties, and this led to the unconscious belief that their duties simply didn't matter. First hearts went, then spirits, then minds, and then hands. All MIA. Negligence and apathy were inevitable.

WHAT IS IMPACT?

Impact is a fundamental precursor to meaning. Meaning cannot exist in a vacuum; it's extremely difficult to find meaning in one's work—especially work that appears routine or mundane—without having a clear sense of how that work affects the outside world.

In fact, meaning and impact are so closely related that when our team first started poring through survey data, we grouped these two together. But then we realized that these two were clearly distinct components of engagement. Meaning is about *purpose*—the "why." Impact is about the *result*—the "what." (Besides, then we would have ended up with MAGC—a pretty lame acronym.)

Survey data clearly showed that individuals could find meaning in what they did, yet still feel like they were making little difference or progress in that meaningful work. The missing piece was impact. Impact can be defined as:

Seeing positive, effective, and worthwhile outcomes and results from your work.

One summer several years ago, I hiked through Zion National Park, Utah, with a group of teens. Over a period of four days, we logged over thirty-five miles of trail, but at about mile six, the group leaders noticed something interesting. When the group trekked into those areas most isolated by majestic canyon walls and heavy forest, although the beauty was certainly apparent, these stretches seemed to go on forever. It felt as if we were hiking the same trail over and over again.

We constantly referred to GPS and trail markings to understand where they were in relation to their predetermined end point. Although our GPS behavior bordered on obsessive-compulsive, the team found that it provided us with relief—and renewed energy—when we knew where we stood in relation to where we had been and what remained ahead. When we could see our progress, we were excited to continue the journey. When progress was questionable, the packs appeared to double in weight. Human beings need to feel that we are advancing and moving forward.

Employee engagement surveys conducted by DecisionWise typically contain the statement:

> Most days, I feel like I am making progress on important work projects or initiatives.

Responses that are strongly in agreement with that statement strongly correlate with employee engagement. That result highlights one way that managers can create a culture of engagement without spending a dime: Give them ways to see progress in their work. Mastery, autonomy, and purpose are tightly linked. Employees need autonomy to feel free to choose an area in which to grow, and gaining mastery in that area in turn makes them feel more autonomous and in control of their work and future. That feeling leads to a greater feeling of purpose, as employees are more empowered to choose the work that's meaningful to them. It's a virtuous cycle that leads to employees who are motivated by what Rosabeth Moss Kanter, writing in the *Harvard Business Review*, calls OPI: opportunity for positive impact.[116]

We all need that sense of progress. We also need to see where we are in relation to where we have been and need to be. What's more, we all need to see that what we are doing makes a difference in an important way. Impact evokes a specific set of emotions and thoughts, such as "I can do my job," "My time was well spent," and "We're making progress." People at all levels need to know that they are more than cogs in a machine over which they have no control. They need to know that what they are doing is having an effect in the world apart from adding to the company's balance sheet.

IMPACT CHANNELS

Having a clear picture of the impact of their work makes people feel worthwhile and valued. Without a clear "impact channel," a window to the world outside work where information on impact is readily available, employees can come to feel that they are on a treadmill, with their efforts yielding little. This is true even if the work is having a massive impact on the company's customers and the world at large.

For instance, you may remember the rash of employee suicides in 2010 at the Foxconn electronics assembly plant in Shenzhen, China. Fourteen employees took their own lives (most by throwing themselves off buildings, which led the company to string nets from the rooftops), presumably due in part to long shifts, poor pay, and working conditions that independent reports described as being like a sweatshop.[117]

Ironically, one of the products the Foxconn workers were assembling was the iPhone, which since its introduction has changed how people live their lives and do business around the globe. Do you think if the workers who took their own lives had been truly aware of the impact their work on the iPhone was having—that they were actually making a difference—some of them might have made a different choice? Impossible to say; perhaps some lives might have been saved.

The issue of choice leads to a critical point: Impact and results are not the same. As with other aspects of engagement, while good leaders provide the essential ingredients, it's up to the individual to choose to engage. I have interviewed countless employees who participate in meetings where, with the best of intentions, the management team projects company financial performance on an overhead screen, presumably thinking that "involving employees in the numbers" will increase overall performance. It's a great theory, and it is important that employees understand the company's (or division's, plant's, department's, team's, etc.) financial objectives. But when it comes to engagement, this does very little. The organization can share all the results it wants, but employees must choose to find both meaning and impact in those results.

Several years ago, I was asked to speak to a group of 450 healthcare professionals about the concept of MAGIC. These were leaders within a healthcare system who were brought together to learn about employee engagement and about how they could better use these five keys in their hospitals. The organization had made significant strides in understanding that the level of patient care was dramatically impacted by their level of employee care. There was no question that the employee experience directly influenced the patient experience.

As I was speaking about the level of impact each of them had on hundreds of patients, a well-meaning nurse supervisor stated, "I understand how, as nurses, we have direct impact on our patients. For me, I find a great deal of meaning through this impact—we're saving lives. But, how does that translate to employees in, say, departments like dietary, transport, or house-keeping? They may not see that level of impact." I saw heads nodding, curious as to what my response might be.

I didn't have to respond. A woman in the far back of the room stood up, grabbing a nearby microphone from one of the facilitators. She stated, with all the fervor of a preacher in a Sunday service, "I work in dietary. My job is to supervise a group of people who are responsible for taking meals to patients three times a day, and sometimes more." Those sitting around her—each of them also from the same department—joined in nodding their heads, followed by an occasional "amen" (this was the southern U.S., after all).

She went on: "None of these patients is at their best when they come to the hospital. While you doctors and nurses are telling them bad news and poking them all day long, my team is bringing them what might be the only joy they experience that day—a good, warm meal. Not only that, every meal is accompanied by a smile and a conversation about *them* as people, not about their health. Now, that's IMPACT." She sat down.

I didn't have to say anything else. The standing ovation she received from 450 audience members said "we get it."

Sometimes they'll see impact in unlikely places. For example, an employee may see no meaning (personal purpose) or impact (personal results) in the company's record-breaking profits for the previous year, but see a powerful impact in how her work on a green energy initiative helped the company reduce its carbon footprint. The impact of the work, in that case, is in direct harmony with her meaning.

Impact helps employees develop a strong inner work life—the emotions, perceptions, and motivations that they experience throughout their workday. Much of this is where spirit comes into the picture.

Does understanding an organization's vision, direction, and performance help create engagement? Of course. Research shows that when employees understand how their work contributes to the realization of the organization's broad vision, they become more engaged and work more effectively to achieve that vision.[118] The inverse is also true: Employees can't have an impact if they don't understand how their work contributes to that vision. If the vision hasn't been communicated, then managers can't align their people or help them understand why their work is important. When employees understand the vision, they also know what tasks are more important than others and how that helps deliver success for the company.

Intuitively, that makes sense. I'm more likely to put my heart and spirit—and therefore my mind and hands—into something that I can see. The data support that. When our researchers looked at the survey question "Most days I feel like I'm making progress on important tasks or initiatives," over 80 percent of individuals who were classified as Fully Engaged responded "Strongly Agree" to this question. This is in stark contrast to the 18 percent of disengaged employees who agreed.

Want to see what happens when a company steps on employees' feelings that they are adding value? Look no further than the fiasco surrounding venerable retailer J. C. Penney. A few years back, new CEO Ron Johnson elected to kill off the company's decades-old sale and coupon culture, attempting to wean customers off what he saw as "artificial prices."

The misguided strategy not only caused sales and profit to collapse, it destroyed employee engagement. Under the new approach, prices were continually being raised and lowered throughout stores, forcing employees into a never-ending cycle of tagging and retagging items. Signage and marketing changed seemingly on a whim, with most of the new signage schemes only confusing shoppers. Johnson regularly introduced complex new merchandising methods without consulting employees who were actually on the sales floor. Often, frustrated workers would abandon the confusing new methods for the old ways that worked.

The end result was chaos. Morale tanked as employees perceived that their extra work was superficial, pointless, and driven by executive caprice instead of some grand strategic plan. Rather than doing any sort of valuable work, they began to see themselves as tools to carry out the latest whim of the CEO. It didn't help that tens of thousands of staff had been let go under the new regime. When the J. C. Penney board finally sacked Johnson, just seventeen months after his disastrous hiring, some employees wept with joy and relief.[119]

In organizations that make it difficult or impossible for their employees to see the impact of their work, you get indifference, frustration, and another example of *learned helplessness*. Employees learn through repeated episodes that in the big picture, nothing they do matters, they are powerless, and management doesn't value their contributions. It's not hard to see how that state of affairs could destroy a business.

EFFORT + IMPACT = ENGAGEMENT

In organizations where high levels of effort pair with high levels of perceived impact, you get an engaged workforce and a stellar employee experience. The combination of effort and impact encompasses many of the key ingredients of employee engagement: satisfying work, a sense of progress, a feeling of community, and confirmation from the employer that the effort is valuable and meaningful. The importance of effort and impact can be seen in this matrix.

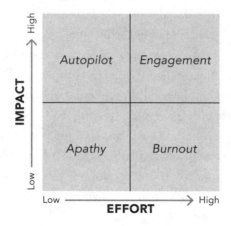

When employees exert their best efforts and find them both valued and meaningful, engagement is the natural outcome. Heart, spirit, hands, and mind? All there. Check.

Low impact and effort breed apathy, but low effort doesn't appear out of nowhere, like a road that starts mysteriously in the middle of a forest. Most employees begin their term of employment giving at least solid effort; they are trying to prove their value, get through a probationary period, or win the approval of their peers, to name a few reasons. But when there's nothing in the impact channel—when they get little or no feedback, recognition, or validation of the impact they are having—effort often wanes and apathy sets in.

Apathy is a state where one lacks interest, caring, or concern. Little feeling is involved. Heart and spirit are absent. Because of this, the individual is unable to find passion in her work. While the mind and hands may carry on in the short term, once apathy truly kicks in the employee is soon saying good-bye to the effort that is so critical to engagement.

"Autopilot" is an interesting category, as some might mistakenly confuse it with "flow." The two are very different, however. The two share a common theme—proficiency. However, *flow* takes advantage of this proficiency to create energy. When an individual who experiences flow finds that he has reached a sense of competency, it is that very competence that leads to enjoyment, pleasure, and performance. A natural outcome is the desire he has to continue to experience that same feeling. He has a desire to continue contributing effort because he can see the impact.

The proficiency that accompanies someone on autopilot, on the other hand, results in the inability to capture the heart and spirit. Simply put, she is bored and lacks challenge. She begins to feel that the effort being put in doesn't result in the type of impact she would like to see. One example of this can be found in the story of music legend Bob Dylan.

During the better part of the 1960s, Dylan was one of the most popular singer-songwriters in the world. He sold millions of albums, performed for sold-out concerts in large venues, and gained the adoration of fans around the world. Who wouldn't be on top of the world? Well, Dylan was not. He was bored and disengaged in his work. After all, he could write a song in his sleep and it would be an instant hit. He needed to make a major key change in his musical direction.

This realization resulted in *Like a Rolling Stone*. After the release of this song and album under the same title, Dylan gave an interview[120] where he described this shift from autopilot to engagement:

Interviewer: "You used to say that you wanted to perform as little as possible, that you wanted to keep most of your time to yourself. Yet you're doing more concerts and cutting more records every year. Why? Is it the money?"

Dylan: "Everything is changed now from before. Last spring, I guess I was going to quit singing. I was very drained, and the way things were going, it was a very draggy situation—I mean, when you do 'Everybody Loves You for Your Black Eye,' and meanwhile the back of your head is caving in . . .

Anyway, I was playing a lot of songs I didn't want to play. I was singing words I didn't really want to sing . . . but 'Like a Rolling Stone' changed it all: I didn't care anymore after that about writing books or poems or whatever. I mean it was something that I myself could dig. It's very tiring having other people tell you how much they dig you if you yourself don't dig you. It's also very deadly entertainment-wise." For Dylan, what began as engagement turned to autopilot, which then gave way to burnout.

BURNOUT AND FEELING VALUED

Then we have *burnout*. Burnout occurs when there is asynchrony between effort and perceived impact—when you're working long hours and late nights over prolonged periods, but seeing little progress and no results. When that happens, it's easy to feel that you're running yourself ragged for no payoff.

But burnout goes deeper than that. Without impact and meaning, the fulfillment that fuels discretionary effort is absent. We're wired to crave validation that we're proficient at what we do and that our work matters. When we don't get that, the emotional tank runs dry. Mental and emotional exhaustion take hold. Suddenly, the reasons we've been expending extra effort don't matter as much as our need to get away from the work and recharge—the definition of burnout.

Employee expectations are impact-dependent. Research on burnout conducted at the University of California–Berkeley found that burnout is a prolonged response to three dysfunctional states in the workplace: exhaustion, cynicism, and sense of inefficacy.[121] If, at the end of performance, there's a means to see impact and results and reap rewards, engagement is likely. If employees feel like nothing they do matters and nothing ever changes, there's a real risk of burnout.

Egghead Alert!

Expectancy Theory is a theory of motivation made up of three factors: expectancy (the perception that effort will lead to performance), instrumentality (the perception that performance will yield results), and valence (the perception that the results will produce a reward of value to the individual). it partially explains why people choose one behavior over others: They believe it will lead to a desirable and worthwhile outcome. At the core of this theory is the individual's belief that he or she is capable of performing at a level of proficiency needed to attain that desired result. This is the hallmark of both high self-efficacy and self-esteem.[122]

Human beings need to feel that in spending our limited time we are purchasing something significant, that we have achieved something worthwhile and valued by the time we go home. Think about the simple pleasure of getting through your to-do list on a given day. In fact, it's such an endorphin rush that if it wasn't on the to-do list, we put it on the list after-the-fact, just so we can give ourselves credit for our accomplishment! If you feel like you've achieved the goals you've set out for yourself, and that the organization values that achievement, you feel efficient, effective, and even powerful. You've made an impact on your world. That's the kind of feeling that can drive engagement for an entire organization.

There's a name for this: *feeling valued*. Engaged employees feel (and are) valued by their peers, superiors, and the organization. That sense of being valued contributes to their sense of self-worth.

Can a manager play a role in helping employees feel valued? Without a doubt. Often, our employee engagement surveys, as well as our 360 degree feedback surveys, will include questions on recognition. Questions like "My manager acknowledges or recognizes our team for strong performance" or "My manager takes the time to provide me with feedback about my performance" typically receive disappointing marks. Most managers simply don't recognize their employees for the value they bring to the organization. Managers who do take the time to recognize and reward generally find increased levels of engagement and stronger team performance.

So, it's about building employees' self-esteem and self-worth through reward and recognition, right? Not quite. While recognition and reward are critical components of engagement, this is not just about making employees feel valued by occasionally throwing a few movie tickets their way. Psychologists refer to this as *contingent self-esteem*: Individuals base their worth on the outcome of events or approval of others. It creates a transactional relationship. It's a dangerous slope.

There's actually little correlation between high self-esteem and high job performance. Organizations are full of employees who have high self-esteem yet perform poorly. They're the ones who spend a good part of their day telling others (including your customers) how good they are at the jobs. They bring up the countless headhunters who are constantly knocking at their door (when everyone knows that they received one random call four years ago, from a not-for-profit looking for someone to move to Mongolia to build yurts). As they say in Texas, they are "all hat, no cattle." They talk a big game and seem to have no shortage of confidence, yet they fail to impact the success of the organization.

The opposite is true as well. Many organizations are full of employees who appear to have a great deal of self-esteem, yet actually have very little. They're masters of disguise. They look to validate themselves through the eyes of others. They are the employees who want to make others think they are indispensable. They build impenetrable fortresses around their roles, convincing others that the organization is circling the drain and they are single-handedly keeping things afloat. Some organizations even begin to believe that these individuals are rock stars without whom the world would stop spinning.

DANGEROUS CONDITIONS

There are two grave dangers present in these situations. First, you have an organization held hostage. Most of these individuals are not as valuable as they have convinced others they are. When our consulting team works with organizations on assessing the talent in their ranks, we often hear of the "untouchables." They are the employees who are so valuable that the organization cannot do without them. We're told that if the employee were to leave, a key customer would quit doing business with the company. Or if the software developer decided to take the job in Silicon Valley, product development would cease and the applications would fall apart. Or there's the assembly-line worker who's the only one who can deal with the temperamental robotics.

As we dig into these cases, we soon find that most of these employees actually have very little impact on the success of the organization. They've just mastered the art of convincing others how valuable they are.

They're like the cross-eyed discus thrower—they don't get much done, but they sure keep the crowd on its toes. If your organization is being held hostage—or you find that you've become one of the hostage-takers—it's time to reevaluate.

The second danger is that these employees are disengaged. It's important to note that some of these fortress builders with low self-esteem are actually strong performers. They are valuable to the organization and are having an impact on success. Their primary purpose is to deliver results, which helps them find validation. They work long hours, often at great personal cost. They take on difficult or undesirable responsibilities and assignments. Organizations love this type of individual. In fact, many Key Contributors fall into this category.

So, why is this a problem? Well, engagement is a 50-50 proposition. Individuals must choose to be engaged, and these employees are not engaged. Engagement involves feeling and acting. These low self-esteem employees may have their minds and hands in the game, but their hearts and spirits aren't along for the ride. So, while they deliver results, having no heart or spirit in their work will eventually cause them to become cynical and skeptical.

Many have seen employees in this situation come to view the organization as an evil monster lurking under the bed, waiting to pounce. They establish unrealistic expectations of others and look for reasons to point out coworker shortcomings. Soon, they're finding fault in customers and bosses. Remember, for these employees solving problems is a validation of their value. If they can point out a problem, they can either resolve it or use it to demonstrate their worth in comparison to others. Either way, they get a quick esteem booster shot. Ultimately, however, they burn out . . . and often take colleagues or customers with them.

CREATING AN IMPACT ENVIRONMENT

In the end, it's about choice. A manager can set the tone for the environment in which an employee can choose to be engaged. The boss can set clear targets, and measure progress against these targets. This allows the employee and the organization to gauge progress, one of the key components of impact. The manager can regularly provide feedback, and recognize and reward performance.

However, the employee must choose to be engaged. The best that any organization can do is recruit well and give employees every opportunity to find meaning in the impact that their work has. Some will not find it with your organization. On the other end of the relationship, if you're the employee who's not feeling valued or that your work is not having an impact, ask yourself why. Are you being provided the window to see the impact of your efforts? If you are, why doesn't that impact resonate with you? If your answers aren't satisfactory, you might not be a good fit for your organization.

Here's an example of an organization creating an optimal impact window. Since its founding in 1973, clothing company Patagonia has demonstrated an unshakable commitment to environmental stewardship as well as a deep, family-oriented corporate culture. But in 2011, the company did something extraordinary that really let its people see the impact of its environmental beliefs: the Buy Less campaign. Patagonia took out a full-page ad in the *New York Times* exhorting people not to buy as much of its outdoor apparel, in order to reduce the industry's environmental footprint. But it didn't stop there. The company also created an online marketplace on Patagonia .com where its customers could buy and sell used clothing items. Apart from burnishing its public image, the online initiative also gave employees an easy way to go online and watch their employer put its money where its mouth is on resource conservation.[123]

By the way, Patagonia's famously intimate and engaged workforce helped sales grow by 33 percent in 2012, a year when overall U.S. apparel retail sales grew by just 2.9 percent.[124]

Another wonderful example of creating an impact-rich environment came from medical-device maker Accellent, whom I mentioned earlier. If you recall, the company began producing posters that told the stories of people who had benefited from their stents, replacement joint components, and other products. It was a wonderful way to evoke meaning in people's work, but an even better way to connect employees to impact that meant something to them personally.

Tricia McCall, Accellent's senior vice president of human resources, explains. "The products we make are helping people live better lives," she says. "Our question was, how does the person on the floor who's making a part that's a tenth of an inch long understand that what they're doing is making a difference? How do we bring that home?

"We determined that we would celebrate how we were helping people closest to home—friends, family—live better lives," she continues. "We publish a magazine, *Accellent News*, and we ran articles there saying that we wanted to hear people's stories. If your story was chosen you would win $500 and if it was published as an 18- by 24-inch poster, it would be at every site in the company. We got nineteen or twenty stories, and we chose ten to become posters.

"We had stories from two employees who had been in horrible car accidents," McCall continues. "One employee's father had a heart attack, and he traced the stent he had back to a part that we made. We also did one additional poster for an individual who had a heart attack at work. The first responders were able to save his life, and he had to have stents put in—which we make. When he came back to work, one of the things he said was, 'I want a poster. I want to tell my story.' He spoke at our quarterly meeting to thank the first responders and to tell people that what we do really does make a difference."

What was the impact of this impact initiative? "It started a conversation. People understood that they were making a difference," says McCall. "Quality and performance improved, and this project is part of that story. We asked, 'How do you get folks to never take a shortcut, to always do their best work?' You help them think about what they're making and how important it is."

THE LAW OF IMPACT PROXIMITY

So, impact turns out to be much more than seeing results on the ground. Under the impact umbrella, you'll find:

- meaningful outcomes of employees' hard work
- consistent evidence that employee effort is making a difference for the company and the customer
- meaningful recognition of employees' proficiency and their value to the organization

This is the *law of impact proximity*. It states that organizations that "close the distance" between work and impact will have higher levels of engagement. These organizations break down the barriers between the work environment and the end results of work so employees can see that their effort is producing something worthwhile.

Medical-device designers post video interviews with patients on the Internet. Factories reward employees who make the greatest contributions to increased energy efficiency. Schools solicit testimonials from former students who get into prestigious universities and put them in the hands of teachers. Engaged organizations find ways to make the work real. They remind employees, "*This* is why you're coming to work every day. This is the difference you make."

Supervisor feedback is another powerful tool for creating impact proximity. When our team consults with an organization, we almost always recommend that they beef up their feedback channels. Our surveys show that 30 percent of employees don't receive regular feedback on how they're doing. Some managers balk because they think if you give someone credit or positive feedback, they'll become complacent. In fact, the opposite is true. People are more likely to become complacent because supervisors aren't providing enough constructive feedback.

Once people do get a pat on the back, they want more. Telling someone "You are on the right track, keep doing that" is a great way to increase performance in the area that you've reinforced.

Are there ways to measure the bottom-line impact of impact? There are. Behavioral economist and author Dan Ariely has done extensive research that strengthens the empirical evidence behind impact and proximity. In one Harvard study, he found that when students putting together Bionicle toys could see the finished toys on their desks as they built other toys, they became more productive, even when their pay decreased with each task and they knew the toys they were building would be destroyed at the end of the experiment.[125] Other students whose toys were disassembled right in front of them—so they were essentially rebuilding the same toy over and over—were not as productive. In fact, the students who could see the results of their work assembled 10.2 figurines versus the other group's 7.2.

In another study with students at MIT, Ariely found that people who felt that their effort in completing a task was unappreciated needed more money to keep doing it than people who felt appreciated.[126] His research team asked college students to find sets of repeated letters on a sheet of paper. A supervisor reviewed the work of only some of the students. Other students watched their work being put through a shredder. Students received 55 cents for completing the first sheet and 5 cents less for each subsequent sheet, and could quit at any time. In the end, the students whose work was acknowledged by the "supervisor" worked longer and for less money than those whose work was ignored or destroyed.

In a Harvard study, researchers found that when students in mock job interviews received even subtle physical cues of approval from their interviewers, such as nodding, smiling, and leaning forward, their performance improved.[127] But the topper may be the study by Wharton School of Business professor Adam Grant. In a 2007 study at the University of Michigan, paid call-center workers had a five-minute conversation with scholarship students who had been directly helped by the school's past fund-raising efforts. They then called potential donors. The interaction with the beneficiaries of past giving was brief, but the effect was profound. One month later, these call-center workers were spending 142 percent more time on the phone with donors than before the study, and donations jumped by 171 percent.[128] That is the power of *impact*.

IMPACT AWARENESS

According to a recent study, 37 percent of consumers and employees want to see the difference they are making by contributing to local causes, 35 percent want to feel it on a national scale, and 28 percent want to have a global impact.[129] That's more evidence that creating an *impact awareness* culture is a powerful competitive tool for any organization.

Office-supply giant Staples has fully embraced this idea. The company has started using an online platform called Profits4Purpose—which lets organizations of all kinds measure and communicate their social impact[130]— to encourage employees to volunteer for the charities that are personally important to them. That's one way to encourage engagement, but Staples takes it a step further. Via the platform, employees can request that the company make a donation to their charities.

Talk about a brilliant engagement strategy: giving employees the means not only to control their level of impact but the power to get others involved. As Profits4Purpose CEO Jason Burns says, "At every level, the best performance will come from people who understand and appreciate this commitment."[131]

At the other extreme are organizations that set up "failure goals." During the Vietnam War, pilots report having risked lives and equipment for the attainment of an immediate goal (as defined by a number or metric), rather than the end objective of winning the war (achieving peace, promoting humanitarianism, etc.). As told by one pilot:

> On a daily level, there was the competition between the air force and the navy, which sometimes led to the misuse of men and equipment, and if not to outright lying, then to exaggerated claims about the damage inflicted during air strikes. One manifestation of the competition was in the sortie rate—a sortie being one round-trip combat flight by one airplane—which was used as a measuring stick to show how hard each service was working to win the war. When a bomb shortage occurred in early 1966, both the air force and the navy sent their planes up with only one or two bombs per plane, to keep their sortie rate high and prevent their competitor from getting ahead in the statistics game. There was constant pressure to show results in the numbers of targets hit.[132]

While our own targets may not be as critical as those in war, they may be critical to our organizational or individual success. But is the sortie scenario a familiar one in your organization or in your own life—hitting a metric while ignoring (or at least not considering) the end goal?

Is the drive for organizational results or the drive to reach your personal numbers getting in the way of real success? Is your organization requiring its employees to fly ineffective—even hazardous—sorties, all in the name of producing photogenic short-term metrics? The result is probably a flurry of low-meaning activity that has little impact on what's truly important.

That's an example of failure goals on both an individual and a team impact level. Individually, diluting impact or encouraging people to create a false impression of their impact harms morale. From a team standpoint (the bomber squadron, in this case), such policies pollute the efforts of team members who are trying to have a legitimate impact.

THE IMPACT OF THE TEAM

Engaged teams must feel that they have a collective impact, and each member of the team must feel that he or she makes a contribution to the team and plays a role in the team's success. Impact is especially critical to team engagement because it's the only engagement key that translates to the collective experience. Think of sports teams that win championships, or search-and-rescue teams that save the lives of lost hikers or mountain climbers. When was the last time you heard anyone talk about a search-and-rescue *person*? Some impact matters only in the context of the team unit.

This gives engaged teams the power to magnify their impact to a degree that even the most engaged solo employee simply can't do. Consider SEAL Team Six. When this elite U.S. Navy squad went into that compound in Pakistan and took out Osama bin Laden, we didn't hear about the individual members. Navy and SEAL culture makes the individual unimportant except in the context of the group; ask a SEAL what he's most afraid of and he won't say dying or being captured. He'll say, "Not being there for the rest of the team."

When the mission was accomplished, it wasn't any single individual who took the immediate headlines; it was the team. Because of the internal concept that the only impact that mattered was the impact the team as a whole made, SEAL Team Six had an impact on the entire world. The impact of a team can profoundly affect an organization.

For a more recent example of the impact of a team, consider the boys' soccer team rescued from a Thai cave in 2018. The rescue was the result of a number of groups coming together from different countries and organizations to accomplish a single purpose—rescue 12 boys stranded in a flooded cave.

The rescue, which took over two weeks, was complicated by fast-moving water, making it clear the boys would have to dive out. First, the teams got together to carefully outline the plan. Next, the experts were sent into the cave to teach the boys to use scuba gear. Each boy was sedated in order to avoid panicking in a delicate situation, and then accompanied on the long trip out of the cave by two divers. Rescuers held the boys' oxygen tanks in front of them, squeezing through narrow tunnels and dangerous passages. The boys were then handed over to a specialist rescue team who helped them until their handoff to awaiting medical teams.

As was the case with Navy SEAL Team Six, the victory was won by many individuals working together. No single individual could have accomplished the miraculous rescue alone. The impact was felt by the entire rescue team, the individuals of that team, 12 young men and their families, and the world.[133]

The inverse is also true: Each team member shares credit for the impact the team makes, regardless of his or her role. When a soccer team wins the World Cup, each player is a champion, even those who didn't play a minute in the deciding game. Simply being part of the team is enough; even role players play a part in success.

CULTIVATING IMPACT

The author Napoleon Hill once wrote, "You must get involved to have an impact. No one is impressed with the won–lost record of the referee." Another factor that makes impact different from all the other engagement keys is that, unlike meaning, autonomy, growth, and connection, it's probably already occurring in your organization. Your people are undoubtedly having an impact in some way on your customers or the world at large. They may not know or appreciate it, or the impact they know about may be impersonal, such as share price or gross revenue. Those figures are important, but they don't strike a chord with most employees. Impact is generally more personal.

The good news is that you don't necessarily have to *create* impact out of thin air. In many cases, you may only need to create impact channels that make your employees aware of types of impact that may be meaningful to them. It's up to them to choose to see the impact they're having.

How to create *impact awareness*? Here's a four-step process that yields results:

Step 1: Measurement

As the Cheshire Cat said, "If you don't know where you're going, any road will get you there." You can't know your impact if you don't have any way of measuring it. You'll only know if you're making progress if you can measure your work against targets.

The mission of some organizations can make measurement easy: If you're a not-for-profit, increased donations can signal big impact, while a sports franchise will probably measure impact by its won–lost record. When the mission is less cut-and-dried, measurement is harder, but it's there and it *can* be measured. If you're a legal aid society dedicated to freeing wrongly convicted death row inmates based on DNA evidence, is your impact defined by the number of convictions you get overturned? Or is it based on freeing a man with a wife and six children versus a man with no family?

Think about how you can measure the impact of your organization. Is it by monetary terms? Customer satisfaction scores? Lower carbon emissions? A higher graduation rate? Or something more ephemeral? What are your targets and how will you grade your progress?

Looking for a good start in measuring impact? Ask your employees how. Not only will they likely come up with some winners, but you will also learn some important information about what's truly important to them.

STEP 2: PROXIMITY

One study found that nurses working in understaffed hospitals with high patient-to-nurse ratios were more likely to experience job burnout, while surgical patients had higher mortality and failure-to-rescue rates.[134] From our experience in working with leaders in these situations, we surmise that this is due, in part, to the nurses' lack of proximity to the results of their work; that is, patients recovering and going home.

Part of the leader's responsibility is creating proximity: putting measures in place to bring impact up close and make it easily accessible. The organization must find ways to connect the workplace to its market, customers, and audience. Putting in place systems and a culture that bridges the gap between work and results can be as simple as putting out an informative in-house e-newsletter, or as complicated as touring an affordable housing project that your company designed. The object is simple: Make it easy for everyone to see, feel, and experience the results of what they do every day. This is how minds and hands connect to hearts and spirits.

Habitat for Humanity is a wonderful example of this. How do you think this charitable organization gets tens of thousands of volunteers to turn out to build houses in the hot sun? Meaning, of course, plays an important role. But it's also because people get to see the fruits of their labor taking shape right in front of their eyes. When you watch a house go up and work side by side with one of the people who'll be living in it, you get an indelible sense of the impact you're having.

Step 3: Context

What's the story of your organization's impact? The leader is the custodian of the narrative, so how are you spinning your organizational story? There's nothing wrong with spin; sometimes it's important to shape a story in a way that helps people see the value of what they're doing.

For example, the P90X workout program is one of the most successful fitness products of all time, having sold more than seven million copies as of 2018.[135] The chief reason for this may be the host, the high-energy trainer Tony Horton. One of Horton's pieces of genius in motivating P90X users is this: Instead of talking about completing a ninety-day workout program—a daunting task for most anyone—he talks only about showing up and "just pushing play." With those simple words, Horton turned simply doing the workout every day into a virtue. Customers felt that by slipping the DVD into their DVD player, they were accomplishing something.

Context and cognitive framing are critical. Manufacturing cold metal medical devices takes on a new importance and meaning when you see that the devices you help build will become part of someone's pacemaker. Tactics like telling the whole story or breaking down complex tasks into smaller chunks so that the chunks become more real can help people really see the impact of their actions.

For example, if you've framed a fitness goal as "I have to lose 30 pounds this year" and halfway through the year you've lost only 10, you're going to feel like you're going backward. But if you reframe the goal as "I'm going to lose 2 pounds a week," not only do most weeks give you a reason to celebrate your positive impact on your health, but if you only lost 1 pound, it's okay! You get a redo!

Step 4: Value

Leaders must also find ways to reward and recognize impact at the individual, team, and organizational level. This is where the 50-50 engagement split really comes into play. You've measured impact, created proximity, redefined the context of the work, and created ways to show people that they are valued and not easily replaced. You've done all you can.

At this point, choosing to find impact becomes the employee's responsibility. Once the means of assessing one's personal impact are available, you must choose to avail yourself of the means—to look through the impact window—and find personal value in what you see. Not all employees will do this. But that's not something you can control. Employees must choose to recognize and value the impact they're having on the world.

Over the past two decades, increased attention paid to employee recognition has given rise to a new industry—the employee recognition business. Why does it exist? Simple. Employees like to be recognized, and recognition can be tied to business results. Estimates are that the market for employee recognition programs exceeds $46 billion.[136] We find, however, that when employees respond to questions regarding whether or not they are regularly recognized by their managers, their responses are typically dismal. What's most interesting is the notion that when employees respond to these questions, they aren't always talking about movie tickets, huge bonuses, and courtside basketball tickets. They're speaking of acknowledgments as simple as a quick "Great job!" or "Thank you!" from the boss. Ultimately, it's not what the employee receives that creates engagement; it's the recognition that something good was accomplished, and that what the individual did actually had an impact.

FIVE QUESTIONS

1. Where does the effort I put into my work exceed the results I get? Where do the results outweigh the effort?
2. Do I generally see the end result of the work I do? Why or why not?

3. In what parts of my work do I feel like I'm making progress? Where am I spinning my wheels?
4. How do I know when I am performing and when I have achieved my goals?
5. What do I do to celebrate my own achievements? What do others (leaders, peers, etc.) do to celebrate our achievements?

RECAP

- Impact and meaning are closely linked. Whereas meaning is purpose, impact is results.
- People need to see progress in their work and that they are making a difference.
- Organizations can create impact channels that allow employees to see the impact of their efforts.
- Understanding how one's impact contributes to the organization's mission improves engagement.
- Without the ability to see the impact of their work, people can feel futile and helpless.
- Impact is not always equal to effort. Someone can be very busy, yet have little impact.
- Impact contributes to the sense of being valued. Value reduces the odds of burnout.
- The law of impact proximity: Organizations that "close the distance" between work and impact have higher levels of engagement.
- Appreciation, feedback, and expressions of supervisor approval improve performance.

CHAPTER SEVEN

CONNECTION

"Communication—the human connection—is the key to personal and career success."
—Paul J. Meyer

LET'S TALK about mangoes. No, that's not a misprint. This story of the mango vendors of Fiji is a wonderful example of the importance of connection. Each morning, local fruit vendors awake before Fiji's sunrise to pack and take their wares to small marketplaces throughout the islands. They toil at the local markets until their supply of goods for the day is exhausted, or until the market closes for the day.

As many as 25 percent of Fijians live below the poverty line, and Fijian fruit vendors know that their ability to support themselves and their families is dependent upon their ability to peddle produce. So, each morning they line up among the other vendors, each seeking to sell enough fruit to, in turn, purchase the goods they need.

Into this situation came HELP International, a not-for-profit organization that was founded to assist individuals, such as those in Fiji, in fighting poverty. Part of what HELP teaches is basic business concepts, and when they came to work with the mango merchants of Fiji, they discovered that they were violating a basic concept: differentiation. In this marketplace in question, the mangoes sold by one vendor were identical in price, quality, size, and everything else to the mangoes sold a mere four feet to the right or left. Next to those carts were similar carts, each selling identical mangoes—most of them from the same origination points. Zero differentiation. Limited sales.

The HELP volunteers proposed a radical idea: What would happen if one of the vendors set up shop the next morning in a location separate from his competitors? By simply moving out of the "mango section" and into another area, the vendor might gain some differentiation by having mangoes available to those who were purchasing, for example, fish. It seemed like a good idea, and they found a vendor who agreed to try it. The next day, he moved his cart to another location, and the strategy appeared to be working.

However, upon arriving at the market the following day, the volunteers noticed that the mango seller had again returned to the area in which his colleagues were located. Upon talking with the vendors, the volunteers learned that the market was, for these individuals, a place where they could connect with others, even if they were competitors. They were more engaged by the social connection—one that had been there for many years—than they were by a monetary exchange, even if it meant fewer Fijian dollars went home that evening. Interestingly, the volunteers did not indicate whether the lone vendor's move had been profitable; it didn't matter. For them, connection was a more powerful motivator.

This need for connection isn't limited to Fijian mangoes. In 2013, the UN released some interesting findings. According to the report, at that time, of Earth's seven billion inhabitants, six billion had cell phones. Not surprising? Perhaps, until you learn that only 4.5 billion had proper sanitation.[137] Is that right? One-and-a-half billion people had cell phones but no toilet or sanitary waste disposal? What does this say about the importance of being connected? Ask your employees (or your local mango vendor). You can probably reach them by cell phone.

WHAT IS CONNECTION?

The last of our engagement keys, connection, is:

The sense of belonging to something beyond yourself.

Connection is a basic human need, residing on Maslow's Hierarchy of Needs just above physical safety. When Robert Reich was U.S. Secretary of Labor and he visited a company to talk with the employees, he would often conduct a "pronoun test" to discover the level of employee engagement. He found that employees who referred to their company in terms of "we" were more engaged than those who referred to the company as "they."

When you're satisfied and pleased with something that your company is doing, you take ownership. You say things like "We're successfully implementing a new program" or "We have great camaraderie, so we get things done." When you're disappointed or unsatisfied, you tend to remove yourself from the equation. You say things like "They don't pay us well" or "They don't get things done."

Reich concluded that an employee who uses *we* feels more integrated into the company, identifies more with the company, and takes more ownership. Presumably, such people are more likely to be satisfied, motivated, and effective in their work.[138]

Connection is the feeling that being part of your organization makes you part of a community of people who are engaged in something that's bigger than any one person. There's a sense of belonging to the organization and the people around you. There's a deep sense not only of social camaraderie but of kinship, of shared culture, values, customers, and mission. Connection doesn't mean having a "best friend" at work, though it's common for connection to come from strong workplace friendships. Connection manifests as the sense that a place is "special," that you and your colleagues are a "band of brothers" who have each other's backs unconditionally. Our team studied a group of more than 363,000 employees across fifty-two international organizations of all sizes and shapes and asked them to rate the statement "I am proud to tell people I work at this organization." Seventy-eight percent of these employees gave a positive response—a relatively high favorability rating. But what's really interesting is that in some organizations, more than 90 percent of employees responded with positive ratings to this question. In these organizations, not only did the employees connect with the organization, the organization connected with its employees.

TYPES OF CONNECTION

The Walt Disney Company is renowned for the seamless experience it creates for its guests at its theme parks around the world. One of the reasons for that seamlessness and consistent quality is the employees that the company calls "cast members." With its many rules and strict appearance and behavior codes, Disney's not an easy place to work, but it's easy to find online communities like AftertheMouse.com where former employees talk fondly about their time working for the Mouse. How many companies can say that?

Clearly, the "cast members" label is about more than just appearances. Employees feel that they are all actors in a huge show intended to surprise and delight children and adults, and as happens in the actual world of theater, the camaraderie runs deep. In general, Disney has created the polar opposite of those toxic workplaces where employees think of their employer as the enemy.

When employees feel a deep, strong connection, they are more likely to expend extra energy for one another, to give more to the organization, and to be more positive in the things they say both at work and away from it. Effort, attention to quality and detail, and morale go up . . . and generally, so do profits. Connection can make a team more than the sum of its parts.

However, connection doesn't happen all at once. It's rare for a new employee to join an organization and immediately feel that he's part of a band of brothers. Instead, people typically pass through a few preliminary stages before achieving connection:

- **Fit.** Fit is similarity to, or a congruence with, an employer's culture or environment. This might manifest as an appreciation for the physical artifacts in the work space, a connection to the social structure, an appreciation for the work environment (digging your cubicle, the break room, etc.), job fit, or a fit with the organization as a whole. A person who fits with an organization may find that the people working there have a background like his own or that the work being done is the kind of work he's trained for and enjoys. He fits in with the company.

- **Belonging.** If fit exists, then the employee may move on to feel that she belongs with the organization—that it's a place that shares her values, where she can enjoy her work and find motivation and reward. Together, fit and belonging produce positive outcomes.

- **Integration.** Once employees feel they belong, they become an integral part of the organization. Rather than being just a part of the organization, the organization is a part of who they are (think Disney cast members).

Connection is an area where spirit plays an important role. When connection exists, energy is generated. Movie producers have picked up on this fact on a couple of levels. Many successful films climb to the top of the box office rankings based on the energy created when people connect: *Hoosiers, Star Wars, Seabiscuit, Rocky, Justice League,* and many others. As characters connect with one another, they apply energy to accomplishing a common goal. Hearts and spirits energize minds and hands. The energy spreads, first among the cast and then to the audience. This same energy is the reason that home-field advantage plays such a strong role in the win–loss records of our favorite sports teams.

This esprit de corps doesn't have to start with a team. It can start with an individual. Movies such as *Slumdog Millionaire* and *Erin Brockovich* are perfect examples of how a single person's dynamic story can capture the energy of an entire audience—and an entire film.

Like satisfaction, fit and belonging are necessary precursors to connection, but they don't *constitute* connection. If our fictional employee finds fit and belonging, he may one day feel that his colleagues "get" who he is and accept him, that the company values him and his work, and that his "they" thinking has changed to "we" thinking. That's connection.

Based on what we've found through our data, research, studies, and experience, we've identified five primary types of connection:

1. **Social connection:** This is the group of people around you, the people with whom you spend most of your time. Social connection is especially important to the group known as "Millennials," workers born roughly

between the late 1980s and late 1990s. Several years ago, we conducted a study on trends of Millennials' hopes, dreams, and aspirations. The responses received through this study were . . . revealing. When describing the ideal boss, one respondent summed up what many were saying when he stated, "He should be honest and open minded. He should be able to guide and should be a friend and coworker."

Friend? Coworker? What happened to organizational hierarchy and authority? Findings in similar studies indicate that 66 percent of Millennial business students agreed with the following statement: "I prefer personal relationships with my bosses."[139] For some people, close relationships with others are their energy source at work.

2. **Organizational connection**: This refers to feeling connected to an organization due to factors like being valued or providing a truly pleasurable work experience. This is identification with an organization that's so deep that the organization becomes a part of who you are. We see this in organizations like Nike, the Peace Corps, and even labor unions. Of course, this can also be a bad thing when connection turns to coercive groupthink, as with Enron.

3. **Mission connection**: You feel connected to the organization's mission and sense of purpose. What you're trying to accomplish as an organization becomes as important as your personal mission, and you'll subordinate your personal needs—at least to some degree—because of your connection and passion for the mission.

4. **Values connection**: You feel that the organization shares and respects your values and works to achieve goals that are congruent with those values. We find this in religious groups, community groups, political parties, and charitable organizations, among others.

5. **Task connection**: You become connected by being in close proximity to other people who are working on the same task. You may be put into a situation where you have little choice but to connect, but you don't have that same connection outside your team. Being part of a team causes a connection to happen. It's opportunistic. Think about the real-life people of the U.S. Army Monuments, Fine Arts, and Archives program, the historical basis for the film *The Monuments Men*. This group, tasked with preserving cultural treasures that would otherwise have been destroyed by the Nazis in World War II, was a blend of Ivy League art professors,

museum curators, historians, artists, and architects.[140] Hardly the type of people you'd want scurrying around the front lines in occupied France trying to save paintings and sculptures. But it worked.

Psychologists John Cacioppo and Louise Hawkley have found that people tend to feel connected in three dimensions: *intimate connectedness*, *relational connectedness*, and *collective connectedness*. Intimate connectedness is uniquely associated with marriage and involves personal satisfaction with the social self. Relational connectedness is about the satisfaction that comes from regular contact with friends and relatives. Collective connectedness is about the satisfaction that comes from voluntary membership in one or more meaningful groups.[141]

WHEN CONNECTION FADES

When connection isn't present, the "they" feeling mentioned earlier sets in. The organization becomes an entity separate from the individual. You get isolation and alienation, two of the workplace conditions most likely to lead to dissatisfaction, resentment, and sabotage. A "How can we stick it to the man?" mentality takes hold.

Here's another interesting finding from our survey database. When asked questions related to connection with one's immediate work group or team, 75 percent respond favorably. In other words, three-fourths of individuals feel a connection to the people with whom they work. It's natural. We're with them more often than we're with our own families.

Now, the rest of the story. This figure drops to just 57 percent when we ask people about their connection to other departments. It doesn't really take a study to tell you this; it's common sense. While it's easy to connect with those around you, it's more difficult to connect with others outside your immediate circle. This sense of connection and trust is tribal. However, this raises issues of trust across departments and functions—an issue that continues to show up as one of the lowest-scoring areas on our employee surveys.

One finance manager summed it up nicely when he said, "My team is great, and I would trust them with my life. But those guys over in Sales . . . wow! Those idiots can't be trusted." Not surprisingly, Sales had the same to say about Finance.

Such fundamental attribution errors (explaining the behavior of others by focusing on internal qualities such as character and work ethic while ignoring external factors and one's own behavior) are indicative of isolation and alienation, two of the most dangerous symptoms of lack of connectedness.

Let's reflect back to our discussion of Yahoo! in the chapter on autonomy. You'll remember that CEO Marissa Mayer issued the mandate that employees would no longer be able to work from home. The announcement dominated a few news cycles and caused some pundits to predict the company's downfall. But the risk of isolation and alienation was surely one of the factors that prompted Mayer to end the company's telecommuting policy. When interviewed about reasons behind the edict, she said, "People are more productive when they're alone, but they're more collaborative and innovative when they're together. Some of the best ideas come from pulling two different ideas together."[142] Mayer rated this quality more important than home worker autonomy.

Mayer highlighted one of the reasons for connection that goes beyond workplace harmony and happiness to the bottom line. Connection fuels collaboration. While people can feel connected at a distance, proximity allows for those chance meetings and creative synchronicities that sometimes breed world-shifting ideas—something not always possible through conference calls, email, and Skype.

THE IRRIGATION EFFECT

In most organizations, a key difference between connection and alienation is *communication*. But this isn't simply a matter of creating conditions under which employees, teams, and the organization as a whole can share information; it's also a matter of avoiding an information vacuum. The physics principle "nature abhors a vacuum" comes to mind. When information and meaning are absent, people won't simply shrug their shoulders and carry on. They will create their own information and assign their own meaning to events.

The trouble, of course, is that the information may be wrong and the meaning may be harmful. This is what I refer to as the *Irrigation Effect*. Picture a farmer's field of grain or corn. As life-giving water enters irrigation furrows, crops thrive. However, where the water in irrigation channels lacks sufficient force to make it to the end of the rows of crops, they will wither and die. In fact, this effect is so evident in drier states that the crops at the beginning of the rows may produce as much as two to three times the harvest reaped from the crops at the end of the rows. That's what happens to connection when communication doesn't make it downstream from the CEO's office all the way to the individual cubicles.

Our survey results clearly show how the irrigation effect plays out in organizations. When asked about organizational communication, the vast majority (more than 90 percent) of executives and senior managers indicate that the level of communication they receive about important events impacting the organization is appropriate. Hardly surprising, given that they are close to (and even may *be*) the source. However, as that water flows downhill, just over 78 percent of mid-level managers report having the communication and information they need to be successful, with just 68 percent of line-level employees responding in the same way.

While the people in the C-suite may think they are communicating (and perhaps they are), the water simply isn't making it to the end of the rows. It's tough to be engaged when one doesn't know what he or she is engaging in.

Spatial closeness is conducive to communication. When our survey results reveal teams that claim they're connected within the team but not outside it, it's often because the necessity to communicate isn't there. If another party isn't physically close or there's not a low-effort means to communicate available, the team probably won't even try to cultivate connection outside the group. There's simply no need. The team becomes sufficient to create that needed sense of belonging, but it's isolated from the organization at large.

Carrying the irrigation effect forward, communication is like water: It tends to seek the lowest possible level. Rarely will the water flow in the opposite direction, and even when managers think they are open to feedback from employees, laws of nature step in. If employees feel connectedness with a group or a mission, they'll exert extra effort to communicate. Until that happens, communication requires conscious effort, easy-to-use tools and channels, and pro-communication policies.

One example of such policy is CHG Healthcare Services' "over-communication." "We're always talking about the culture," says CHG's SVP of administration, Kevin Ricklefs. "We tie what other people would call business messages into the cultural message. For example, our Grand Rapids office closed because of weather. Some people would send out an email saying the office is closed. We say, 'Because we value the safety of our employees, the office will close today.' Things like that are constant small reminders that we care.

"Also, every message, every communication has a story attached to it," Ricklefs continues. "We just want to make sure you understand that we care. We try and take factual messages, such as how we did in the last fiscal year, and tie them to how we're successful because of our culture, our beliefs, and so on. It's a continuous conversation with the employees. We do a lot of surveys and focus groups where we ask employees about issues that affect them.

"You have to maintain open, honest, two-way communication. For example, every February we do our employee survey. We post the whole survey online so everyone can see every result. That's over-communication. We don't want people to say things that make everybody feel good; we want to ask for help with things that aren't going well. If we want to change something, we'll get a group of employees and ask their opinion. We've been a highly successful company culturally and financially based on having this open, organic two-way communication. It's just what we do. It's part of our fabric."

Egghead Alert!

Leader-Member Exchange Theory (LMX) focuses on the two-way ("dyadic") relationship that exists between supervisors and subordinates. LMX posits that there are in-groups and out-groups in most organizations and teams. In-groups are favored by the manager and tend to receive more frequent and clearer communication. Because of this (in part), they tend to be more engaged and perform more effectively. Out-groups are less favored by their superiors. Out-groups receive limited communication, development opportunities, and assignments. As a result, they tend to be less competent and are less engaged.

It's not hard to see how a group that is cut off from the communication that is the lifeblood of connection and engagement would simply create its own information, meaning, and reality, which could do real harm to the mission of the organization.

Few examples illustrate this unpleasant reality better than the story of how "stack ranking" did irreparable harm to the mighty Microsoft. Stack ranking (or forced ranking) is the practice of ranking employees in comparison to other employees, much like the "grading on a curve" we all learned to despise in high school. By the mid-2000s, the Redmond, Washington, giant had become lumbering, paralyzed, and seemingly unable (or unwilling) to innovate. At the heart of its increasingly poisonous culture was this stack-ranking process. A *Vanity Fair* piece describes stack ranking and its impact on the decline of Microsoft as follows:

> At the center of the cultural problems was a management system called "stack ranking." Every current and former Microsoft employee I interviewed—every one—cited stack ranking as the most destructive process inside of Microsoft, something that drove out untold numbers of employees. The system—also referred to as "the performance model," "the bell curve," or just "the employee review"—has, with certain variations over the years, worked like this: every unit was forced to declare a certain percentage of employees as top performers, then good performers, then average, then below average, then poor.
>
> "If you were on a team of 10 people, you walked in the first day knowing that, no matter how good everyone was, two people were going to get a great review, seven were going to get mediocre reviews, and one was going to get a terrible review," said a former software developer. "It leads to employees focusing on competing with each other rather than competing with other companies."

Spooked by the stack-ranking system, Microsoft employees started retreating into isolated worlds. Top engineers would not work with other top engineers for fear they might be outperformed. Teammates sabotaged each other trying to ensure that someone else would get the poor review—and probably be fired. Denied information on their value or impact on the company, employees created their own alternate reality, a *Hunger Games*–like battle to keep their jobs. Innovation and collaboration stopped completely. This set the stage for companies like Apple, Facebook, and Google to sprint right past the foundering software pioneer.[143] It's difficult to imagine an environment more corrosive to connection . . . or a clearer example of the damage that a connection vacuum can inflict.

Earlier, when I discussed the concept of satisfaction, I referred to the issue of physical safety. Physical safety does not cause engagement to occur, but when that safety is taken away an employee quickly disengages. Emotional or psychological safety is similar.

When an employee doesn't feel he or she is emotionally safe in an organization, disengagement occurs. We see this with organizations where employees are constantly fearful for their jobs, or are not treated with dignity and respect by their supervisors. However, when you feel connected to the organization, a task, fellow employees, or the mission and values of the organization, you feel emotionally safe. Whether it's the organization that has your back, or your partner on the police force who's watching out for you, that sense of belonging allows you to open your heart.

THE KEY DRIVER

For many, connection may be the key driver of engagement. Why? Two reasons. First, it's the one element of MAGIC that employees project outward toward others. Meaning, autonomy, growth, and impact are introspective qualities arrived at through extremely personal processes. You're not likely to grab a colleague in the office and gush, "Let me tell you why I find making these photocopies *so* meaningful!" But connection, by its nature, is collaborative. It's communicative. It's fundamentally about reaching out to others.

Because of this, connection has the greatest potential for either stunningly positive or grotesquely negative impacts, as we saw with Microsoft. Deep connectedness or total lack of connectedness are both contagions; they can make either goodwill and positive energy or dysfunction and dissatisfaction go viral throughout an organization.

The study of network contagion is a clear illustration of this power. Let's step outside the corporation for a minute, and look at something seemingly unrelated—obesity. Researchers Nicholas A. Christakis and James H.

Fowler discovered that obesity (among other things) is influenced by a person's social network. This makes sense. We often surround ourselves with people of similar interests and habits (and, quite possibly, size!). No surprises there. However, their research showed that even if a twice-removed friend who lives on the other side of the country gains weight, you're likely to gain weight too. It sounds crazy and counterintuitive, but the pair has found the same effect in Germany with such phenomena as suicide, politics, and back pain.[144] This strange effect appears to be real: Via shared social cues, pressures, subtle messaging, and a host of other under-the-radar channels, simply having a distant social connection to someone can profoundly influence behavior. Social media makes this even more prevalent.

The other reason that connection is so important is that connection is the only engagement key that can directly encourage people to choose meaning, autonomy, growth, and impact. A culture that encourages engagement and communication can give employees the push they need to seize growth opportunities, choose to find meaning and impact in their work, and be more autonomous.

For these reasons, it's vital to take steps to cultivate a connected organization. Even some of the world's largest companies are getting hip to this idea. Unilever Corporation, the third-largest consumer goods company in the world, allows close to 100,000 of its 170,000 employees (everyone but factory workers) to work wherever they want, whenever they want, as long as the work gets done. It's all about *what*, not *how*.

The program, called Agile Working, was implemented in 2008 in the wake of a massive reorganization that led to enormous layoffs that shattered both employee morale and job satisfaction. The company's HR team developed a pilot program that allowed workers to use technology like smart phones and Skype to collaborate, making flexibility the order of the day. Now, it might seem odd to make a program designed to let employees see one another *less* often the centerpiece of a *connection* strategy, but Unilever had to find a way to let its people know it was paying attention to their needs.

There were also compelling potential financial benefits. Unilever, the architects of the program said, would save on business travel, need less office space, reduce health-care costs (a study of workers in Best Buy's Results Only Work Environment program revealed that they exercised more, slept better, and were less likely to come to the office when they were sick), improve employee satisfaction, reduce turnover, and dramatically improve recruiting effectiveness. The bosses took the bait.

In 2008, Unilever rolled out its Agile Working pilot program with 250 employees at an office in Englewood Cliffs, New Jersey. Within a few months, workers said that they were more productive and better able to meet professional and personal demands. The pilot group's survey scores in key areas reflecting engagement also signal the program's success:

- Eighty percent cited increased personal productivity.
- Thirty-four percent said they were more satisfied with their jobs.
- Twenty-nine percent were more likely to stay with Unilever.
- Eighty-six percent preferred the Agile Workplace to a traditional workplace design.

Since then, the entire company has implemented Agile Working. Despite the decrease in face-to-face contact with colleagues, worker satisfaction continues to increase.[145]

THE POWER OF CULTURE

This seems almost contradictory—the idea that being apart actually increases connection. A contradiction, that is, until you realize that for Unilever, connection was not just about proximity or working shoulder to shoulder with one's coworkers. Connection can also hinge on feeling connected to an organizational culture that shares your values and listens to your needs. That's what took place at Unilever. Connection is more than being able to high-five your office mate; it's feeling that you're a valued part of a bigger team rowing as one toward a common goal.

Counter to the conventional wisdom that says losing physical connection with fellow employees will make people lazy and depressed, workplace flexibility appears to enhance many aspects of working life. Fifty-eight percent of telecommuters are likely to put in more than forty hours in a workweek, compared to just 28 percent of those working in a traditional office.[146] Creative workers (writers, designers, etc.) working remotely are 11 to 20 percent more productive than workers engaged in repetitive tasks.[147] In fact,

79 percent of surveyed workers say they would like to work from home at least part of the time.[148]

Let's look at JetBlue again. More than 1,900 of JetBlue's fifteen thousand "crew members"—mostly booking agents—work from home, most of them around Salt Lake City, where one of their support centers is located.[149] A quick search on websites such as Glassdoor.com reveals that while this works for a good percentage of new hires, it doesn't agree with all. JetBlue works to ensure that they hire those with whom this type of work arrangement agrees. They also put their agents through a four-week training course, during which agents learn both the day-to-day tasks of reservations and the elements of the company's culture, such as its customer care philosophy. Jet Blue also goes to great lengths to ensure that these work-at-home crew members feel they are part of the company. For this segment of JetBlue's population, it works.

The point is, what works for JetBlue may not work for Yahoo! or another organization. Many (and, quite possibly, most) organizations would struggle with a policy similar to that of Unilever or JetBlue. Many employees would also find this a difficult work environment, despite some superficial advantages. In the end, regardless of where employees work, engagement requires a culture of connection.

Culture may be as crucial to connection as face-to-face communication. An organization built upon on an underlying soil of respect for employee needs and open, attentive communication will foster that "we" feeling even if person-to-person communication is more limited due to people working more often from remote locations. Imagine the level of engagement in a workplace with a highly interactive on-site workforce *and* a culture of connection and participation!

We don't have to imagine it. We've seen the powerful impact of a rich, deep, authentic company culture. But just what is culture? We know that it's not what the company does. We know that it hinges in part on the congruence of individual and company values—the organization cares about what you care about. We know it also hinges on liking the people with whom you work. Even in organizations with many remote workers, a social connection to people is important.

Culture could be described as the social operating system of the organization, the underlying environment that shapes social interaction and shapes the emotions involved in the company and its work toward a specific end. Simply put, it's "the way we do things around here." The culture of Apple is based on beauty and creating incredible experiences, while the culture at Google is built around personal autonomy and solving the world's problems. Employees connect around those cultural assumptions. They are a fabric that everyone can grab a piece of, binding the organization together.

If your organization were a person, how would you describe it? Conservative? Edgy, with multiple body piercings and tattoos? Compassionate? Hardworking? Fun? Stuffy? If we think of organizations as people, we get a clearer idea of the implications of culture. Employees *do* think of their organizations as organisms (there's a reason both words share the same Latin root). They *do* have personalities, needs, and desires. Culture is a potent force that can become a driver of engagement on all levels . . . if it's done right. People must connect with that culture, whatever it might be.

DOING CULTURE RIGHT

How do you do culture right? First of all, culture depends on narrative and story. What is the narrative of the organization? How did it begin? What were the motivations behind its creation and what are its motivations today? How does it impact the world? How do its customers feel about it? What's its purpose? Do the employees play a role as custodians of the organizational story?

At one extreme you have Unilever and Apple. At the other you find companies that develop software offshore. These organizations rely on contract programmers who often dwell in places like Lithuania and Russia. They've never met, often don't speak the same language, and have little shared culture. So, while they're great at following instructions, there's no collective story that connects them. These virtual teams will never surpass their instructions, never innovate based on collective inspiration. It's not in their DNA.

Another factor is pride. Is there pride in the organization? Any organization must have pride in its people, mission, and identity. History and brand also matter to culture. Where has the organization been? How has it lived up to its stated values in the past? What is its brand promise? What words are widely associated with its brand according to surveys of its customers?

The formation of a strong culture also requires the placement of "anchors"—social, intellectual, environmental, inspirational—that serve to consistently communicate the culture to employees. These could be things like Google's free cafeteria food or 20 percent personal time policy— ever-present features of the office that send a specific message about the nature of the workplace and the employee's place in it.

Physical signs that reflect the personality of the organization—these are known in the social sciences as **artifacts**—are some of the most powerful anchors. No, this doesn't mean ping-pong tables; it's about meaningful pieces of the physical space that make a statement about the nature and character of the workplace and the people who work in it. These are satisfaction elements, not cultural artifacts. In some companies, that might mean edgy urban warehouse design with exposed concrete and corrugated metal. In others, it might mean an open, bullpen-style office where brightly colored couches and "playpens" have replaced cubicles.

Take audio-products maker Skullcandy. A few years back, after they went public, the leadership team realized that the company was losing the youthful, streetwise aspects of the culture that got them where they are today. They needed to figure out their new corporate values and determine their narrative, physical environment . . . and the artifacts that would embody their culture in that environment.

They created an amazing workplace environment based on a hip skate culture, outfitted it with things like functional skate ramps and skateboard ing memorabilia, and crafted a culture built around performance-based flexibility, an open environment for collaboration, and lots of incentives. Today, it's not uncommon to see Skullcandy employees skateboarding around the offices, fully connected to a culture that "gets" who they are. Skullcandy also allows its employees to take a half day off each time it snows more than a few inches—a regular occurrence in its home base, the beautiful mountain town of Park City, Utah.

This doesn't mean that your company culture has to mimic the hip cultures I just described. In fact, for many organizations, a shift toward similar practices as those we described would be seen as disingenuous—at the very least, out of place and inappropriate. Perhaps most important, culture must be authentic, and employees should be able to play a role in shaping it. Imagine the clumsiest corporate attempts at creating employee culture you've ever heard about—theme cruises, the famous Hawaiian-shirt-day scene from *Office Space*—and it's not hard to imagine the internal monologue of employees dealing with management's attempts to "keep it real." *Lame. Clueless. They just don't get us at all.* Cue the eye roll and knock some points off the engagement score.

If culture is to be a tool for connection, then it can't be akin to one of those awful faux downtown "entertainment districts" you find in some cities. You know the ones: collections of dining and entertainment venues organized into a streetscape that was designed by committee to look "edgy" and "urban." They're awful. They're the furthest thing from a real urban district like Brooklyn's Williamsburg or LA's Silverlake. And everyone who goes there knows it.

Inauthentic, canned culture does more harm than having no prevailing culture at all. It tells employees that not only does management not understand who you are and what you care about, management would rather hire a consulting firm to come up with a canned "culture plan" than spend time learning who you are and what you care about. Employees aren't able to connect. Cultural shifts work because they are based on a deep, personal understanding of what makes employees tick. When you build that kind of cultural environment, connection flourishes.

A MATTER OF TRUST

The final core component of connection is *trust*. In the most engaged organizations, trust is deep and mutual. Employees trust their leaders and vice versa. Trust is the currency of connection. It's a basic building block of culture, because an effective culture is one that evokes thoughts like "I can trust this company to align with my tastes and interests and to represent me, and what I care about, to the larger world." The organizations in which we all work are proxies for us; saying, "I'm an employee at [insert your company name here]" means something. For culture to be positive, employees need to trust that the organization's "halo effect" will continue to be something they can be proud of.

Trust is the absolute knowledge that your words reflect your future actions. It's the unquestioned belief that you will do what you say you will do. It's the seed for the "band of brothers" feeling that informs the best teams. It's the unshakable belief that you have my back. It precedes connection. You can't have connection without it.

In looking at Microsoft and its stack-ranking debacle, we've already seen what lack of trust can do to an organization. Because of this, trust requires evidence. I need you to prove to me that I can trust you. Once you prove to me that I can trust you, I will have a connection with you as long as you continue to meet my expectation of trust. So, trust is transactional. You must continue to perform. You have to keep earning it. Sorry, that's the way it goes.

There is also a difference between *earned trust* and *granted trust*. Earned trust is built over time and is based on your experiences and interactions with a person or an organization. If, over time, the other party has given you reason to believe that it will back up its promises with deeds, you will begin to develop trust. Granted trust is given based merely on position or circumstance. It's not earned. Parents grant trust to an emergency-room physician who's working on their child. A man accused of a crime grants trust to the public defender assigned to keep him out of prison. We all grant trust to the pilot when we fly in a plane.

What destroys trust? Hypocrisy is one way to do it. Failure to do as you say—to fulfill the promise behind your words with action—is another. The loss of trust due to nonperformance can be incremental. If you drop the ball once, I might let it go. I might still trust you. If you do it more often, I might start to question whether I can trust you or not. Of course, the upshot is that if you have to question whether or not you have trust . . . you don't have it.

In our surveys, when we've asked about trust, the answers often boil down to "I can trust this person to represent my interests, even when I'm not around." That's the level of trust that breeds a deep sense of connection, when individuals trust that their fellows will function as a "proxy self" and do what is best not only for themselves but for everyone, for the team. Another behavior that kills trust is purely self-interested behavior, where people look out for their own interests before that of their colleagues.

Trust is vital where people are expected to put team needs above individual needs. Take the 1988 Los Angeles Dodgers, the American baseball team that sportscaster Bob Costas called the worst team on paper ever to play in the World Series.[150] Still, the seemingly overmatched Dodgers beat the superior Oakland Athletics in five games. How? In part, trust. Apart from its outstanding pitching staff, the team was mostly a ragtag collection of wild-eyed role players epitomized by the bench corps known as the

Stuntmen. They joked, rode other teams' players, and played with a reckless abandon that inspired the entire squad.

With a team composed mostly of regular Joes, the Dodgers knew they had to have one another's backs. They had to trust that if one player failed, another would lift him up. That's exactly what happened.

Contrast that with the U.S. Olympic basketball team's shocking loss to Argentina in a semifinal game in the 2004 Summer Olympics. The so-called Dream Team was made up of the best players from the NBA, and was expected to cruise to a gold medal. However, they were not a team in the true sense. Players who had never played together before were hastily thrown onto a squad and expected to dominate. They didn't. They couldn't. How do you trust someone you've never worked with to have your back? How do you act with confidence that if you run to Point A, your teammate will have the ball there waiting for you? It's no wonder that Argentina beat the U.S. team, 89–81.[151]

Trust, like connection, needs to be cultivated and grown over time. It's fragile. That's why it's so important to create an ecosystem where trust, culture, communication, and connection can flower.

CULTIVATING CONNECTION

All aspects of engagement have to be chosen by the employee; that's part of the even-Stephen nature of engagement. But for organizational leaders, cultivating connection is both easy and challenging. Easy because people want to connect, so basic connection may require nothing more than putting people in close proximity and encouraging them to communicate. In fact, it's a basic psychological need. Difficult because you can't manufacture the ingredients of connection like you do the parts of a car. If people perceive communication, culture, and trust to be phony and inauthentic, they'll reject them and start looking at the organization with cynicism. True connection is organic.

However, as with all the other drivers of engagement, the organization has a role to play in creating the fertile soil where employees can choose to connect. These are some of the ways they're doing it:

- **Prescreening hires.** The Association for Talent Development, the leading professional association for people in employee development and talent, has prospective new hires complete a thirty-minute online simulation of the organizational culture before they progress through the hiring process. Many choose to opt out and walk away after completing this. It's an effective way of winnowing candidates to weed out those who simply won't respond to the organizational culture.

- **Tapping into cultural interests.** Smart organizations listen to their people about what matters to them—their tastes in music, art, and design; the causes that motivate them; their interests in books, movies, and politics. For example, Nike is located near Portland, Oregon, a beacon of sustainability and environmental concern. So, when the company decided to revamp its sustainability policy, it solicited employee input. They worked with employees on scenario planning and found that their current footprint was not sustainable. The result was a new sustainability initiative complete with employee participation.

- **Planting core beliefs.** Beliefs inspire actions. Actions, backed by beliefs, cultivate meaningful success. They also cultivate admirers, who become a company's best advertisers. But what are your organization's core beliefs? Do you know? Do you care? Do you operate in accordance with your organization's values? Discovering your organization's core values and weaving them into every aspect of daily operations increases the odds that your people will choose to connect with the organization on a personal, emotional level. There are three steps to creating consistent core beliefs and generating meaningful success:

  1. Take the pulse of your current corporate culture and values. Use an employee survey or other form of assessment to find out whether or not your employees perceive a system of beliefs in your company. Do they see a foundation of beliefs? Do they work in accordance? Do they agree with your organization's values? Do they reflect core values in interactions with your customers?
  2. Define your vision of the future and your idea of an ideal corporate culture. Through words, images, quotations, or any other medium, describe the corporate culture you envision. How will you carry your organization's values through every aspect of your business?

As we coach leaders and individual contributors, we often find that they are disconnected from the vision, or simply don't know what that vision is.

3. Outline the progression from the current corporate culture to the belief-based ideal. How will you move from Point A to Point B? How will your employees go from Point A to Point B?

This holistic, employee-centered, deeply authentic way of creating culture and connection is finally taking root in the command-and-control-obsessed corporate world. For evidence, simply look at a study by IBM. Based on a look at more than 1,700 CEOs from sixty-four countries and eighteen industries, a growing wave of executives are embracing openness, transparency, and employee empowerment. According to the study:

> . . . Companies that outperform their competitors are 30 per-
> cent more likely to identify openness—often characterized by a
> greater use of social media as a key enabler of collaboration and
> innovation—as a key influence on their organization. Outperform-
> ers are embracing new models of working that tap into the collec-
> tive intelligence of an organization and its networks to devise new
> ideas and solutions for increased profitability and growth.

Managers and executives are turning eagerly to social networks and similar tools—connection channels that are available to anyone and encourage open, candid communication—instead of using email and phone calls as primary ways to connect with customers, partners, and employees. Perhaps most promising, the survey shows that CEOs see collaboration, communication, creativity, and flexibility as essential drivers of employees in what is evolving into more interconnected working world.[152]

That's a far cry from the old desire that employees simply be loyal, work hard, and keep their mouths shut. Things are changing. Minds are changing. From the newest hire to the C-suite, everyone in organizations across the spectrum of human enterprise is realizing that a connected, engaged workplace is a win for everyone.

FIVE QUESTIONS

1. What type(s) of connection—social, organizational, mission, values, or task—is/are most important to me? Where do I get this in my job, and where is it missing?
2. Do I feel like I belong in my role? On my team? In my organization? Why or why not?
3. Where am I part of the in-group, receiving frequent and clear communication and interaction with others? Where am I part of the out-group, receiving limited communication or opportunities? What is *my* role in this?
4. What about the culture of my organization do I resonate with? Where is there a disconnect?
5. Do others trust me and feel connected to me? What evidence do I have of this?

RECAP

- Connection is the sense of belonging to something bigger than yourself.
- It's about "we" rather than "I" or "they."
- Fit, belonging, and integration are stages of connection.
- There are five types of connection: social, organizational, mission, values, and task.
- Lack of connection leads to isolation and alienation.
- Connection can be tribal: one department not connecting with another.
- The *irrigation effect* refers to communication that does not reach all the stakeholders downstream from its originator.
- Having in- and out-groups can breed communication ghettos that tear organizations apart.
- Connection also requires that an organization be emotionally and psychologically "safe."
- Connection doesn't always rely on proximity. Shared values and culture can create it even if workers are scattered in many locations.
- To foster connection, culture depends on anchors, authenticity, and trust.

PART THREE

Engaging People™

CHAPTER EIGHT

The Engaging Individual

"There are only three measurements that tell you nearly everything you need to know about your organization's overall performance: employee engagement, customer satisfaction, and cash flow."
—Jack Welch

Engaging People™. It's a phrase with multiple meanings. As an adjective, an *engaging* individual describes one who draws interest. We have all worked with people who are, by nature, engaging individuals. They draw us in. They have engaging personalities. They have engaging conversations. They are people who can create action through others, causing us to want to make something happen.

As a verb, an *engaging* individual is one who both feels and does. We give our hearts and spirits (the feeling), as well as our minds and hands (the doing), to our work. We personally engage in what we do. Engaging individuals act, meaning that rather than sitting back passively, waiting to feel something, they go out and do something. They also bring others along with them, inspiring others to act as well.

Engagement begins with the individual employee. If the organization—corporation, not-for-profit, university, sports team, what-have-you—is the entire organism, then each employee is like a single cell. Change may appear on the scale of an entire organism, but change begins at the level of the single cell. In this chapter, we'll begin our look at the process of growing a more deeply engaged organization by looking at the role that you—you, the employee—play in your *own* engagement.

At this point, your position and title are irrelevant. Even if you occupy a glass-walled office in the C-suite, you are first and foremost an individual, working for the benefit of a wide range of stakeholders: your colleagues, shareholders, customers, and family members, to name a few. Even if you are at the managerial or executive level and have the power to shape and set organizational policy, your greatest impact on the level of engagement within your organization will be how engaged you are personally—how strongly you find meaning, autonomy, growth, impact, and connection in where you work and with whom you work.

To that end, it's worth reiterating a critical point about engagement:

Engaging is a choice.

Even if you are the policymaker, engagement doesn't just happen. Remember, the organization's job is to create the conditions optimal for its members to engage with their work, their mission, and each other. Once that fertile soil has been laid down, it's each individual's responsibility to say, "Yes. I will trust, I will commit emotionally, and I will embrace opportunities to flourish in my organization." It's important to remember that engagement involves hearts, spirits, minds, and hands. This means that you must choose to both feel and act.

Sometimes, if the conditions aren't right for an individual to engage, that also means speaking up and saying, "This is what I need if I'm going to engage." A number of years ago, there was a bright young woman working on our assessment team. She was a stellar performer and an active contributor to our success. However, in regular one-on-one discussions about her development, we learned that she saw her position as a short-term opportunity to earn an income before pursuing what she really got passionate about. The year prior, she had earned a degree in exercise physiology, but she hadn't been able to find work in that field before she joined our team. She explained that she would continue to contribute actively (the mind and the hands were certainly there), yet her heart and spirit were not in her work. Committed? Yes. Engaged? No.

We discussed the fact that most of the MAGIC keys were there, but meaning and growth were lacking, or at least diminished. She was growing professionally and personally, and added some valuable bullets to her resume. But she wasn't growing in the areas in which she wanted to grow. Similarly, she found meaning in what she did, but it wasn't in the area in which she wanted to find meaning. Regardless of what the organization was doing, she knew that she found purpose and the opportunity to grow around exercise physiology, not administering assessments for our team.

We puzzled over this for a while. She was certainly satisfied. She enjoyed her work. We valued having her with us, as she was an important part of our team. If only we could find a way for her goals and ours to intersect in a way that would create that excitement that she found in her work in exercise physiology.

She came up with the solution.

"What if I were to continue to act as a personal trainer for a couple of clients at a time in the mornings before I got to work?" she asked. It sounded reasonable to us, and we happily agreed. After that, her creative juices started flowing.

"What if *you* were to start a corporate wellness program for *our* company?" we asked. As spending time eating in hotels didn't always agree with our traveling consultants' waistlines, this would be a real benefit to them, we reasoned.

To make a long story short, we all agreed, and within a week, she had set up a wellness program that not only engaged her, but brought health benefits to the entire team. It was a creative win-win that worked for both a valued employee and the organization.

THE ENGAGEMENT RESISTANCE CURVE

That's an example of the conscious nature of engagement. No organization can "reach out and grab you" and make you become engaged. Business isn't *Field of Dreams*. You can't "build it and they will come." That ethos may work for baseball, but it's probably not going to get you hearts, spirit, minds, and hands in the "real" world. Engagement is a choice.

While some of the keys to engagement are based on innate qualities that are not always under your conscious control—you probably don't have complete control of what you will find meaningful—how you choose to act on those stimuli is very much a conscious choice. That's why, in any organization, all employees fall somewhere along what we call the engagement resistance curve.

Some individuals engage more easily and eagerly than others due to both innate personality characteristics (autotelic personality, high self-esteem) and learned behaviors (high levels of trust, past positive workplace experiences). Others engage grudgingly, if at all, due to the same factors, from poor self-esteem and cynicism to issues like undiagnosed anxiety disorders. Simply put, some people are wired for engagement, while others aren't. Most of us, however, fit somewhere between these two extremes. We choose to be engaged (or disengaged) based on the environment we are in and where we find the MAGIC—meaning, autonomy, growth, impact, and connection—in that environment. It's a 50-50 proposition. The organization builds the playing field, and we choose to bring our hearts, spirits, minds, and hands to the game.

Most of us approach engagement with varying degrees of resistance. The engagement resistance curve doesn't rank people's current levels of engagement, but their propensity for *becoming* engaged. It looks like this:

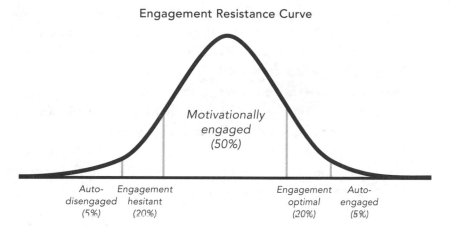

Engagement Resistance Curve

Motivationally
engaged
(50%)

| Auto-disengaged (5%) | Engagement hesitant (20%) | Engagement optimal (20%) | Auto-engaged (5%) |

- **Auto-disengaged:** These are the lost causes, the people who are unlikely to engage regardless of what the organization does. This employee cannot view work as anything more than a paycheck, and he is likely to hold an adversarial view of his employer, whether that attitude is justified or not. He is cynical, critical, suspicious toward his employer's motives, and a negative, indifferent clock puncher.

- **Engagement hesitant:** This employee would rather not engage, but is not opposed to it, either. She is likely to regard her job as something that pays her expenses and nothing more, and she is likely to regard efforts at engagement with a jaundiced eye. Relationships with organizations are transactional—quid pro quo. She will respond to engagement efforts only if they are persistent and personal, and she tends to step in and out of engagement. She tends to be naturally somewhat jaded and pessimistic about work.

- **Motivationally engaged:** A good portion of us will fall into this category. These employees are willing to engage if their motivational and satisfaction needs are met—if they are paid fairly, given appropriate perks, feel emotionally safe in their roles, shown potential paths of advancement, and so forth. They are not always cheerleaders, nor are they saboteurs. They are potentially effective employees who fully engage and deliver excellence under the right conditions.

- **Engagement optimal:** This employee does not engage as instantaneously as the auto-engaged employee, but he does not require a great

deal of encouragement to do so. He will respond positively to organizational opportunities to engage, provided they are authentic and
promises are backed by action. He also tends to be optimistic, confident, self-aware, and enthusiastic, if not on quite the same "walking
on sunshine" level as the auto-engaged person.

- **Auto-engaged**: This employee is innately inclined to find meaning,
  purpose, connection, and fulfillment in almost any work. She quickly
  and easily embraces organizational efforts to increase levels of engagement. She tends to be optimistic, confident, self-aware, and enthusiastic. In short, she will be engaged in nearly any environment.

YOU ARE THE OFFICE JERK

Where do you fall on the engagement resistance curve? Why? Our experience conducting more than 30 million engagement surveys tells us that
the number-one determinant of personal engagement is you. People who
can't or won't engage may make a fundamental attribution error and blame
their employer, but more often than not, they are the reason they don't
become engaged.

Behavioral finance consultant Dr. Daniel Crosby describes it this way:

Take a moment to consider your dating life. As you look back over
the people you've dated, what patterns emerge? All too often, as I
coach frustrated young (or not so young) executives, they bemoan
the fact that, "I always date weirdos." After some initial empathic
listening, I typically try to get the conversation back to them. After
all, you are the only consistent link in this chain of bad relationships.

The psychology of this is well understood but underemphasized
in the workplace. The tendency to excuse our own bad behavior
and vilify others for theirs is known as the "fundamental attribution
error." The FAE goes like this, we tend to excuse our own bad behavior on the basis of extenuating circumstances rather than anything
deep-seated and personality based. If I'm a jerk to my coworkers, it's
not because I'm a bad guy, it's because I haven't had my coffee yet . . .

. . . Let's realize that if every place we have ever worked is stale
and oppressive, we just might have something to do with that. Do

you know what is the best predictor of employee satisfaction? I'll give you a hint, it's not foosball tables, casual Fridays or a Wii in the break room—it is what shrinks like me call "individual differences." YOU are the best predictor. Foosball is great, but unhappy people are unhappy with or without the perks.[153]

I call this the "Wherever you go, there you are" phenomenon. Remember, you are the only constant that you take with you from situation to situation. The auto-disengaged person in one organization will be the auto-disengaged person in her next organization. DecisionWise research teams have found some interesting facts to back up this idea. The teams looked at the engagement survey responses of over 350,000 employees in various organizations. As the team followed these employees across a five-year period, we were curious as to whether these individuals shifted across the four engagement categories (Fully Engaged, Key Contributors, Opportunity Group, and Disengaged). In other words, if I'm a Key Contributor this year, does that change two years from now?

As you learned earlier in this book, the results were fascinating. Yes, they did move from category to category, with one big exception—the Disengaged. Less than five percent of disengaged employees moved from the Disengaged category to the Fully Engaged or Key Contributor categories within a two-year period of time. In other words, only five percent of those who were disengaged in their jobs became engaged while working for the same organization.

Some well-meaning organizations would say, "We need to help these disengaged employees and find ways to engage them." As cold as it may sound, the better response might be, at least according to the research, "Let us help you find a place outside of our company that might better match what engages you."

You are responsible for your ability or inability to engage, regardless of your position within your organization or your organization's efforts to "get employees engaged." The truth is that some people will find a way to engage *no matter what*. The interesting thing here is that workplace engagement often spills over to home-life engagement. While we may try to separate work and personal lives, the fact is that we are whole individuals, rather than tidy segments; home life, community life, work life, social life, and so forth all flow into one another. If you are disengaged at work, chances are you'll be disengaged in other areas of your life as well.

"You are the office jerk" means that if you want to solve the galling riddle "Why can't I get as engaged as some of the people I work with?" you should look in the mirror. Engagement may be a 50-50 proposition between employer and employee, but the individual has as much power to drive employer engagement initiatives as the top decision makers do. You can't wait for your employer to come to you, because doing so presupposes that your employer (1) understands engagement; (2) realizes that you and others are not engaged; and (3) knows the unique factors that will engage you, the individual.

Do you simply knock on your superior's door, complain that you're not feeling engaged, and demand (whether implicitly or directly) that he do something about it? Of course not. The process begins with you, not your employer. This is why there is an abbreviated ENGAGEMENT MAGIC® Self-Assessment at the end of this chapter. A more extensive version of this assessment is available online at www.engagementmagic.com/self-assessment. When you finish reading chapter eight, take a few minutes to complete this assessment, as well as the free online version. When you know more about how engaged you are, you'll have a much clearer idea of how engaged you wish to become and what to do about it.

When you complete the assessment, you'll end up with three scores for each of the five engagement keys: *experienced engagement, desired engagement,* and *engagement gap.* Your experienced-engagement score reveals the levels of all five MAGIC keys that you are currently experiencing in your organization. Think of it as today's engagement report card.

Your desired-engagement scores show the levels of meaning, autonomy, growth, impact, and connection that you would *like* to be experiencing at work. Your desired-engagement scores are your goals—assuming you want to meaningfully increase your level of overall engagement.

Your engagement gap is the difference between your experienced engagement and desired engagement for each part of MAGIC. Think of these numbers as an aspirational list showing you how far you need to go in order to become truly engaged in what you do—to enjoy your work more, find it purposeful and meaningful, and help your organization become more successful. The engagement gap is critical, because it shows you the areas of greatest need.

The math is pretty clear: The larger the difference between your experienced and desired scores, the more dramatic the change that has to occur for you to become completely engaged. If there are only one or two points between experienced and desired engagement in, say, Impact, then a few small tweaks are probably all that's necessary. But if there's a twenty-point chasm between your experienced level of connection and the level of connection you desire, you're going to have to take radical action—and insist on the same from your employer. A large gap might not even be bridgeable; you might have to accept that you won't get the level of engagement you want in your current situation.

Increasing your level of engagement and connection at work could improve your health. Social isolation has been linked to increased risk of disease, lack of control over higher mental functions, higher levels of stress hormones, insomnia, and accelerated age-related decline. Further investigation reveals that lonely people are actually different at the genetic level, with under-expression of genes involved in immune response, healing, and combatting inflammation, among others. It appears that perceiving yourself as being isolated and alone is dangerous to your well-being, and that engaging with others and feeling connected is beneficial.[154]

ENGAGEMENT IS NOT ABSOLUTE

Even flawed attempts at encouraging engagement are preferable to doing nothing. Some engagement is always better than none. However, engagement is not binary. It's not a matter of flipping a switch: engagement ON, engagement OFF. You, the individual, may be the means by which engagement is propagated through an organization, but you're also a complex being with your own unique motivations, behaviors, and needs. Engagement on a personal level is not cut-and-dried. It's complex. Because of this, it's important to look beyond your spot on the engagement resistance curve and understand some deeper truths.

For one thing, engagement is a spectrum, not an absolute state. You are not going to feel engaged all the time in your work or personal life. Can you imagine feeling exalted and in the flow when you're, say, changing a toilet-paper roll in the office bathroom? Of course not. That's absurd. But it's an illustration of the fact that you will not feel 100 percent engaged 100 percent of the time. No one does. Your level of engagement will rise and fall from moment to moment depending on:

- What you're doing
- How you're feeling physically and emotionally
- Your life outside work and its relationship to your work
- How well your satisfaction and motivational needs (compensation, perks, physical security, etc.) are being met
- The levels of meaning, autonomy, growth, impact, and connection present in your organizational culture at the time

Those are all volatile states, so at a given point in time the snapshot of your engagement level will also be volatile. That doesn't matter. What does matter is your level of engagement over the long term. Over months and quarters, the ups and downs even out and a clear picture emerges. Patterns take shape: Your work brings you strong meaning, but you have few mechanisms to determine your impact. That's correctable, and as long as your level of engagement is generally positive and trending upward, it's fine if on a given day you don't feel like an employee in a company where you are racing around on a scooter, listening to house music, and celebrating your stock options.

Google has created an interesting environment—one that is, perhaps, uniquely suited to Google. Google will feed you, do your laundry, run your errands via Google Shopping Express, and give you five months of paid maternity leave. In return, you'll work long hours and exhibit a creative, problem-solving brilliance that's almost impossible to find in any other organization. There's a reason that Google's hiring process is excruciatingly rigorous: They need the best of the best, people who are worth the investment in the culture.

For Google, it works, and their business success is largely a result of this investment. Bottom line, it's a great company. It's no wonder that, when we compare Google's perks to the perks, benefits, and environment offered within our own walls, we start to see flaws in our own organization. How many times a day do you think employees at other Silicon Valley tech companies mutter, "Well, at Google, they offer [insert your favorite lusted-after Google amenity here]." Yet, according to payroll consultancy PayScale, the median employee tenure at Google is just over one year.[155] It's easy to take the best of what we see elsewhere and compare it to the worst within our own world.

WHAT DO YOU NEED TO ENGAGE?

So, do you need to have all five MAGIC keys present in order to be engaged? The simple answer is "yes," but that's incomplete. There are a few points that are critical to understand in response to this question:

- **Every variation of the MAGIC keys need not be present in order for you to engage.** Let's look at Autonomy, for example. When our engagement consultants work with our client partners on their engagement journeys, we spend a good deal of time on-site in their facilities. Because of this, our spatial and temporal autonomy is restricted—we are where our client partners need us to be, when they need us to be there. We have some degree of control, but that's limited by client needs. Are we disengaged? Not by a long shot. We have a great deal of task autonomy, as well as social autonomy. In fact, that's part of the reason we're in the business we are. While it's important that each MAGIC key be present in order for you to engage, these keys can be present in different ways.
- **For most people, different MAGIC keys carry different weight.** For you, connection may be critical. For others, the idea of social connection is actually disengaging ("I hate company parties!"). The socially reticent person may still find organizational connection to be important. However, the real reason he works here is because of the meaning he finds in his work.
- **What engages you will not necessarily engage another person.** Company engagement initiatives that try to impose engagement on employees are doomed for the simple reason that while a corporate plan to have employees volunteer at local homeless shelters may resonate with *some* employees, it won't resonate with *all* of them. Some may even resent the implication that they can be told what to care about and find the efforts to be manipulative. Remember, engagement isn't something that is done *to* you, it's a choice—your choice.

- **With engagement, frequency and intensity matter.** Do you find meaning in what you do every day, or only on occasion? Is the work you do deeply meaningful to the degree to which it feels like your life's mission, or is it something you merely feel is important until something better comes along? The greater the frequency and intensity with which you experience the five MAGIC keys, the greater your level of engagement will be.

Wise organizations simply put the conditions in place under which employees can choose how they will engage, then step back and let the process proceed more or less organically. If you are in the kind of organization that takes a one-size-fits-all approach to the employee experience, remember that you are not obligated to find meaning, autonomy, or connection in the same place as your colleagues. On the other hand, if you are in an organization that allows employees to express what engagement means to them, feel free to express what matters to you without worrying about what others are doing or saying. Eventually, you will figure out what gets you truly engaged.

When you do, keep one more truth in mind: The things that engage you and the needs of your organization will not always align. Sometimes the differences are irreconcilable. Sometimes you will need to find another organization into which your definition of meaning, growth, and all the rest can fit more harmoniously. Sometimes companies and individuals just don't fit. Better to see that clearly and move on to brighter horizons. You may bring your mind and hands to the job each day, but without the heart and spirit, soon the mind and hands will begin showing up less frequently as well.

THE RESPONSIBILITY TO ENGAGE

However or wherever you reach a level of engagement that suits who you are, you have a responsibility to become as fully engaged as possible. Why? Because engagement is contagious, as is disengagement. Each fully engaged individual makes an organization stronger; each disengaged individual weakens it.

In the case of engagement or disengagement, persistent examples of a culture and belief system in action tend to breed more of the same. This is hardly limited to the workplace—consider the example of former Los

Angeles police chief William Bratton and his Broken Windows policy. Bratton, a former NYPD chief, became the chief of the notoriously racist and reviled Los Angeles Police Department in 2002 and quickly set about making Broken Windows a central part of policing.

The idea behind Broken Windows is simple: a zero-tolerance approach to small crimes such as vandalism, graffiti, and yes, broken windows. When you allow such crimes to proliferate, the theory says, you send a message to the community that no one is watching—no one cares. This encourages more serious crime. Bratton's approach did the opposite, dedicating police resources to reducing even minor crimes and community damage. To be sure, that wasn't his only strategy; expanding the LAPD and encouraging more constructive dialogue between white officers and members of the black and Latino communities played a big role as well. What we do know is that by the time Bratton left the LAPD in 2009, violent crime was down 54 percent over the final year of Bratton's predecessor, and surveys showed that 83 percent of Los Angeles residents rated the LAPD as "good" or "excellent," up from 71 percent just two years earlier.[156]

Egghead Alert!

Emotional Contagion is the tendency for individuals to synchronize their emotions with the emotions of those around them, whether consciously or unconsciously. We mimic others' emotions, even if we aren't aware of it. This mimicry can take a long period of time to develop, or it can manifest in a matter of seconds. For example, one study found that students living with depressed roommates became increasingly depressed over a three-month period of time.[157] Similar studies found that employees' positive emotions impact customers' perception of the quality of service,[158] and also affect how much people tip.[159] Emotional Contagion affirms that we are both impacted by and impact the moods, attitudes, and general emotions of those we are with.

The difference between even one deeply engaged individual and that same individual being cynically, apathetically disengaged is the same as the difference between an urban neighborhood filled with flowers, antique streetlamps, and food carts versus one filled with graffiti, broken sidewalks, and trash. Both encourage people to behave in certain ways, but one form of behavior is desirable and beneficial while the other is harmful.

Which does your commitment to engagement make you, a broken window or a renovated house? Do your actions encourage others to become more engaged or less engaged? This is why you have a responsibility to discover what engages you and to pursue it to the best of your ability. That same MAGIC for which you turn to others is the same MAGIC for which they are looking to you. Do people choose to connect with you? Is part of their social autonomy a choice to work with *you*? Your willingness to choose engagement will impact others' willingness to do the same.

Are you familiar with the concept of the first follower? It's the idea that in any social situation, there's always one person who decides to risk looking foolish by being the first one to try something—the most common example being the first person to step into an open field at a music festival and start dancing. At the start, everyone else stands around and watches, not wanting to be the first person to validate what the lone dancer is doing and risk disapproval from the crowd. However, once a second person joins the first dancer—a first follower—that quickly opens the floodgates. The implied approval of a second dancer brings everyone into the field, and before you know it you have a flash mob.

Personal engagement gives each of us the chance to be that first follower—the one who acts on the organization's efforts and chooses to engage. You have an obligation to *yourself* to be engaged. This is the one time when we say, "Forget the organization, forget your coworkers, and think of yourself." Do you really want to show up, day after day, to a job to which you don't (or can't) bring energy and passion? If you do, your actions will soon reflect your state of engagement. So will the engagement levels of your colleagues. Accepting that obligation and acting on it—choosing engagement—creates a win-win-win for you, the people around you, and your organization as a whole.

PERSONAL ENGAGEMENT MAGIC® SELF-ASSESSMENT

Here's where the rubber meets the road. Below is an abbreviated variation of the Employee Engagement Assessment we've given across the globe. It's different, however, from our employee surveys in that it focuses specifically on you and your level of engagement, not your company. At this stage, it will be helpful to complete this assessment so you'll have a clearer idea of how engaged you are today and how engaged you could become in the future.

This assessment is simple and should take only about ten minutes. The online version (www.engagementmagic.com/self-assessment) is more comprehensive and will take a little longer, and will give you additional insight into your own MAGIC. Once you're finished, if you think you would value even more probing reflection on your own engagement, you can find a set of thought-provoking questions in the Appendix of this book.

INSTRUCTIONS

The self-assessment below will help you evaluate your MAGIC—where it's strong, and where it could use a boost.

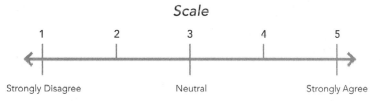

As you respond to the questions below, indicate your agreement with the statement by placing a score from 1–5 (1= Strongly Disagree; 5= Strongly Agree) on the line next to the question. Once you have completed the assessment, go back to each section, add up the score for the section, and write the score on the "Score" line—"M" for Meaning, and so on. On the "Desired" line for each section, indicate the score you would desire from that section, with 25 points being the highest possible for the entire section or key. Those MAGIC keys that are most important for you will have the highest "desired" scores. Once you have both your actual score and your desired score, the difference between these two scores is the "Gap." A gap can be either positive

Self-assessment

		Score	Desired	Gap

MEANING

1. My work is an integral part of who I am as a person. _____
2. My job provides me with a sense of meaning and purpose. _____
3. I am proud of the work we do in this organization. _____
4. My job inspires me. _____
5. For me, this is more than "just a job." _____

M _____ _____ _____

AUTONOMY

6. I have the authority I need to do my best work. _____
7. I am generally able to choose how to best perform my job. _____
8. I am given the freedom to fully use my talents and abilities in my current position. _____
9. My supervisor trusts and empowers me to get my work done in the way I see best. _____
10. I am able to be creative and innnovative at work. _____

A _____ _____ _____

GROWTH

11. There are people here who see my potential, and work to help me acheive it. _____
12. I regularly feel challenged and stretched in my job. _____
13. My job offers enough variety that I am learning new things. _____
14. My job helps me grow both individually and professionally. _____
15. I receive regular performance feedback and coaching. _____

G _____ _____ _____

IMPACT

16. There are clear objectives here by which I can measure my success. _____
17. I can clearly see the results of the work I perform. _____
18. The work I do has a direct impact on the success of the organization. _____
19. Most days, I leave work feeling like I was able to accomplish what I needed. _____
20. Most days, I can see that I am making progress on important work projects. _____

I _____ _____ _____

CONNECTION

21. I am a good fit with the company's culture. _____
22. I enjoy the people I work with. _____
23. I feel like I belong here. _____
24. I can embrace the mission, values, and ideals of this organization. _____
25. I trust the people I work with. _____

C _____ _____ _____

SATISFACTION

26. Overall, the compensation and benefits I receive here are fair. _____
27. I have the tools and resources I need to perform my job. _____
28. I feel that what I receive from the organization is aligned with the effort I put in. _____
29. At work, I am treated with dignity and respect. _____
30. In my job, I feel emotionally and physically safe. _____

S _____ _____ _____

ENGAGEMENT

31. I love my job. _____
32. My heart is in the work I do. _____
33. It is easy to become absorbed in my work. _____
34. I feel happy when I am intensely working in my job. _____
35. At work, I feel strong, energized, and vigorous. _____

E _____ _____ _____

Self-assessment Results

Element	Low	Moderate	High	Experienced Score	Desired Score	Gap
M	5 10 15 20 25			_____	_____	_____
A	5 10 15 20 25			_____	_____	_____
G	5 10 15 20 25			_____	_____	_____
I	5 10 15 20 25			_____	_____	_____
C	5 10 15 20 25			_____	_____	_____

Element	Low	Moderate	High	Experienced Score	Desired Score	Gap
S	5 10 15 20 25			_____	_____	_____
E	5 10 15 20 25			_____	_____	_____

(you have an abundance of this particular MAGIC key) or negative (you lack in this area, and need more than you currently find in your work).

Sections for both Satisfaction and Overall Engagement are also included.

RECAP

- Engagement is a matter of personal choice. No one can impose engagement on you, nor can you impose engagement on someone else.
- Engaging individuals both feel and *do*.
- If all the basics for engagement are present, but it just isn't happening, then the things that speak to heart and spirit are probably absent.
- The engagement resistance curve measures your propensity for becoming engaged—how hard your organization and colleagues will need to work to capture your heart, spirit, mind, and hands.
- You may be the office jerk. You are the common factor in all your workplace (and social) situations.
- Your engagement gap measures how far you have to go in order to reach the level of engagement you desire.
- Engagement doesn't have an on/off switch. You don't have to experience all the keys at their maximum to be engaged.
- Frequency and intensity matter.
- Engagement is a gift you give yourself.

CHAPTER NINE

THE ENGAGING MANAGER

"Management is doing things right; leadership is doing the right things."
—*Peter Drucker*

YOU'RE MOST LIKELY a member of multiple organizations. Community groups, alumni associations, church groups, the PTA, the bowling league, a family, the Rotary Club, the singles scene, the NRA—you name it. This means that you must take responsibility for your engagement in each organization. In the case of a business, you're an employee. That's true no matter what it says on your business card. But you may also be a manager, and as a manager you do have some responsibility for the engagement of others. If so, this chapter is for you.

Most of what we've talked about so far isn't what you would typically expect to find in a university management program or a management training workshop. This book isn't filled with wisdom on how to calculate quick ratios and EBITDA. I haven't told you how to implement a Six Sigma program, or held forth on the implications of carrying costs on warehousing. But I'm well aware that those topics can be critical to management and organizational success.

After all, the success of an organization is measured by outcomes. Is our business profitable? Are we developing new products? Did we make enough bricks? Is our livestock healthy? Are our patients receiving the lifesaving treatments they need?

Despite what they may say in mission statements, few businesses exist exclusively to "Provide for our employees' well-being." That would be naïve. Ultimately, stakeholders care about engagement only if improved engagement enhances performance and delivers improved results. Fortunately, that's precisely what it does.

That's why a significant portion of this book is devoted to outlining how engagement and performance are interconnected. And that's why, at this point, it's appropriate to discuss how engagement impacts both you, the manager, as an individual and the teams and departments you are charged with leading.

Managers are accountable for the outcomes of the organization in which they work. They aren't hired simply to make sure employees feel good and are happy. They are expected to deliver results. Organizations reward (or punish) managers for outcomes. While this is obviously appropriate (managers should be accountable for organizational performance), it's only half the equation. *What* gets done is as important as *how* it gets done.

In the autonomy chapter, I discussed the fact that management should help employees understand *what* needs to be done, but that *how* they go about getting results is where autonomy really kicks in. Of course, I also took care in pointing out that the *how* must occur within appropriate boundaries. For our purposes, a manager can be defined as anyone with supervisorial responsibility over a work group, team, or department who does not possess the powers of an executive; that is, to set and enforce overall organizational strategy. You, the manager, are the one responsible for enforcing the boundaries—for keeping employees coloring inside the lines while ensuring that within those lines, they're free to be unabashedly creative.

Managers are at the heart of what we do because you're the glue of the organization. At one extreme, we have the senior executives, who are focused on the "big picture": developing and implementing broad strategies, dealing with public relations and politics, managing complex finances, and so on. At the other, we have the rank-and-file workers who perform the tasks that create products, serve customers, ship goods, and keep the company running day-to-day.

In between lie managers. If the dwellers of the C-suite are the brain of the organization and the front-line employees are the hands, you're the nervous system connecting the two. Without you, nothing gets done. You're the sergeants. Think about a military post. Who makes things run? The sergeants. They've seen it all, done it all, know the shortcuts, and know how to motivate people. Remove the officers from a military base and, chances are, things will continue to run just fine for a time; take away the sergeants, and things will grind to a halt in a matter of days. Managers drive, and are accountable for, outcomes. And, if you don't have the word *manager* on your business card? Read on. Whoever or whatever you are, you're likely currently playing a role as a leader somewhere, have been a leader in the past, or will be one in the future.

THE PROMOTION PROBLEM

Here's where we run into one of the most common problems with effective managers: They keep getting promoted. In our coaching practice, our consultants often report experiences with "promoted doers." In traditional organizations, employees considered good "doers" (people who have a talent for getting the job done) form the pool from which supervisors choose new managers when promotions come around. Now, that's perfectly appropriate. However, it also creates a problem.

When a former "doer" is abruptly handed a manager or supervisor title, he or she may not have the tools to lead. He or she may be an excellent software developer but lack the skills, background, tools, and learning needed to excel in a management role. Usually, one of three things happens: (1) This person adapts and gains the qualities needed to become a solid leader; (2) the new manager takes what he or she knows from experience and becomes a "super-doer," forgetting that it's now his or her job to lead and inspire others, not do everything; or (3) the newly promoted fails miserably, taking his or her team down with the ship.

Fortunately, much of the time the first scenario plays out—the manager learns, adapts, succeeds, and leads. Perhaps you have experienced this in your own career or worked alongside those who have. However, the second and third scenarios are all too common. As many organizations work to pull themselves out of their managerial death spirals, they do so by focusing on results—and, possibly, results at any cost. After all, results are what the organization rewards. Right?

DO AS I SAY, NOT AS I DO

Earlier, I mentioned the concept of 360-degree feedback. This type of assessment uses a survey to understand the performance and behaviors of individual managers and employees. A group of raters—typically peers, supervisors, and subordinates—is asked to provide confidential online feedback about a manager, and the results are reported back to the manager.

Several years ago, our research team was asked to work with a major cereal manufacturer whose leadership was concerned that many of the company's managers were failing. The managers in question had been with the company for some time and had risen through the ranks, and while the company was doing well overall, the leadership suspected that their managers had the potential to have a more positive impact on the company's success. In order to see what was really going on, we began by gathering data.

Our team started with both an annual performance evaluation, which had already been in place for years, and a 360-degree feedback assessment. The annual performance evaluation measured operational outcomes—how much cereal was manufactured, quality, safety, and so forth. Additionally, it provided input from each manager's boss on how well he or she was meeting specified objectives. In other words, similar to most companies, it measured key operational metrics and outcomes—*what* got done.

The 360-degree assessment, on the other hand, asked supervisors, peers, and subordinates about behaviors. Did the manager communicate well, build the team, recognize, and reward? Was he or she perceived as ethical, trustworthy, inspiring, skilled, and knowledgeable? While the annual performance appraisal measured what got done, the 360 measured *how* it got done. We wanted to understand the entire picture of each manager's operational performance, as well as how he or she was leading the team.

We got more than we bargained for.

We soon recognized that this study would take some time—three years, to be exact. Over this period, we followed 147 managers as they moved within the ranks of the company. We had access to the managers' annual employee performance evaluations and their 360-degree feedback, so this was a good start.

In assessing the effectiveness of a manager, it's generally assumed that those who score well on traditional annual evaluations will also score well on the 360-degree feedback assessment. That's logical, right? If the *how* is in line, then the *what* will also be in line, and vice versa. Makes sense.

However, to everyone's surprise, it didn't work out that way. After following these managers for three years, we statistically compared the results of each one's annual performance evaluations with the same manager's 360-degree feedback assessments over the same time period. The findings? There was no correlation whatsoever. None. Zip.

This result contradicted much of what we were taught in business school. Weren't we told that good leaders are well rounded in their approach, considering more than simply the end result? Hmm. We dug deeper and found that managers could hit their operational metrics and get results, yet *not* be regarded as good leaders.

In fact, as we looked at the managers who were scoring well on their annual employee evaluation while flopping in their 360-degree assessments, we found that they were getting results at the expense of customer and employee relationships. Remember, EX = CX. It was no surprise that turnover among the employees on their teams was nearly *five times* the average turnover in the company as a whole. In short, these managers were hitting objectives but leaving a trail of bodies as they did so.

Still, these managers were getting results, right? They were delivering, and isn't that what the organization wanted, despite the collateral damage? Even though they came at the expense of customer relationships and employee well-being, their results still looked darned good on a financial statement.

This shortsighted approach didn't work for long. The average tenure of the results-at-any-cost manager in this particular plant was just under eighteen months, compared to an average tenure of over seven years for other managers. During this period, not only did the managers' results steadily decrease, their relationships with customers and subordinates deteriorated. Of the 147 managers included at the beginning of the study, forty-two were no longer with the company by the third year, with most of them leaving due to performance or customer issues.

What did those forty-two managers who left the company have in common? You guessed it: They were part of the results-at-any-cost cohort. But even worse than their level of attrition was the way they decimated entire teams on their way out the door. By the end of the third year, the data had become so clear that we could often predict a team's level of engagement by looking at the behavior of its manager.

What did we learn? First, many managers are put into positions where they are expected to lead without knowing how to do so. We promote doers into managerial roles and expect that they will know how to lead by . . . osmosis? Instead, we have removed a skilled doer from a position where he was highly effective and set him up to fail. We have failed to recognize that leadership demands a completely different set of skills. Now, we've lost a line worker who got great results, and we have a manager who's foundering and, quite possibly, a disengaged team.

We also learned that while managers can get operational results, some go about it in a way that is shortsighted and dangerous to the long-term success of the organization. This type of management is unsustainable and damaging. Finally, we got a reminder of just how important strong leadership is to engagement. If engagement is a 50-50 employee–employer proposition, much of the employer's 50 percent falls squarely on the manager's shoulders.

In fact, it's probably not an exaggeration to state that the primary responsibility of an effective manager is to ensure that his or her direct reports are as engaged as possible. As we've seen, results and positive outcomes tend to run downhill from there.

ENGAGING MANAGERS = ENGAGING TEAMS

You may be like the managers in the above scenario—a valuable individual contributor promoted into a position of leadership without the proper guidance or tools. Hopefully, you're the manager who gets it. You get results and lead a strong, engaged team on the way to success. In either case, here's a humbling reminder: 78 percent of managers rate themselves higher on 360-degree surveys than do their direct reports. A good percentage of us are legends in our own minds.

Let's look back at the "Engaging People" concept and apply it to managers. First, a leader can be an engaging (as an adjective) individual. He or she may possess certain skills, personality traits, or abilities that naturally draw people to the engaging environment. But there are also certain things these engaging managers do to create an environment in which others choose to engage.

Whatever situation you're in, as a manager you have influence over the engagement of the people you supervise. While they must still choose to be engaged, you have more influence than probably anyone else in your organization. So, no pressure. The good news? Our research shows that the more engaged you are as a manager, the more engaged your subordinates are likely to be.

As critical as managers are to the health of an organization, it would be surprising if the engagement level of managers didn't impact the engagement level of the employees working under them. In fact, in research we conducted to see if there was a relationship between the engagement level of managers and the engagement level of their subordinates, we found that the more engaged managers are in their work and workplace culture, the more engaged their teams are.

Our research teams reviewed data files containing employee engagement survey results from twenty-two companies. After removing the results from all managers with fewer than four subordinates, we were left with survey responses from 2,300 managers and 18,913 rank-and-file employees. Careful analysis of the engagement scores of both groups revealed that:

- Within the manager category, 35 percent of people fell into the Fully Engaged category, 50 percent were classified as Key Contributors, 13 percent fell into the Opportunity Group, and only 2 percent were Fully Disengaged.
- The employee surveys showed a similar distribution—27 percent of employees were Fully Engaged, 49 percent were Key Contributors, 20 percent of employees were in the Opportunity Group, and 5 percent were Fully Disengaged.
- The percentage of employees who are Fully Engaged increases by 50 percent when the manager is Fully Engaged instead of merely being a Key Contributor. The increase in engagement is even greater when compared with the teams of managers who are either in the Opportunity Group or Fully Disengaged: We see a 157 percent jump in the percentage of employees Fully Engaged in both categories.

Boiled down, the results of our research show that (1) engaging managers do affect the engagement levels of their teams; and (2) engaging leaders have more engaged teams.[160]

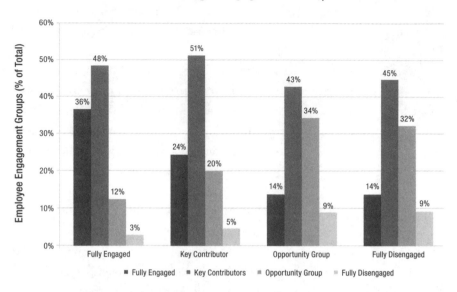

Manager's engagement (horizontal axis) compared to employees' engagement (vertical axis).

HOW ENGAGED ARE YOU?

The good news is that managers and executives seem to be increasingly more engaged than in the past. In 2017, managers and executives showed the highest engagement levels of any position category, and we saw their engagement jump considerably over the previous five years. The bad news is that not enough managers understand just how critical their own engagement is to that of their teams.

As a follow-up to our 2016 research on the impact of a manager's engagement on that of their team, our researchers' 2018 findings emphasized just how critical that relationship is. These researchers found that when a manager's own level of engagement increased just one percentage point from one year's survey to the next, we could expect to see a 213% increase in the odds of that manager's employees engaging in their work.

Let's translate that. If I'm a manager taking an employee engagement survey, and my average response (on a five-point favorability scale) to the items on that survey is one point more favorable than on last year's survey (say, from an average of 3.4 to 4.4), the odds of my employees engaging in their work more than doubles!

How engaged are you as a manager? This question is really two questions: (1) how engaged are you; and (2) how engaged are the people you manage? Your engagement level is crucial, but if it doesn't lift up the engagement levels of the people who report to you, you're probably not as effective a manager as you think you are. After completing the self-assessment in chapter eight, you already have a jump on evaluating your own level of engagement. Given what you've just read, and knowing your own current level of engagement, what does that tell you about how likely your team is to be engaged? Rather than speculate about that, get some data. How? Ask for It! Have the people who report to you complete the same chapter eight self-assessment that you completed. It only takes a few minutes, and you can make them comfortable with the task by directing everyone to leave their names off the surveys. Or, better yet, ask them to take the online version of the assessment at www.engagementmagic.com/self-assessment. They can complete the assessment confidentially and print out their own results.

Before you start having your people take assessments, however, it's worth your time to finish this chapter. You see, the dynamic between managers and line employees is not as complex as people think. That's one of the things our team has learned in compiling more than 30 million employee engagement surveys from organizations around the world.

In assessing your effectiveness as an engaging manager, there are five key questions to ask:
- How engaged are you both as an individual employee and as a manager?
- Am I both feeling and doing?
- How engaged do your subordinates think you are?
- How engaged do you think your subordinates are?
- How engaged do they feel?

Whatever tools you use to assess engagement, it's critical to discover the gaps. Does your team see you as less engaged than you think you are? Do you feel your team is more engaged than they say they are? These disparities can be useful guides for helping you improve team engagement.

You don't have to conduct a comprehensive organization survey to understand what engages your team. Many times, finding this out is a matter of opening communication. Unfortunately, most boss-to-subordinate conversations are about metrics: "How do your monthly sales look? Did you meet with the new vendor? Were you able to reconnect the conduits on the heat tunnel?" Few, however, are about engagement: "What makes you feel energized on the job? Do you have any interest in working from home? Are you interested in taking on a new challenge?"

The objective is to empower you to help your people find delight, energy, and personal fulfillment in their work and make your team or department a more productive, profitable part of your organization. We find that few managers have what we refer to as "engagement conversations" with their employees. These are conversations in which a manager discusses the employee's engagement and that of the team, and they're of vital importance. But before you can initiate such essential dialogue, you need to have a clear understanding of what it means to be an engaged manager.

WHAT IS AN ENGAGING MANAGER?

As I've already said, being engaged as a manager is not the same as being engaged as an employee. The forces that drive your personal engagement will be the same as for any other individual: meaning, autonomy, growth, impact, and connection. But an engaging manager is more than an engaged employee.

For many managers, engaging means "getting you to do what I want you to do." If you comply, you are engaged. Congratulations. Except that's wrong. An engaging manager doesn't coerce by bringing to bear either real or perceived threats of penalty, loss of privilege, termination, and so on. Remember, we're trying to engage hearts and spirits, and no one ever brought their heart or spirit to the table based on threats or fear.

The engaging manager is responsible for putting in place the conditions that will empower employees to *choose* engagement: open communication, rewards and recognition, proximity to the impact and meaning of work, hygiene factors such as pay and benefits, respect and listening, and effective teaching, to name a few.

The engaging manager tills the soil for his direct reports, creating the same conditions that helped him engage in work and workplace culture. He then encourages employees to find engagement in the ways that are unique to that employee, based on what he knows about their passions, interests, and needs. The disengaging manager, on the other hand, either doesn't know what motivates his people or doesn't care. It's about management by authority, threat, and inertia.

There's a psychological principle called the Pygmalion effect, which suggests that managerial attitudes, expectations, and treatment of employees will explain and predict both behavior and performance.[161] In short, if you as a manager set high expectations for an employee's performance, and communicate those expectations in an affirming way ("I have complete confidence that you can do this"), the employee is likely to perform up to your expectations. Well, there's also something called the Golem effect, named after not the character from *The Lord of the Rings* but the mythical creature from Jewish folklore.

The Golem effect is the opposite of the Pygmalion effect: the negative side of the self-fulfilling prophecy. The disengaging manager expects less from his or her people—or outright expects them to fail—and his or her people work down to those lower expectations.[162]

In either case—Pygmalion or Golem—the manager's expectations stem directly from his level of engagement. If a manager is engaging in the workplace, he's likely to have a positive view of what his team can do and to communicate that belief in an empowering, encouraging way. A disengaging manager, dissatisfied with the organization and indifferent about his job, "infects" his team with his apathy, negativity, and belief that the work doesn't matter. His team's performance reflects it.

Egghead Alert!

A variation on the Pygmalion effect is the observer-expectancy effect, also called experimenter's bias. It says that an experimenter or observer—for example, a teacher testing children in a classroom—will often communicate unconscious cues that will cause the subjects to perform in accordance with the observer's bias. A manager who believes a subordinate incapable of performing well in a given task may unintentionally communicate cues that harm the subordinate's confidence or otherwise impair her performance. The opposite is also true. [163]

ENGAGEMENT IS A COMPETENCY

As my colleague, Matthew Wride, and I sat down to put the finishing touches on our book, *The Employee Experience*, he proposed an interesting concept. As we reviewed the data from employee surveys, 360-degree surveys, and various manager psychometric assessments, we noticed a pattern—managers with engaged employees appeared to have some commonality in the way they did certain things. Engaging managers behave differently than other managers. These behaviors, as my colleague described them, were actually competencies, meaning areas in which a manager developed certain skills or abilities.

As we pored through the data with our consulting teams, it was clear he had hit on something. Engagement is a competency.

Competencies (areas in which we are competent) can be learned. They can be taught. They can be practiced and perfected. They can be measured. We can also hold managers accountable for these competencies, and even expect managers to develop these competencies if they are to lead teams. This is where the second part of the "Engaging People" concept comes into play. Engaging managers are engaged, but they also have the ability to draw that out in others.

We began to measure this competency of engagement with numerous managers, and found that there are behaviors common to engaging managers. These include:

- **Values alignment**—Engaging managers act in ways that reflect company values and help employees align personal values to the mission of the organization.

- **Inspiring others**—Engaging managers share an inspiring vision that challenges and excites the team, and leads them in a way that supports that vision.

- **Delegation, empowerment, and accountability**— The MAGIC key of Autonomy means little if employees don't have the ability to make things happen, while being held accountable for results. Engaging managers align expectations, expect subordinates to own their work, and hold people accountable. They get out of the way and empower others with the resources and authority they need to succeed.

- **Invest in and strengthen the team**—Engaging managers accurately assess performance, provide feedback, seek to develop employees, and provide challenging assignments to stretch the team. They see and invest in the potential of others, recognizing their success along the way.

- **Personalize impact**—Focus on the end result is key in any organization. An engaging manager clarifies the end goal, then works to help employees understand their role in contributing to that end result. They help others see how their work matters.
- **Building relationships**—Consistent in the outcome of every survey we run is the theme that relationships do matter (yes, even to the guy that hasn't talked to anyone in the three years he's been on the line). An engaging manager is emotionally intelligent, builds rapport, facilitates teamwork, listens, and promotes a culture in which everyone feels safe in speaking up.
- **Takes care of the Satisfaction elements**—Engaging managers consider the basics of satisfaction as non-negotiables. They take the hygiene factors off the table by ensuring they are covered. Areas such as safety (physical or emotional), appropriate compensation, dignity and respect, reduction of stress, and providing proper tools and resources are "givens." Respect for work-life balance is clear.
- **Personal engagement**—Engaging managers engage personally, and others see it.

ENGAGEMENT IS VIRAL

Managers are the sergeants of the organization. While they may not shape policy on a global level, nobody is more instrumental in implementing policy. Changes in a company's culture, deploying new channels to learn about the impact of one's work, promoting opportunities for growth such as training and development initiatives—the manager is at the front lines of them all. You, as a manager, have a powerful effect on how engaged your organization will ultimately be.

You see, engagement is ultimately a *viral* phenomenon. True, the word is terribly overused in a time when everyone's talking about viral marketing, viral memes on social networks, and so on. But it makes sense when you're talking about an organization—a living organism in which every employee is a cell. Inside the organization, ideas, emotions, and attitudes spread in the same way that a virus spreads from cell to cell in the body.

Remember, an organization can't say, "You will now be engaged." Beyond choosing to be engaged herself, however, a manager can (and should) create conditions under which engagement can thrive and then step back and see who "catches" the "engagement bug." It's a very organic process.

As a manager, you have a great deal of influence over this process. By virtue of your own level of engagement—what you say and do rather than the orders you give or the memos you write—you can help create an environment in which people will choose to be engaged or choose to be cynical and indifferent. You're the boots on the ground, and your performance as a leader can have a far greater impact on organization-wide engagement than decrees from the C-suite. After all, if you go all-in, your followers are more likely to do the same.

For example, our manager engagement research showed us something interesting: for the most part, a manager's own engagement isn't directly correlated with their employees' engagement. Our statistical analyses (linear regression) found that a manager's engagement (high or low) accounted for about 5% of their employees' engagement. In other words, just because a manager is engaged, it doesn't mean that his or her employees will also be engaged. However, when we ran additional analyses (Chi-square), we found that Fully Engaged managers had a 50% higher-than-expected level of Fully Engaged employees, and half the expected percentage of Opportunity Group and Fully Disengaged Employees. The opposite trend was demonstrated for Opportunity Group and Fully Disengaged managers (i.e., half the expected Engaged and double the expected Disengaged). So, while an engaged manager doesn't necessarily mean engaged employees, engaged managers are far more likely to act in ways that create an environment in which their employees can choose to engage. Simply being engaged is not the key to a manager's success; it's what that manager does as a result of his or her engagement that affects employees' engagement.

Clearly a manager's engagement is critical, but it's not as simple as hoping your engagement transfers to someone else like a common cold. In short, your people want to engage, and they will respond to a manager who has found meaning, autonomy, growth, impact, and connection in her work and wears those qualities on her sleeve for all to see. The point is, engagement is the innate default setting of the great majority of human beings. We naturally crave it, and we will stretch to find it even in circumstances where it is not made readily available.

What is a manager's role in engagement? First of all, be transformational, not transactional. When we see articles that talk about this or that company's engagement programs and go into detail about awarding cruises to high-performing personnel, we want to bite our pencils in half. Rewards are important, but they don't equal engagement. Rewards are transactional. If I give you a cruise to the Caribbean this year, what happens when I don't give you a cruise on the Rhine next year (remember the adaptation principle back in chapter one)? Engaging managers help their people *become* better—more fulfilled, more skilled, more autonomous.

Beyond this, and in addition to the specific competencies mentioned earlier, our research on engaged teams and engaging leaders has consistently revealed six common things that good managers do to create engaged teams:

1. **They are personally engaged.** Not only do these managers preach engagement, they live it. They are engaged as both individuals and managers. They bring their hearts, spirits, minds, and hands to their work. It's contagious.
2. **They are involved.** "Management by exception" is common, which means the only time a subordinate interacts with her leader is when she does something well or really steps in it. Engaging managers are there day-to-day, taking the temperature of everyone, learning what people need to be inspired to give discretionary effort.
3. **They hire wisely.** You may not have total discretion over hiring for your team or department. But you probably have influence. The engaging manager does whatever he or she can to ensure that new hires are people likely to get on board with the organization's engagement environment.
4. **They bring the MAGIC.** They understand the components of engagement, and don't try to substitute imitation satisfaction factors for what's truly important. They understand and accurately assess their employees' engagement, and take action to ensure that the environment enables their employees to choose to be engaged.
5. **They don't mess it up.** When your team is fully engaged, sometimes your job is just to get out of the way and adjust the sails. Elite managers exhibit real skill at managing the zone of proximal development,

the zone where people are comfortable taking on new challenges with the aid of a teacher or mentor. Beyond it, people can cross the eustress/distress threshold and experience anxiety that can inhibit growth. Being a great teacher—knowing when to push people toward growth and when to back off before anxiety sets in—is the mark of a great, fully engaged manager.

6. **They lead by example.** More than anything, the engaging manager's role is to lead by example. In the words of Gandhi, "Be the change you wish to create."

HOW DO YOU KNOW IT'S WORKING?

Engagement surveys are valuable ways to understand levels of employee engagement and how to address them. Additionally, engagement conversations are powerful tools for starting a conversation that will provide insight into what engages (and disengages) your team. There are also some more organic ways to determine whether you and your team are fully engaged in work and culture:

- **Team engagement indicates manager engagement.** If you see your people exceeding expectations and putting in discretionary effort, then it's likely that they and you have high levels of engagement. It's rare to find engaged teams with disengaging managers.
- **You're producing results.** Is your team exceeding its goals? Are your people happy, energetic, creative, and innovative? Is your department a center of efficiency, productivity, and customer satisfaction? Odds are, your people are deeply engaged in what they're doing.
- **You can "feel" the difference.** A good manager reads signs in real time. Are people late for work constantly, absent, or sloppy? Are there customer service issues? How do people carry themselves? Is there excitement and energy in the workplace or is there always some reason to be negative?
- **You can manage less and lead more.** Engaged employees don't need to be *managed* in the strict sense. They don't need to have their supervisor over their shoulder, because they enjoy what they do. They don't

need you to set goals for them, because they set their own. You're free to inspire, share the narrative, teach, listen, and facilitate communication. You're free to lead, rather than to manage.

The best way to learn about your team's or department's level of engagement—and thus your own—is not to rely on surveys or reports. It's to be in the thick of the action, talking, listening, and learning. This is "action research." Talk to your people, watch what they do, and watch for patterns. Look for telltale signs of engagement: high energy, extra effort, ownership, employees having one another's backs, no complaining, and so on. What you learn may well improve you as a manager and your organization as well.

RECAP

- Engagement isn't often taught in business school, but fostering it might be a manager's most important skill.
- The manager's job is to enforce the boundaries that channel and direct people's creative energies. Managers are the glue of the organization.
- Promoting "doers" to leadership roles without training them to lead causes serious problems in organizations.
- Managers who get good results are not necessarily engaged leaders.
- Research shows that engaging managers improve the engagement level of their teams.
- Engagement is a competency. It can be learned, practiced, taught, measured, and developed. We can (and should) hold leaders accountable for being "engaging managers."
- Managers should be having more "engagement conversations" with their people.
- The Pygmalion effect says that people will live up to others' positive expectations. The Golem effect says they will also live down to negative expectations.
- The best way to help people engage is to exhibit engagement yourself. Your actions will follow. Engagement is viral.

CHAPTER TEN
The Engaging Organization

"The achievements of an organization are the results of the combined effort of each individual."
—*Vince Lombardi*

FINALLY, WE REACH the organizational level, where everything comes to fruition. This is a deliberately short chapter because, frankly, engaging organizations is what this whole book is about. So, let's cover some facts that are unique to organization-wide engagement, wrap things up, and go home.

It's important that we be realistic. I realize some employees are simply saying, "Look, Tracy, I'm just trying to put food on the table. These are nice, but engagement doesn't pay the bills. I work because I have to." Some managers in organizations may read this book and say, "Hey, most of our employees show up for work each day, do their jobs, and go home. They earn barely above minimum wage, and this stuff is beyond what they need and what we can give. This is all nice, but it's for people in offices working cushy jobs. Can my employees really relate to this?"

For the past number of years, my wife and I have had the opportunity to travel to Germany, where I have taught in an international MBA program. It has been interesting to teach the concept of engagement to an international group, often representing ten or more countries in each cohort.

Most of these students, many of them coming from leadership positions in countries where poverty is the norm, clearly resonate with the importance of engagement. However, each year I am approached by students wondering how these concepts apply to their particular situations. Some will return to their countries where employees are doing all they can to survive and are just grateful to be able to provide a meal for their families. The idea of "engaging" in their work is a "completely foreign concept" (that phrase has multiple meanings). Others will return to positions in which they supervise a team of line-level workers who "put in their eight hours and go home."

"Beyond a paycheck," they ask, "why would an employee choose (or need) to engage?" That question is usually followed by another: "And why would a company care about engaging employees when all the company really needs is to have people to show up and do their work?"

The truth is, I can't disagree with this sentiment. In fact, a significant part of the workforce today is in exactly this position. For those of us who have basic needs and a little more taken care of, we're truly fortunate. However, most of us work because that's how we pay for life. A few things to consider, by way of reminder:

FOR THE EMPLOYEE

- When we're engaged at work, we're much more likely to be engaged at home and in other areas of our lives.
- Engagement feels better than disengagement, is psychologically healthier, and helps us have a better outlook on life and ourselves.
- Disengaging employees are far more likely to experience stress-related health issues than are engaged employees.
- We all have a basic human need for success and fulfillment. At the most basic level, we have an innate need to engage.

FOR THE ORGANIZATION

- Engaging organizations are more profitable, have greater market share, deliver higher quality, take better care of customers, and are more innovative.

- People want to work for organizations in which they can engage. Employees will choose to be engaged when the environment supports it.
- Engagement is a foundational leadership responsibility.
- Creating a culture of engagement is, quite simply, the *right* thing to do.

So, to those of you simply putting in your time, wouldn't you rather experience meaning, autonomy, growth, impact, and connection than punch a time card with little purpose beyond taking home a paycheck? You have a choice.

For those organizations that believe the concept of engagement falls into the category of "soft stuff," for which you have little patience, consider the hard facts. Simply put, engaging organizations produce more and cost less. That's fact, not opinion.

CREATING THE ENGAGING ORGANIZATION

In engaging organizations, executive leadership takes proactive steps to create a culture and an environment that, while it cannot impose engagement on anyone, removes the barriers to engagement and provides a clear path for those employees who choose to become more engaged. At the level of the entire organization, it is the responsibility of leadership teams to develop and enable systems that create that "fertile soil" I've spoken about in this book. These can include:

- communication strategies that connect workers with the results of their work
- clear vision and direction
- a corporate culture that reflects and promotes a set of widely held values
- inviting and acting on employee ideas and feedback
- attention to satisfaction factors such as compensation, perks, and physical security
- programs that help employees develop new skills and pursue innovative ideas without the fear of failure

- allowing employees to better control the conditions of their environment

This list is a drop in the bucket. There are as many strategies and tactics that can inspire employees to engage as there are different kinds of organizations, and not all need to be radical or costly. In fact, sometimes simple steps are the most effective—provided they are based on an intimate knowledge of what employees care about, what motivates them, and what they hope to get from work beyond a paycheck. Some examples:

- Recreational Equipment, Inc. (REI), one of the nation's leading outfitters for outdoor sports and activities, has created a "company campfire" social network, where employees and managers are free to gather, debate, and even argue on even terms. Nearly half the company's eleven thousand employees have used the tool to gain a clearer voice in issues affecting the company and their jobs.[164] Engagement keys increased: *autonomy and connection.*

- CUNA Mutual Group, a Wisconsin-based insurer, wanted its employees' opinions to shape its Corporate Social Responsibility (CSR) campaign. So, it asked them what they thought. Through internal websites, surveys, social media, and meetings, leaders asked more than nine hundred employees to identify the kinds of volunteer work and charitable giving that they found most meaningful. They found that more than 90 percent of CUNA employees cared deeply about sustainability. More important, leaders used this insight and further employee participation to develop a company-wide sustainability and conservation program.[165] Key increased: *meaning.*

- The hotel business can be a grueling one that wears dedicated employees down. Not at the boutique Kimpton Hotel chain, however. The chain has become famous for providing guests with "Kimpton Moments"—authentic, in-the-moment service for its guests—since the company's inception. Kimpton fuels the esprit de corps necessary for such dedication by maintaining an open, informal, fun workplace: annual Housekeeping Olympics, an open-door policy at every level of the company, and an annual $10,000 prize for the employee providing the best "Kimpton Moment," to name a few.[166] Engagement keys increased: *autonomy, impact, and connection.*

- The Mahindra Group, a $20 billion emerging-markets company based in Mumbai, employs over 240,000 people, in 100 countries, across several dozen industries. The company focuses on creating a culture based on a common purpose—providing unity amid diversity. Mahindra claims that it is "many companies united by a common purpose—to enable people to rise." Over one-third of the company's employees participate in planning and leading service projects under the "Rise for Good" mission, including education, athletics, healthcare, agriculture, and the arts.[167] Engagement keys: *meaning, impact,* and *connection.*

- TOMs shoes, famous not only for their shoes but also for their One for One* program, focuses on employee engagement through social engagement. The program provides help (shoes, sight, water, safe birth, bullying prevention, and other forms of assistance) to those in need each time a product is purchased. In addition, employees are invited to submit ideas for a charitable project that inspires them personally. Each month, the company votes. Those submitting winning ideas are given time off of work and $10,000 to make their ideas reality.[168] Keys increased: *meaning, autonomy, growth, and impact.*

I could go on and on with examples of extraordinary employee engagement programs. But for now it's sufficient to see that none of these organizations made inroads by requiring employees to engage. That doesn't work. What they did do, however, was make engaging so irresistible that only the most hard-bitten, skeptical workers—the lost causes—refused to get on board the bus. As a result, these organizations, and others like them, have enjoyed the benefits of healthy, widespread engagement: increased revenues and profits, better retention, and higher customer satisfaction scores, for starters.

WHEN MANAGEMENT DOESN'T GET IT

Those organizations and those like them are, however, the best of the best. There are plenty of other enterprises—corporations, not-for-profits, universities, churches, sports franchises—that have a dangerous misunderstanding of what engagement is and its importance to the bottom line.

We know that organizations own 50 percent of the engagement equation, which means that organizations can impact engagement positively or negatively.

Recent studies looked at companies that went through wrenching downsizing and found that (no surprise) these layoffs severely damaged morale and engagement. Again, we didn't need a study to tell us that, right? These studies found some interesting additional points, however. First, the number of employees who actually exited the organization was not limited to those who were laid off. In fact, the number of employees who left was actually *five times* the number laid off.[169] Once the initial layoff wound was inflicted, employees no longer trusted the motives or intentions of the organization, let alone its stability. Not only were engagement needs not met, but the organizations in the study actively undermined even the basic components of employee satisfaction.

In examining the effect of layoffs and attrition in greater depth, our research team found not only a similar phenomenon, but also something potentially even more damaging. Typically, those who left an organization of their own volition after the layoffs occurred were those who were skilled and valuable enough that they could quickly find employment elsewhere. Those who remained were often composed largely of two groups: the dedicated employee, and the less employable, disengaged worker who was unable to find a place in another organization.

While the former group was certainly desirable, the latter basically "quit and stayed." The cream of the crop was skimmed off, leaving the weaker personnel behind. Unfortunately, that remaining group often spread their disengagement "contagion," corrupting and disengaging much of the rest of the organization in what often became a downward spiral. That's one example of what can happen when an organization's leadership misunderstands engagement.

WHAT ENGAGING ORGANIZATIONS DO

Reward programs and perks can be effective tools to help promote engagement, but not in a vacuum. Goodies like company trips to Disney World or Las Vegas or cash bonuses work only when they are part of a larger strategy that tells employees they are valued and clears the way for them to find meaning in what they do, see the impact of their work, and grow as people.

Elaborate vacations or other ultra-perks as the culmination of, say, a program to see which employee can come up with the most innovative new product idea are highly engaging and worthwhile. Lavish prizes simply to reward hitting goals, with nothing else behind them, become baubles. Eventually, employees can develop a dangerous sense of entitlement. When budgets get slashed or there's a changing of the guard and the extras vanish, they feel cheated and vengeful—not the qualities you typically look for in an Employee of the Year.

So, if engagement-friendly organizations aren't the ones offering the best motivational extras, what do they have in common? A few of the key characteristics of the best organizations:

- They focus on both engagement and satisfaction. Like love and marriage, you can't have one without the other. Satisfaction factors are the price of admission to engagement; they don't constitute engagement, but you can't have it without them. Engaging organizations make sure that things like compensation, benefits, perks and extras, physical work spaces, and recognition programs are on the leading edge for their industries.
- They believe that engagement is a shared responsibility. It's not entirely the organization's job to make engagement happen . . . but that doesn't mean the burden is completely on the employee, either. Remember, engagement is a 50-50 collaboration. Leaders in an engaging organization know that they have to put the basics in place, and that they can't coerce employees into doing their part. They also accept that some people will never engage, no matter what, and focus their efforts on attracting employees who are more likely to become engaged.
- They pay attention to the five keys that unlock the power of engagement—meaning, autonomy, growth, impact, and connection—even if they don't have formal programs in place to cultivate them all just yet. The five keys form the backbone of any successful engagement strategy.

Most important of all, engaging organizations treat their people like people, not cogs in a vast command-and-control machine. They listen to them. They respect their needs. They value those who are valuable. They make room for life away from work. They expect and demand the best from everyone, and then make it possible for them to deliver. They accept that human beings want challenge—want to grow and excel and develop mastery. They treat people as what they are: the powerful secret weapon behind any great enterprise.

Research bears this out. A recent study examined this chicken-and-egg question: Which comes first, engagement or job performance? British psychologists looked at 755 employees of a large bank for four years and considered results in two areas: financial performance and customer satisfaction. The results? The organization's commitment to encouraging employee engagement led directly to better job performance, not the other way around.[170] At the end of the day, engaged, passionate people—not perks, awards, or technology—are what make great companies great and good companies better.

MAKING MAGIC HAPPEN

Consider the classic story of the cathedral: Three masons are chipping granite from a block. A passerby asks each mason what he's doing. One says, "I'm hammering rock." The next says, "I'm building a wall." The last says, "I'm building a great cathedral." Identical task, but the story behind the task shaped each man's perception of the impact of his work. The difference in motivation can be dramatic. Remember the man putting the switch plates on the world's biggest indoor stadium?

The organization's leaders must safeguard the company narrative—the "why we do what we do" story. The story is all about purpose and framing, and it helps people find meaning in their work. Engagement also comes from open, caste-free communication. Open-door policies are the way to go, and I'm not just talking about hanging up a copy of the organization's open-door policy as you close your office door. The guy in the mail room should feel free to walk into the CFO's office with a concern. Secure employee social networks encourage sharing of ideas and connection away from the office. Regular "straight talk" sessions, in which anything (within reason) can be said as long as the intent is constructive, promote honesty and prevent secrets and grudges from building up like toxic sludge.

Doing engagement right also may mean changing the reason that you hire people and the tools you use in hiring. Instead of hiring someone based only on a set of skills and perhaps an education, what if hiring were based on a pre-interview test to assess whether or not the prospective employee has the personality characteristics to thrive in the company's engagement environment? Skills can be taught; character can't.

Finally, organizations that are successful at creating an engaging employee experience are those that empower their employees to act in ways that the employees find ethical, moral, fair, sustainable, and just. Every employee is a human being with a sense of right and wrong and a desire to be purposeful and feel good about their place in the world. Engagement is powerful. It simply requires the right keys to unlock that power. The organization that gives its people the tools, encouragement, and freedom to become the best people they can be—to really, truly *engage*—will also find itself rising to unimagined heights of success.

Being an engaging organization, an engaging manager, or an engaging employee doesn't happen overnight. It's an iterative process, meaning it's a journey of ups and downs, not a periodic event. But every move in the right direction counts.

Engagement is a choice. It's about hearts, spirits, minds, and hands. Meaning. Autonomy. Growth. Impact. Connection. Work your MAGIC.

Appendix
Further Questions

THROUGH CAREFUL STUDY of the MAGIC keys, you have discovered the factors that lead to engagement. For those interested in further understanding and increasing your own levels of engagement, the following questions may help get you started. Enjoy the journey!

1. What do I love versus what do I do?
   - What type of work am I passionate about, and how close does the work I'm doing now come to that?
   - Is there a realistic, practical way to close the gap between what I love and what I do? Can I transform my job?
   - Is it possible to bring some element of what I love that's currently unrelated to my work into my workplace? (Example: a passionate hobbyist musician offering music lessons to employees during lunch breaks)
   - If not, how can I balance the need to love my work with the need to be a productive part of an organization? Do I need to leave? Can I learn to fulfill my passion in the work I'm doing today?
   - Can this passion be fulfilled outside work, while simultaneously doing work I can still engage in? (Example: the assembly-line manager who coaches the soccer team after work)
2. What about my work leaves me feeling energized?

- Conversely, what leaves me feeling drained?
- What do the activities that leave me feeling energized (or those that leave me drained) have in common? Do they have themes that could be used in other settings, projects, activities, and so forth?
- Which strengths do these activities take advantage of?
- Are there ways to maximize time spent on what energizes me, while also reducing what sucks the energy from me? Remember, we all perform tasks that don't necessarily energize us. That's life. The important thing here is balance.

3. Where am I giving my all and where am I not giving my all? Why?
   - What fuels the disparity in my effort? Is it motivation like pay, or the threat of punishment? Or is it being emotionally involved in the work?
   - Do I feel that I should be compensated more when asked to do work that I don't enjoy? In other words, do I have a transactional view of my work?
   - When was the last time I felt in "flow" and what combination of factors put me there? How could I recreate them?
   - What things are important to me in my life and how can I express them in my work?

4. What do I need to have more of?
   - Meaning—What would give my work greater meaning and sense of purpose? What constitutes purpose and meaningful work for me?
   - Autonomy—What does autonomy mean to me? Which of the factors of autonomy are "must-haves" for me, and which aren't especially important to me? Are there areas in which I could have more autonomy, and even benefit the organization, if I were to make some changes?
   - Growth—What am I looking for in order to fully develop as a person and a professional? What kind of growth is meaningful to me—intellectual, emotional, financial, and so forth? What kind of growth opportunities could my employer make available that would help me reach my goals for self-actualization?

- Impact—What kind of impact do I want to make? Why does it matter to me? Whom do I care most about having an impact on—customers, the community, the world? What methods of connecting me with the impact of my work would I most appreciate? What's possible and practical for my employer?
- Connection—Do I enjoy interaction with others? What do I get from it? What does it take from me? Does the benefit outweigh the cost? What am I looking for from my workplace relationships? What would make me feel that I am part of something bigger than myself? Does my employer need to cultivate trust? Transform culture? Empower communication?

5. What have I done in the past to foster my own engagement? What have I done in the past to resist employer attempts to help me engage? Using the "Wherever you go, there you are" concept, if I did make a change, what would be the realistic result?
6. What are the top three actions that I need to take?
7. What are the top three actions that my organization needs to take?
8. Is engagement going to happen at my current role/workplace or do I need to change/leave?
9. Am I engaging? Do I both feel and do?

APPENDIX
ENGAGEMENT CONVERSATION

MOST MANAGERS ARE WILLING to have conversations with their teams about engagement. Most employees welcome the conversation, if done correctly. However, most of us don't know where to begin. The following questions will help get the conversation rolling.

1. What does a good day at work look like for you?
2. What does a bad day look like?
3. What do you like about your work?
4. What do you wish were different?
5. Do you have fun at work?
6. How do you feel at the end of the day?
7. MEANING
   - What about your job gets you out of bed in the morning?
   - Where do you find meaning in your work? Where is it missing?
   - How does your job help you accomplish what's most important in your life? How does it detract? What's missing?
8. AUTOMONY
   - What type(s) of autonomy is/are most important to you? Where you work? With whom you work? When you work? What you work on? Any others?
   - Where is that autonomy present, and where is it missing?

- How do you feel about the level of direction and support you receive from me? From others?

9. GROWTH
    - Where do you feel you are growing in your job? Where do you feel stagnant?
    - Are there areas outside what you do each day that you would like to be involved in? Where would you like your career to go, and how can we support that?
    - What interests or talents do you have to contribute that we're not fully recognizing or using in your current role?

10. IMPACT
    - Where do you feel your work has the greatest impact (on whom, what, etc.)? Where do you feel you're spinning your wheels?
    - When people evaluate your performance, what do you think are the key areas they look at? What's going well? What's getting in the way?
    - Where do you see yourself currently making a difference? Where would you like to see yourself making a difference?

11. CONNECTION
    - Tell me about the people you work with. Do you enjoy working with them?
    - What type(s) of connection is/are most important to you?
    - Do you feel like you belong here? Why or why not?

12. Where is our organization letting you down? Where is it lifting you up? What needs to change in that area?

13. Where am I letting you down as a boss? How am I helping you? What needs to change in our relationship?

14. If you won the lottery tomorrow and left your job, what would you miss most?

15. What keeps you here? What might entice you away from our team today?

Notes

1 Brenda Kowske, *Employee Engagement: Market Review, Buyer's Guide, and Provider Profiles* (2012), https://www.bersin.com/News/Content.aspx?id=15735 (page no longer available)

2 http://finance.yahoo.com/news/Wells-Fargo-Plans-Layoffs-zacks -1940186693.html

3 http://www.bbc.co.uk/news/uk-england-devon-18276195

4 https://www.shrm.org/resourcesandtools/hr-topics/compensation/pages/ short-term-pay-incentives-at-private-and-smaller-companies.aspx

5 PayScale.com, "2013 Compensation Best Practices Report."

6 Terry Waghorn, "How Employee Engagement Turned Around Campbell's," http://www.forbes.com/2009/06/23/employee-engagement-conant-leadership -managing-turnaround.html

7 Gallup, Inc., *State of the Global Workplace: Employee Engagement Insights for Business Leaders Worldwide* (2013).

8 Brickman, P., Coates, D., & Janoff-Bulman, R. (1978). Lottery Winners and Accident Victims: Is Happiness Relative? *Journal of Personality and Social Psychology, 36*(8), 917–927.

9 William H. Macey, *Employee Engagement: Tools for Analysis, Practice, and Competitive Advantage* (New York: Wiley-Blackwell, 2009).

10 https://www.cia.gov/news-information/featured-story-archive /2012-featured-story-archive/CleanedUOSSSimpleSabotage_sm.pdf

11 http://blogs.wsj.com/source/2012/11/25 /five-ways-to-be-happy-and-productive-at-work/

12 I. B. Mauss, M. Tamir, C. L. Anderson, and N. S. Savino, "Can Seeking Happiness Make People Unhappy? Paradoxical Effects of Valuing Happiness," *Emotion* 11, no. 4 (August 2011): 807–15.

13 Roy F. Baumeister, Kathleen D. Vohs, Jennifer L. Aaker, and Emily N. Garbinsky, "Some Key Differences Between a Happy Life and a Meaningful Life," *Journal of Positive Psychology* 8, no. 6 (2013): 505–16.

14 Maylett, T., & Wride, M. (2017). *The Employee Experience: How to Attract Talent, Retain Top Performers, and Drive Results.* San Francisco: John Wiley & Sons, p. 179.

15 D. MacLeod and N. Clarke, "Engaging for Success: Enhancing Performance Through Employee Engagement: A Report to Government" (London: BIS, 2009), http://www.berr.gov.uk/files/file52215.pdf

16 Corporate Leadership Council, "Driving Performance and Retention Through Employee Engagement" (2004).

17 Towers Perrin, "Towers Perrin 2004 European Talent Survey: Reconnecting with Employees: Attracting, Retaining, and Engaging."

18 McLean & Company, "Identify & Reengage the Disengaged" (2011), http://hr.mcleanco.com/research/ss/hr-identify-flight-risks

19 Kenexa, "The Impact of Employee Engagement" (2008).

20 Corporate Leadership Council, "Driving Performance and Retention Through Employee Engagement."

21 Roger Connors, Tom Smith, and Craig Hickman, *The Oz Principle*: *Getting Results Through Individual and Organizational Accountability* (New York: Portfolio, 2004).

22 Future Workplace, "Multiple Generations @ Work" (2012).

23 Tony Hsieh, "Your Culture Is Your Brand," *Zappos Blogs*, January 3, 2009, http://blogs.zappos.com/blogs/ceo-and-coo-blog/2009/01/03 /your-culture-is-your-brand

24 Evan Kirkpatrick, "Lessons Learned from Tony Hsieh's $350MM Downtown Project in Las Vegas," *Forbes*, February 13, 2013.

25 Semuels, A. (2018, February 14). Why Amazon Pays Some of Its Workers to Quit. Retrieved August 3, 2018, from https://www.theatlantic.com/business/ archive/2018/02/amazon-offer-pay-quit/553202/

26 Sarah Goodyear, "We're in This Together: What the Dutch Know About Flooding That We Don't," *Atlantic,* January 9, 2013, http://m.theatlanticcities.com /politics/2013/01/were-together-what-dutch-know-about-water-we-dont/4355/

27 CNNMoney, "100 Best Companies to Work For," http://money.cnn.com /magazines/fortune/best-companies/2013/snapshots/7.html

28 E. Deci and R. Ryan, 2002 (Eds.). *Handbook of Self-Determination Research* Rochester, NY: University of Rochester Press

29 Transport Accident Investigation Commission, Aircraft Accident Report 79-139.

30 Teresa Amabile and Steven Kramer, "Do Happier People Work Harder?" *New York Times Sunday Review*, September 3, 2011.

31 J. Stuart Bunderson and Jeffery A. Thompson, "Measuring the Meaning of Meaningful Work: Development and Validation of the Comprehensive Meaningful Work Scale" (CMWS), *Group & Organization Management* 37, (October 1, 2012): 655–85.

32   William A. Kahn, "To Be Fully There: Psychological Presence at Work,"
     Human Relations 45, no. 4 (April 1992): 321–49.

33   Tierney Plumb, "Are Architects Necessary?" *WorkDesign*, November 2013,
     http://workdesign.co/2013/10/office-design-by-employees

34   Chartered Institute of Personnel and Development in cooperation with the
     Public Sector People Managers' Association, "Leading Culture Change: Employee
     Engagement and Public Service Transformation," (November 2012).

35   Wayne Drash, "On Crippled Cruise Ship, Icky Jobs Fell to 'Amazing' Crew,"
     CNN.com, February 17, 2013.

36   Abe Arkoff, *The Illuminated Life* (New York: Pearson, 1994).

37   Douglas LaBier, "Why It's Hard to Find Your 'Life Purpose' in Today's World,"
     Psychology Today; The New Resilience (column), May 24, 2011.

38   Tyler F. Stillman, Roy F. Baumeister, and Frank D. Fincham, "Alone and Without
     Purpose: Life Loses Meaning Following Social Exclusion," *Journal of Experimental
     Social Psychology* 45, no. 4 (July 2009): 686–94.

39   Alex Davies, "South African Mercedes-Benz Workers Made This Car for Nelson
     Mandela When He Was Released from Prison," *Business Insider*, December 6,
     2013.

40   Teresa Amabile and Steven Kramer, "To Give Your Employees Meaning, Start
     with Mission," *Harvard Business Review*, HBR Blog, December 19, 2012.

41   http://www.itraineeship.com/profiles/sony/; http://www.sony-europe.com/article
     /id/1178278971157

42   http://www.volvo.com/investors/finrep/ar06/eng/fundamentalvalues/pops
     /printable/6_vision_mission.pdf (page no longer available)

43   http://exxonmobil.com/Benelux-English/about_principles.aspx.

44   Daniel Goleman, "Make the Mission Meaningful," http://www.linkedin.com
     /today/post/article/20121220212057-117825785-make-the-mission-meaningful

45   *Office Space*. Dir. Mike Judge. Perfs. Ron Livingston, Jennifer Aniston, Stephen
     Root, Gary Cole. 20th Century Fox, 1999.

46   "The Beat Goes On," *CBS Sunday Morning*, March 29, 2009,
     http://www.cbsnews.com/news/the-beat-goes-on

47   E. L. Kersten, "Why They Call It Work," *Harvard Business Review*, February 2006.

48   Alice M. Isen and Barbara Means, "The Influence of Positive Affect on Decision-
     Making Strategy," *Social Cognition* 2, no. 1 (1983): 18–31.

49   C. M. Haase, M. J. Poulin, and J. Heckhausen, "Happiness as a Motivator:
     Positive Affect Predicts Primary Control Striving for Career and Educational
     Goals," *Personality and Social Psychology Bulletin* 38, no. 8 (August 2012):
     1093–104.

50 J. Boehm and S. Lyubomirsky, "Does Happiness Promote Career Success?" *Journal of Career Assessment* 16, no. 1 (February 2008): 101–16.

51 "Iconic Figures from Sept. 11: Where Are They Now?" NBCNews.com, http://www.nbcnews.com/id/39038466/ns/us_news-911_nine_years_later/ns /us_news-911_nine_years_later?GT1=43001#.Updm2xbogdI

52 Susanne Craig, "9/11 Through the Emotional Lens of Cantor Fitzgerald," NYTimes.com, September 11, 2013, http://dealbook.nytimes.com/2013/09/11 /911-through-the-emotional-lens-of-cantor-fitzgerald/?_r=0

53 http://www.rrdonnelley.com/about/lakeside-classics/home.aspx

54 Roy F. Baumeister, Kathleen D. Vohs, Jennifer L. Aaker, and Emily N. Garbinsky, "Some Key Differences Between a Happy Life and a Meaningful Life," *Journal of Positive Psychology* 8, no. 6 (2013): 505–16, doi:10.1080/17439760.2013.830764.

55 Baumeister et al., "Some Key Differences."

56 "How Tough Is Too Tough?" *Inc.* (February 2014): 47.

57 R. Nauert, "Worker Autonomy Can Lead to Greater Productivity, Satisfaction," *Psych Central* (2011).

58 http://solutions.3m.com/wps/portal/3M/en_WW/History/3M/Company /McKnight-principles/

59 http://web.mit.edu/invent/iow/frysilver.html

60 http://investor.jetblue.com /phoenix.zhtml?c=131045&p=irol-newsArticle&ID=1820150&highlight=.

61 Frost & Sullivan, "The Homeshoring Phenomenon" (2012).

62 M. Fleshner, S. F. Maier, D. M. Lyons, and M. A. Raskind, "The Neurobiology of the Stress-Resistant Brain," *Stress* 14, no. 5 (September 2011): 498–502.

63 Peter Northouse, *Leadership: Theory and Practice*, 6th ed. (Thousand Oaks, CA: Sage, 2012).

64 Barry Schwartz, *The Paradox of Choice: Why More Is Less* (New York: Harper Perennial, 2004).

65 Daniel Pink, *Drive: The Surprising Truth About What Motivates Us* (New York: Riverhead Hardcover, 2009).

66 http://www.prestashop.com/blog/en /prestashops-employees-help-redesign-u-s-offices-workplace-mecca/.

67 A. Erez, J. Lepine, and H. Elms, "Effects of Rotated Leadership and Peer Evaluation on the Functioning and Effectiveness of Self-Managed Teams: A Quasi-Experiment," *Personnel Psychology* (2002).

68 Frederick Winslow Taylor, *The Principles of Scientific Management 1910*, monograph, 1911.

69   Herbert A. Simon, *Models of My Life* (New York: Basic Books, 1991), xvii.

70   http://haradamethod.org/?p=62 (page no longer available)

71   Gabe Newell. *Forbes*. Retrieved June 1, 2017 from https://www.forbes.com/profile/gabe-newell

72   David Rock, "Managing with the Brain in Mind," *Strategy + Business*, Autumn 2009, http://www.strategy-business.com/article/09306?pg=all#authors

73   N. R. Carlson et al., *Psychology: The Science of Behaviour*, 4th Canadian ed. (Toronto: Pearson Education Canada).

74   M. E. P. Seligman, *Helplessness: On Depression, Development, and Death* (San Francisco: W. H. Freeman, 1975)

75   James Bandler with Doris Burke, "How Hewlett-Packard Lost Its Way," CNN.com, May 8, 2012, http://tech.fortune.cnn.com/2012/05/08/500-hp-apotheker/

76   http://money.cnn.com/2013/02/25/technology/yahoo-work-from-home/

77   John Simmons, "IBM, a Pioneer of Remote Work, Calls Workers Back to the Office," https://www.wsj.com/articles/ibm-a-pioneer-of-remote-work-calls-workers-back-to-the-office-1495108802

78   http://qz.com/115831/googles-20-time-which-brought-you-gmail-and-adsense-is-now-as-good-as-dead/.

79   http://searchengineland.com/google-earnings-156219

80   Bob Thompson, "Lean, Not Mean—3 Reasons Why Southwest Wins with a Culture That Empowers Employees," Customerthink.com, http://www.customerthink.com/blog/lean_not_mean_how_southwest_wins_with_a_culture_that_empowers_employees

81   Adrian Campos, "Why Costco Is Beating Wal-Mart," *USA Today*, December 2, 2013.

82   http://www.syracuse.com/news/index.ssf/2013/11/walmart_asks_workers_to_donate_food_to_fellow_employees_for_thanksgiving.html

83   Mig Pascual, "Zappos: 5 Out-of-the-Box Ideas for Keeping Employees Engaged," *U.S. News & World Report*, October 20, 2012.

84   Ellen Messmer, "Young Employees Say BYOD a 'Right' Not 'Privilege,'" *CIO*, June 19, 2012.

85   https://www.gensler.com/

86   Craig Knight and S. Alexander Haslam, "Your Place or Mine? Organizational Identification and Comfort as Mediators of Relationships Between the Managerial Control of Workspace and Employees' Satisfaction and Well-Being," *British Journal of Management* 21, no. 3 (2010).

87 Rosemary Batt, Virginia Doellgast, and Hyunji Kwon, "The U.S. Call Center Industry: Strategy, HR Practices, and Performance. National Benchmarking Report," Cornell University ILR School (2005).

88 http://www.bus.miami.edu/news-and-media/recent-news/2008/ften.html

89 H. A. Murray, *Explorations in Personality* (New York: Oxford University Press, 1938), 164.

90 L. F. Obukhova and I. A. Korepanova, "The Zone of Proximal Development: A Spatiotemporal Model," *Journal of Russian and East European Psychology* 47, no. 6 (November–December 2009).

91 Jeremy P. Jamieson, Wendy Berry Mendes, and Matthew K. Nock, "Improving Acute Stress Responses: The Power of Reappraisal," *Current Directions in Psychological Science* 20, no. 10: 1–6

92 http://online.wsj.com/news/articles/SB10001424052970204301404577171192704005250 (page no longer available)

93 Hans Selye, *Stress Without Distress* (Philadelphia: J. B. Lippincott Company, 1974), 171.

94 Mark Le Fevre, Gregory S. Kolt, and Jonathan Matheny, "Eustress, Distress, and Their Interpretation in Primary and Secondary Occupational Stress Management Interventions: Which Way First?" *Journal of Managerial Psychology* 21, no. 6 (January 1, 2006): 547–65.

95 Amos Tversky and Daniel Kahneman, "The Framing of Decisions and the Psychology of Choice," *Science*, New Series 211, no. 4481 (January 30, 1981): 453–58.

96 Michael Farris, *From Tyndale to Madison* (Nashville, TN: B&H Books, 2007), 37.

97 Edwin A. Locke, Gary P. Latham, Ken J. Smith, and Robert E. Wood, *A Theory of Goal Setting & Task Performance* (Upper Saddle River, NJ: Prentice-Hall, 1990).

98 Elliot Aronson, Timothy D. Wilson, and Robin M. Akert, *Social Psychology* (Boston: Pearson, 2012), 150.

99 Chip Heath and Dan Heath, *Switch: How to Change Things When Change Is Hard* (New York: Crown Business, 2010).

100 Justin Kruger and David Dunning, "Unskilled and Unaware of It: How Difficulties in Recognizing One's Own Incompetence Lead to Inflated Self-Assessments," *Journal of Personality and Social Psychology* 77, no. 6 (1999): 1121–34.

101 Tom Rath and James K. Harter, *Wellbeing: The Five Essential Elements* (New York: Gallup Press, 2010)

102 Glassdoor, Harris Interactive, "The Age of Social Recruiting."

103 Beverly Kaye and Julie Winkle Giulioni, *Help Them Grow or Watch Them Go: Career Conversations Employees Want* (New York: Berrett-Koehler Publishers, 2012).

104 Jacquelyn Smith, "What Employers Need to Know About the Class of 2012," *Forbes*, April 3, 2012.

105 H. A. Simon and W. G. Chase, "Skill in Chess," *American Scientist* 61, (1973): 394–403.

106 Pink, *Drive.*

107 Mihaly Csikszentmihalyi, *Flow: The Psychology of Optimal Experience* (New York: Harper & Row, 1990).

108 Csikszentmihalyi, *Flow.*

109 W. L. Robinson, "Conscious Competency—The Mark of a Competent Instructor," *Personnel Journal* 53, (1974): 538–39.

110 R. Rosenthal and L. Jacobson, *Pygmalion in the Classroom* (New York: Holt, Rinehart & Winston, 1968).

111 Fox News, "Air Force Strips 17 Officers of Power to Launch Intercontinental Nuclear Missiles," May 8, 2013, http://www.foxnews.com/politics/2013/05/08/air-force-reportedly-strips-17-officers-power-to-launch-intercontinental/

112 Robert Burns, "Nuclear Officers Napped with Blast Door Left Open," Associated Press, October 23, 2013.

113 http://www.af.mil/News/ArticleDisplay/tabid/223/Article/468806/34-icbm-launch-officers-implicated-in-cheating-probe.aspx

114 "A Look at Nuclear Force Lapses Revealed So Far," *Washington Post*, April 5, 2014, http://www.washingtonpost.com/national/a-look-at-nuclear-force-lapses-revealed-so-far/2014/04/05/0580982a-bc98-11e3-9ee7-02c1e10a03f0_story.html

115 Fox News, "Air Force Strips 17 Officers of Power."

116 Rosabeth Moss Kanter, "Three Things That Actually Motivate Employees," *Harvard Business Review*, HBR Blog Network, http://blogs.hbr.org/2013/10/three-things-that-actually-motivate-employees/

117 "Light and Death," *Economist*, May 27, 2010.

118 Stephanie T. Cato and Jean Gordon, "Relationship of the Strategic Vision Alignment to Employee Productivity and Student Enrollment," Walden University (March 2012).

119 Kim Bhasin, "J. C. Penney Pricing Disaster Destroyed Employee Morale," *Huffington Post*, May 2, 2013, http://www.huffingtonpost.com/2013/05/02/jcpenney-pricing-disaster-morale-n_3196037.html

120 http://www.interferenza.com/bcs/interw/66-jan.htm

121 Christina Maslach, "Job Burnout: New Directions in Research and Intervention," *Current Directions in Psychological Science* 12, no. 5 (October 2003): 189–92.

122 https://wikispaces.psu.edu/display/PSYCH484/4.+Expectancy+Theory

123 Kyle Stock, "Patagonia's 'Buy Less' Plea Spurs More Buying," *BusinessWeek*, August 28, 2013.

124 MarketLine, "Apparel Retail in the United States," February 27, 2013.

125 http://www.fuqua.duke.edu/news_events/archive/2008/ariely_legos/#.UrW8K6XogdI

126 James Heyman and Dan Ariely, "Effort for Payment: A Tale of Two Markets," *Psychological Science* 15, no. 11 (2004): 787–93.

127 Karim Kassam, Katrina Koslov, and Wendy Mendes, "Decisions Under Distress: Stress Profiles Influence Anchoring and Adjustment," *Psychological Science* 20, no. 11 (November 2009): 1394–99.

128 Adam M. Grant, Elizabeth M. Campbell, Grace Chen, Keenan Cottone, David Lapedis, and Karen Lee, "Impact and the Art of Motivation Maintenance: The Effects of Contact with Beneficiaries on Persistence Behavior," *Organizational Behavior and Human Decision Processes* 103, no. 1 (May 2007): 53–67.

129 Cone Communications, 2013 "Cone Communications Social Impact Study."

130 https://profits4purpose.com

131 http://profits4purpose.wordpress.com/tag/corporate-volunteering-2/

132 Zalin Grant, *Over the Beach: The Air War in Vietnam* (New York: Simon & Schuster, 1986), 112.

133 All 12 boys and soccer coach rescued from Thai cave: Live updates. (2018, July 10). Retrieved August 13, 2018, from https://www.cnn.com/asia/live-news/thai-cave-rescue-live-intl/index.html

134 L. Aiken, S. Clarke, D. Sloane, J. Sochalski, and J. Silber, "Hospital Nurse Staffing and Patient Mortality, Nurse Burnout, and Job Dissatisfaction," *JAMA* 288, no. 16 (October 23–30, 2002).

135 Podcast 104, An Interview with Steve Chou. How Tony Horton Started P90X and Sold Over 7 Million Workout DVDs. Retrieved August 13, 2018, from https://mywifequitherjob.com/tony-horton-p90x/

136 Bersin, J. (2012, July 03). New Research Unlocks the Secret of Employee Recognition. Retrieved from https://www.forbes.com/sites/joshbersin/2012/06/13/new-research-unlocks-the-secret-of-employee-recognition/#21427d575276

137 http://newsfeed.time.com/2013/03/25/more-people-have-cell-phones-than-toilets-u-n-study-shows/

138 Pink, *Drive.*

139 Andrea Hershatter and Molly Epstein, "Millennials and the World of Work: An Organization and Management Perspective," *Journal of Business and Psychology* 25, no. 2 (June 2010): 211–23.

140 Nicola Lambourne, *War Damage in Western Europe: The Destruction of Historic Monuments During the Second World War* (Edinburgh: Edinburgh University Press, 2001), 124.

141 Louise C. Hawkley, Michael W. Browne, and John T. Cacioppo, "How Can I Connect with Thee? Let Me Count the Ways," *Psychological Science* 16, no. 10 (2005).

142 http://tech.fortune.cnn.com/2013/04/19/marissa-mayer-telecommuting/

143 Kurt Eichenwald, "Microsoft's Lost Decade," *Vanity Fair*, August 2012.

144 Nicholas A. Christakis and James H. Fowler, "The Spread of Obesity in a Large Social Network over 32 Years," *New England Journal of Medicine* 357, (July 26, 2007): 370–79.

145 Robert J. Grossman, "Phasing Out Face Time," *HR Magazine,* April 2013.

146 Jennifer L. Glass, University of Texas; Mary C. Noonan, University of Iowa.

147 E. Glenn Dutcher, University of Innsbruck.

148 TeleworkResearchNetwork.com.

149 http://blog.jetblue.com/index.php/2013/09/05/unpacked-working-from-home/

150 Scott Ostler, "This Is One Incredible Stunt They're Pulling Off," *Los Angeles Times,* October 20, 1988.

151 http://sports.espn.go.com/oly/summer04/basketball/news/story?id=1869300

152 IBM Institute for Business Value, "Leading Through Connections" (2013),

153 http://incblot.org/uncategorized/you-are-the-office-jerk/

154 John T. Cacioppo, "It's Time for a Science of Social Connection," Psychologytoday.com, July 26, 2010, http://www.psychologytoday.com/blog /connections/201007/its-time-science-social-connection

155 http://www.bloomberg.com/news/2013-07-29 /why-are-google-employees-so-disloyal-.html

156 http://www.city-journal.org/2013/23_1_william-bratton.html

157 M. J. Howes, J. E. Hokanson, and D. A. Lowenstein, "Induction of Depressive Affect After Prolonged Exposure to a Mildly Depressed Individual," *Journal of Personality and Social Psychology* 49, (1985): 1110–13.

158 Douglas S. Pugh, "Service with a Smile: Emotional Contagion in the Service Encounter," *Academy of Management Journal* 44, no. 5 (2001): 1018–27.

159 W. C. Tsai, and Y. M. Huang, "Mechanisms Linking Employee Affective Delivery and Customer Behavioral Intentions," *Journal of Applied Psychology* 87, (2002): 1001–8.

160 DecisionWise & Brigham Young University, "Do Engaged Managers Have Engaged Employees?" Intern study, Marriott School of Management, Brigham Young University (December 2013).

161 R. Rosenthal and L. Jacobson, *Pygmalion in the Classroom*

162 E. Y. Babad, J. Inbar, and R. Rosenthal, "Pygmalion, Galatea, and the Golem: Investigations of Biased and Unbiased Teachers," *Journal of Educational Psychology* 74, (1982): 459–74.

163 Donald H. Meichenbaum, Kenneth S. Bowers, and Robert R. Ross, "A Behavioral Analysis of Teacher Expectancy Effect," *Journal of Personality and Social Psychology* 13, no. 4 (December 1969): 306–16.

164 Sylvia Vorhauser-Smith, "How the Best Places to Work Are Nailing Employee Engagement," *Forbes*, August 14, 2013.

165 http://www.ibmadison.com/Blogger/Smart-Sustainable-Biz/June-2013 /CUNA-Mutuals-brilliant-approach-to-employee-engagement-leads-to -increased-focus-on-sustainability/

166 http://www.hotelnewsnow.com/Article/7619 /Hotels-acknowledged-for-employee-engagement

167 http://www.mahindra.com/about-us

168 Buchanan, L. (2016, April 27). Toms' Secret Recipe for Improving Its Employees' Quality of Life. Retrieved from https://www.inc.com/magazine/201605/leigh-buchanan/toms-employee-culture-programs.html

169 Charlie O. Trevor and Anthony J. Nyberg, "Keeping Your Headcount When All About You Are Losing Theirs: Downsizing, Voluntary Turnover Rates, and the Moderating Role of HR Practices," *Academy of Management Journal* (April–May 2008).

170 Silvan Winkler, Cornelius J. König, and Martin Kleinmann, "New Insights into an Old Debate: Investigating the Temporal Sequence of Commitment and Performance at the Business Unit Level," *Journal of Occupational and Organizational Psychology* 83, no. 3 (2012): 503–22.

Index

ENGAGEMENT MAGIC® Resources
FROM DECISIONWISE

Visit **www.EngagementMAGIC.com** to access:
- ENGAGEMENT MAGIC® self-assessments
- Manager resources for engagement
- Personal resources for increasing engagement
- Whitepapers, articles, and the latest in engagement research
- ENGAGEMENT MAGIC® blog

Would you like to experience ENGAGEMENT MAGIC® in your organization?

Contact us to learn more about our proven engagement interventions, based on the research from the book:
- Onsite, in-house, and open-enrollment workshops
- Team engagement workshops
- Executive coaching
- Keynote addresses
- Employee engagement surveys

About DecisionWise
Since 1996, DecisionWise has been helping leaders and organizations around the world unlock the power of employee engagement. As an organization development firm, DecisionWise conducts employee engagement surveys, provides in-depth analysis, consults with executive leaders, and trains leaders and employees in over 70 countries on the Employee Experience.

ENGAGING PEOPLE™

www.decision-wise.com | info@decision-wise.com | +1.801.515.6500 (USA)